PRAISE FOR *MOTHERING EARTH*

"In *Mothering Earth*, Julia Rockwell beautifully puts words to the transformation that takes place on a sustainability journey and what it feels like when you're no longer stuck in the game of 'doing things perfectly' but let yourself sink into a new life rhythm. One with more meaning, joy, and peace of mind—for yourself and your family! She will guide you through very concrete and actionable steps that will take you out of your old mindsets (without shame) and into new ones that are better for you and for the planet. Conscious parenting is not an easy task, but Julia will show you how it's not only possible—it's the foundation for a whole new kind of life. And one that you don't want to miss out on."

Anne Therese Gennari
Author of *The Climate Optimist Handbook*

"*Mothering Earth* is the approachable, accessible guide I've needed to move from overwhelm to action. Julia skillfully outlines the small, simple changes my family can make to live more sustainably and create a stronger planet."

Jill Koziol
Cofounder & CEO, Motherly

"We all want to make the right decisions in our household and as consumers to reduce our footprint as well as encourage companies to act ethically and set an example for our children. Julia has done incredibly thorough research coupled with her dedicated experience and testing in order to offer a wide host of solutions for every aspect of domestic life. This book will be an incredibly valuable resource for parents and nonparents alike as we all seek to lighten our load on Mother Earth!"

Danielle Jezienicki
Director of Sustainability, Grove Collaborative

"We all know we should lower our carbon footprint and create less waste, but the shift always feels daunting and un-fun, best left for another day when we finally have time to do the research and buy all those specialty products. A busy mom of two, Julia knows what works for modern families and shares accessible and affordable swaps and strategies to reduce waste without sacrificing style, time, convenience, or fun. Positive impact on the planet AND your family? Yes, please!"

Jenna Zimmerman Robinson
Emmy- and James Beard Award–nominated writer, producer, and director

"As an ecologist, the immensity of global change is on my mind every day. Julia's tips and ideas for living more gently on our earth while living our busy lives are a breath of fresh air. It's wonderful to have reminders and new ideas on how we can take action and help our children put the planet first in their choices as they learn and grow."

Kara Moore O'Leary
Ecologist & Conservation Biologist

"Julia's book connects the dots between climate change and the prevailing notion that one must consume their way to being a good parent. She reframes the sustainability conversation in a way that provides families space to move forward into a lifestyle change that's enriching and regenerative for weary parents and a weary planet. I'm glad for this accessible and practical guide to *Mothering Earth*."

Maura Dilley
Reuse Designer, Cascade Circular

"Julia understands the challenge of combining a busy family lifestyle with the desire to protect and improve the planet for our kids' future. She is insightful and fresh and most importantly never smug or alienating. She's a role model who breaks it down into manageable parts, allowing any interested parent to feel good about their progress!"

Alison Mountford
Founder & CEO, Ends+Stems

"Julia is that fun friend who shows you how living sustainably doesn't require big sacrifices, but rather how small choices can have big impact."

Sandra Velasquez
CEO & Founder, Nopalera

"*Mothering Earth* is the encouraging and empowering guide busy parents are looking for to help them embrace sustainable living. Wherever you fall on the spectrum of sustainable living, this book has practical tools to bring more joy, presence, and compassion to your family and the world."

Kristi Yeh
Marriage and Family Therapist & Founder of Parent Self-Care

"*Mothering Earth* is an inspiring and informative book that offers simple solutions to help readers live more sustainably. Readers can use this book as a sustainable living guide, jumping around to various chapters that spark interest and implementing these easy eco-actions at their own pace. The perfect read for a busy eco-minded parent!"

Jessie Stokes
Founder, Tiny Yellow Bungalow

MOTHERING EARTH

MOTHERING EARTH

THE BUSY FAMILY'S GUIDE
TO SAVING THE PLANET

Julia Rockwell

imagine!

At the time of publication, all URLs printed in this book were accurate and active.
Charlesbridge and the author are not responsible for the content or accessibility of any website.

The pages of this book are printed on SFI-certified, responsibly forested paper.

An Imagine Book
Published by Charlesbridge
9 Galen Street
Watertown, MA 02472
(617) 926-0329
www.imaginebooks.net

Library of Congress Cataloging-in-Publication Data
Names: Rockwell, Julia, author.
Title: Mothering Earth: the busy family's guide to saving the planet /
    by Julia Rockwell.
Other titles: Busy family's guide to saving the planet
Description: Watertown, MA: Charlesbridge, [2023] | Includes
    bibliographical references and index. | Summary: "How sustainable
    living can simplify life, help us make healthier choices, and save the
    planet."—Provided by publisher.
Identifiers: LCCN 2022057095 (print) | LCCN 2022057096 (ebook) |
    ISBN 9781623545574 (hardcover) | ISBN 9781632892515 (ebook)
Subjects: LCSH: Green movement. | Sustainable living. | Home economics.
Classification: LCC GE196 .R636 2023 (print) | LCC GE196 (ebook) |
    DDC 640.28/6—dc23/eng20230320
LC record available at https://lccn.loc.gov/2022057095
LC ebook record available at https://lccn.loc.gov/2022057096

Display type set in Galvji
Text type set in Photina MT
Printed by Maple Press in York, Pennsylvania
Jackets printed by JP Pow in Boston, Massachusetts
Production supervision by Jennifer Most Delaney
Designed by Nicole Turner
All jacket imagery courtesy of the author

Printed in the United States of America
(hc) 10 9 8 7 6 5 4 3 2 1

To my children

CONTENTS

PREFACE

"Mom, look! It's a 3-in-1 dinosaur. This is the one I wanted!" My six-year-old quickly tears open the box to his "new" Lego set and pours the pieces onto the table where we begin building together. It's moments like this that I treasure: him, focused on a project; me, sitting by his side as we chat and tell jokes.

The fact that the Lego kit is secondhand doesn't take away from his zeal or how much I cherish this time together. In fact, it makes it better knowing that these precious moments don't have to come at a cost to the environment or my child's future. While I am well aware of the plastic problems that plague our planet, our family's "no *brand-new* plastic" rule is one that we try to enforce, not just with kid's toys but with everything we bring into our lives. We shop secondhand for the majority of things now, plastic included. And this isn't the only earth-minded swap we've made since we started living sustainably years ago. We went through a complete eco-overhaul, and now sustainable living is our *new normal*.

Before our *green* lifestyle began, I'd always thought I was an earth-friendly gal. Like many other San Franciscans, I drove a Prius, carried a refillable water bottle, and voted for representatives who supported green initiatives. I worried about climate change, but it seemed like something out of my control. It felt like a problem that existed down the road and was up to politicians to figure out. However, a few months after the birth of our second child, my views of myself and the world changed in an instant.

I was sitting in bed, scrolling through news articles with my milk-drunk baby asleep across my lap when I came across a headline that plunged me into an all-consuming state of panic. It read "UN Says Climate Genocide Is Coming. It's Actually Worse Than You Think." The impact of those words took the breath out of my body and cracked open my entire reality. From that moment forward, my life could not continue as usual.

I was having what I like to call an *eco–life crisis*. Here are signs you may be having one, too:

- You're too young for a midlife crisis.
- You define *plastic surgery* as cutting plastic out of your life.
- Instead of worrying about hot flashes, you're concerned about the hottest days on record.
- You find your partner utterly irresistible when they order a vegan hot dog.
- You believe that happy hour should only include biodynamic wine.
- You traded in your gas-guzzling car for a used electric vehicle.
- The only type of silicone you're interested in is for food storage purposes.
- Your bucket list is filled with trash from your beach cleanup.

If any of those sound familiar, welcome to the club. My eco–aha moment hit me by complete and total surprise. I hadn't been living under a rock; global warming was not news to me. But in that lightning-bolt moment, everything clicked into focus. It finally hit home that it was just a matter of time before climate change would threaten the lives of my children. Climate emergencies weren't some hypothetical, futuristic occurrence. They were already happening across the globe and here in the United States. The truth: climate change was going to be detrimental to my children unless something changed, quickly! And that change needed to include me. To find my way out of the feeling of despair that consumed me, I knew I needed to transform my eco-angst into eco-action.

OPERATION *CLIMATE CARETAKER* BEGINS

In the weeks that followed my climate breakdown, I couldn't shake the thoughts of death, famine, meteorological disasters, economic collapse, and an end to life as we know it. However, as I researched deeper into what I could actually do as one individual, my hopelessness shifted to hopefulness. I realized that we, the parents of the world, possess so much more power than I ever imagined just in the choices we make every day. As the lead consumer in my household, I recognized my own accountability in the problem, too. Even with my *green* choices, I had been unknowingly perpetuating a lot of earth-damaging habits. It was clear: there was so much more I could do.

During late-night breast-feeding sessions and those precious moments when both kids were napping, I became a research addict. I devoured studies and spent hours understanding the data. I started listing all the actions we could take to reduce our footprint, and it was during this time that I found my way to zero-waste living. I had heard the term before but thought that to be zero-waste you needed to fit a year's worth of trash into a single Mason jar. As I learned more, however, I came to understand that zero-waste living is not just about focusing on how much you throw away. It's also about looking at the entire life cycle of a product and considering its impact, both environmentally and ethically, from its origin through to its disposal. I was taken by the idea of reducing how much we consumed, particularly our plastic and trash footprint, so we started living zero waste.

My husband supported my newfound mission and embraced the lifestyle, too. Together, within six months, we effectively reduced our family of four's trash by 90 percent and our recycling by 75 percent. Online shipping boxes were no longer exploding out of our weekly recycling bin. I felt so much pride staring into the depths of our garbage can on trash day and seeing just a few pieces of trash scattered on the bottom. I found zero-waste living to be motivating; there was an allure to being able to clearly measure our success through "stuff" (or lack thereof). And while it was clear that there was no true *zero* in zero waste, I enjoyed the process of finding swaps and shifts that allowed us to consume less plastic and generate less trash.

I knew it was important not to get spellbound by just the physical impact I was making. I needed to be cognizant of my carbon footprint as well. So I paired ideas from the zero-waste movement with those of climate activism. We sold my husband's old gas-guzzling car for a used electric vehicle (saving us over $600 a year, even with our newly added car payments). We cut down on meat and decided to take family vacations closer to home. When making decisions, we no longer just weighed cost and time as factors, we also considered the full environmental impact of our choices. Within a year, we had down shifted our overall ecological footprint by two-thirds.

LIKE A PHOENIX RISING FROM THE GARBAGE

When we first started living sustainably, it felt like the weight of the world hung on every choice I made. While my "wins" made me feel like a sustainability superstar, my inevitable "fails" left me disheartened. Small daily trip-ups left me feeling lost and like my efforts were futile. While I understood on an intellectual level that my actions alone were not going to solve the environmental mess we're in, the perfectionist gal that I am had a hard time embracing unavoidable mishaps. As time went on, though, my constant self-criticism slowed. I began to see my place in the world differently.

Stilling my negative self-chatter began when I started bringing mindfulness to my everyday actions. By slowing down, I found a deeper connection to the world around me. Tiny mundane tasks held a greater sense of purpose. My shopping lists were filled with meaning. There was no longer a false sense of joy when acquiring "stuff." The pleasure I was now finding was derived from making choices that made the world—and people's lives—a better, safer, and healthier place. I saw how everything I touched, ate, wore, and brought into my home was a statement on the type of world I wanted to promote. My choices were living proof of my values. Connected to something greater, my reason for being here was to protect it for future generations.

It was during this time that my black-and-white thinking about sustainability began to fade, as I came to see that there isn't just one way to live an eco-lifestyle. I saw that sustainability exists on a scale. I let go of my guilt for driving places when public transportation (or timing) didn't align, and I did not freak out when the secondhand clothes I ordered for my kids came shipped in plastic mailers. I was finally able to internalize that it was about doing the best I could, given my circumstances.

While our transition into sustainability may have been bumpy, eco-living steadily became routine. In time, life felt simpler and I found I had more time for myself. Sustainable living had streamlined our life. Our family schedule slowed to a calmer, more enjoyable pace than we had ever known. We prepared meals and cooked together. Straightening up the house was quicker for me and my husband because less stuff now meant more time. We sought the outdoors and took deeper recognition of the beauty and wonder that surrounded us. It became evident that sustainable living had led us to make different choices about how we spent (and appreciated) our days. The constant emotional cycle of chasing *more* began to melt away. For the first time, I was chasing the idea of *less*. We were saving money, our sanity, and the planet.

TALKING RUBBISH

When we started living sustainably, my newfound passion was all I wanted to talk about. I was an annoying zealot who literally did not want to talk about anything but beeswax wraps and carbon offsets. After a few awkward interactions, it was clear I needed to shift my approach. I cooled it with the soapbox and decided to share our eco-adventures on social media. This allowed friends to come to it if and when they were ready—and what a game changer. In the months that followed, friends and people I had never met were reaching out regularly with sustainability questions, eco-swaps, and a desire to learn more. I found that parents, mothers in particular, were consuming my message with urgency. In time, I started writing more about sustainable living. The growing demand was such that I started hosting workshops and swap 'n' socials and was invited to give talks at schools in our area. Within a few years, I had pivoted my career to helping families live more sustainably.

And so here I am. A mom on a mission. Stepping up and furthering my small part in this larger global story. In the process, I have become passionate about helping other families do the same. I believe that you are an agent of change. You have the ability to make a meaningful impact and I am excited to help you on your journey. May this book guide and inspire you and your family to lead a more sustainable life.

INTRODUCTION

What if you could simplify your life, make healthier choices for your kids, and save the planet—all at the same time? That's sustainable living.

YOU CAN MOVE MOUNTAINS

Whether you're interested in reducing your carbon footprint or cutting down on plastic, or are overwhelmed by the idea of adding "save the planet" to your already overflowing to-do list, you have come to the right place. By picking up this book, you are joining together with other parents who share your concern about the environment, climate change, and our children's future. Welcome. This is a safe, empowering place to be.

As a parent, you are a cultivator of life. To give birth, adopt, use a surrogate, foster, or to have a chosen family—how you become a parent comes about in many ways, but parenthood isn't about how we arrived in this role. *To parent* is a verb involving love, action, and responsibility. We do our best to support, teach, feed, clothe, heal, protect, and care for our children. We want the world for them, but right now, that world is in jeopardy.

The facts around the climate crisis are downright terrifying. According to the United Nations, we have until 2030 to fight climate breakdown before we reach the "point of no return." Also by 2030, it is estimated that drought alone could displace 700 million people worldwide. Add in microplastics and the fact that mass extinction is occurring at an alarming rate, and it may be tempting to bury your head in the sand. But there is good news: hope is not lost. However, we must act now while we have a choice, or the choices will be made for us. We are on the front lines as the last generation of parents who can do something to fight this crisis.

If you're a mother and your concern over the state of the planet brings out your momma bear instincts, you are not alone. Nine in ten mothers feel that it is their moral duty to create a safe and healthy environment for their kids, with 81 percent of moms saying they are worried about climate change. In fact, research has shown that mothers hold greater concern over the climate crisis than any other group.

And while I know the idea of defeating the greatest threat that has ever jeopardized human existence may feel insurmountable, there is a lot we can do. And you don't need to wait another day to start. You can help create a livable future for your children through your daily deeds. Your individual actions are not inconsequential. You are an essential thread in the fabric that makes up society. If we begin to pull on that thread, you will see that the whole world is connected.

> "The world's not going to change unless we are willing to change ourselves."
>
> **—RIGOBERTO MENCHÚ TUM**
> *activist, Nobel Peace Prize laureate, mother*

Mothers, fathers, grandparents, caregivers—we can all create meaningful change—and you can do so without sacrificing convenience or comforts. No matter your experience making sustainable choices, I promise to meet you where you are and take your sustainability efforts to the next level, at your own pace and without judgment. Never recycled a day in your life? No problem. Do you carry a refillable water bottle but aren't sure what else you can do? I've got you covered. Whether you are expecting your first child or have a teenager who is ready to fly the nest, I have hundreds of tips to help you and your family lead a more sustainable lifestyle—today. And to do so, you . . .

- do **not** need to carve out separate time to focus on sustainability
- do **not** need to spend more money
- do **not** need to partake in DIY projects
- do **not** need to be perfect
- do **not** need to get rid of all the plastic in your home
- do **not** need to turn your family's life upside down
- do **not** need to feel guilty (you didn't create this mess we are in)
- do **not** need to live off the grid

Through simple swaps, small habit shifts, and harnessing your unique interests and skills, I will guide you to make realistic, practical, and meaningful changes to your daily routine that will save you time and money and are better for the planet.

THE MOTHERLOAD

While sustainable living might sound great in theory, the reality of it may feel monumental, particularly with kids in tow. (I get it. I've got two kiddos myself.) As parents, we already have a lot on our plates. Not only are we raising the next generation, we are doing so while managing a household, a career, and a life outside the home. *Busy* would be an understatement. Groceries, laundry, meals, cleaning, paying the bills, homework help, emotional support for your children, healthcare, the family calendar, replenishing the wardrobe of your ever-growing child, signing the kids up for extracurricular activities, teacher communication, gifts, holidays, planning the family vacations, school breaks, and summers off . . . Being a parent is not a full-time job. It's an *all-the-time* job. Top that with the gravity of climate breakdown, microplastics, and endless waste, and it can feel like too much to bear. Solving the earth's woes may feel like more than you have the capacity to take on, but if I have learned anything in my years of living an eco-lifestyle while raising children, it's that sustainable living is not something "extra" you need to add to your schedule. In fact, it creates more time and space for what truly matters.

THE TIES THAT BIND US

As we start to peel back the layers of sustainable living, you will see that our health is deeply linked with the health of our planet. Pesticides are not just destroying insect populations; they're also harmful to humans. Red meat isn't just correlated with an increased risk of heart disease, stroke, type 2 diabetes, and cancer; it's also one of the main drivers of climate change. Overconsumption isn't just overwhelming our kids and their bulging toy boxes; it's depleting the world of its natural resources. Social issues such as racism, gender equity, poverty, education, and tribal sovereignty aren't isolated matters. They are deeply linked to each other, the climate crisis, and our capacity for climate resilience. So when we pause and take a look at the interconnection between the breakdown of the planet and our health, both individually and collectively, we see that they're frequently one and the same. The first step in healing these ruptures is through connection—connection to the planet, to each other, and to ourselves. Living sustainably is one way to help repair the fractures in how we relate with each other and the world around us.

WOMEN + THE CLIMATE

On the surface, one might not correlate women's rights to the climate, but the reality is climate change is not gender-neutral. Globally, including here in the United States, women and girls are disproportionately impacted by the crisis. Statistics put forth by the United Nations indicate that 80% of people displaced by climate change are women. And while we are seeing these disparities play out in developing countries, we must also acknowledge our deficits here at home.

In the wake of Hurricane Katrina, the devastating impacts of gender inequality could not have been more evident. According to the National Resource Defense Council (NRDC), "Eighty-three percent of single mothers were unable to return home after Hurricane Katrina for a full two years after the storm. It's estimated that two-thirds of jobs lost after Hurricane Katrina were lost by women." And while these figures highlight women and mothers, it would be remiss not to acknowledge that race, income, sexual orientation and gender identity, disability, and age also determine those who are disproportionally impacted during and after natural disasters.

Despite the fact that women are more negatively affected by the crisis than men, we see time and time again that it's women and other marginalized groups who step up as organizers to help build back communities in the aftermath of climate emergencies. This fortitude is just one example of how women are essential to climate action and resilience. Female leadership, rights, and empowerment are also imperative in the fight against the crisis:

- **In Business:** One study looked at around 2,000 companies in 24 sectors and found that when a business had a 1% increase in female managers, it correlated to a .5% decrease in carbon emissions. Additionally, businesses that have greater gender diversity show a 5% decrease in CO_2 emissions overall than firms with predominantly male leadership.

- **On Our Ballots:** A 2012 study found that "$CO_{(2)}$ emissions per capita are lower in nations where women have a higher political status."
- **In Our Closets:** Fashion is one of the most polluting industries and it is also infamous for exploiting female workers. Buying ethical or secondhand clothes isn't just better for the environment, it also supports women's rights.
- **In Our Wallets:** Women in the United States control or influence 85% of household purchases. including new homes (91%), cars (65%), food (93%), bank accounts (89%), and vacations (92%). With a spending power of $2.4 trillion, what and how women consume is an everyday weapon against the climate crisis that should not be overlooked.
- **In Our Past + Present:** Patriarchy, racism, and colonialism all contain one common principle: that the planet and/or people are here for exploitation. All three systems of oppression can be linked back to the root of the climate crisis. And thus, we are coming to see climate change not as an independent issue, but rather as a culmination of transgressions. As we seek to dismantle these systems, our efforts not only tackle social issues; they also address the underlying cultural sources of the crisis.

Environmental action is a feminist issue. Narrowing the gender gap, combating racism, ending poverty—all are pieces of the climate resilience equation. So if we are to talk about fighting climate change, women and other marginalized groups must be part of the conversation. And while that work is essential within leadership roles in business and government, it must also be included in our everyday lives at home, in the office, on our ballots, and with our purchases. It is through the lens of our choices and habits that we must examine the systems we are upholding and the ones we are rejecting. Leading a sustainable lifestyle is an assertion of human rights and is part of a larger revolution to create a world that we want for ourselves and our children.

Sustainable living = Human rights

It must be noted that the act of mothering the earth cannot be left to women. It requires everyone to nurture and protect (or "mother") this precious home we share. Caring for the earth is NOT something connected to gender, but rather, a way in which we approach tending and connecting to the planet and one another.

Just one person can make a difference. While your actions alone are not going to fix everything, what you do is part of a larger picture. As Americans, we, in particular, must recognize our need to change. Fact: the United States is disproportionally responsible for climate change. As a nation, we make up just over 4% of the world's population but generate 15% of the total worldwide greenhouse gas emissions. For perspective, as of 2020, the average carbon footprint of an individual in the United States is over 14 tons, while the global average per person is closer to just 4 tons. I don't tell you this to make you feel guilty but to clarify the importance of our choices as Americans, and the power and weight our decisions carry.

WE ARE ALL ECO-ACTIONISTS

Change makers come in a lot of different forms—and you are one of them, even if the idea of being an "environmentalist" feels like a leap. I recall the first time my husband called me an environmental activist. I looked at him quizzically as the term just didn't sit right with me. I was a mom trying to live more sustainably so that my children would have a future. What I quickly came to realize is that to lead a sustainable life, you do not need to conform to "environmentalist" stereotypes. Nor do you need to quit your day job to be a full-time activist. You can be who you are and continue leading your life, doing what you do, and still reduce your footprint. We all have the power to become an "eco-actionist"—someone who uses their daily habits, choices, and routines as tools for change. In the wise words of Dr. Rachel Naomi Remen, "It's about healing the world that touches you." So by considering the environmental impact of your everyday decisions, you too can influence change. And you do not need to be perfect. It's all about making informed decisions and doing what you can, given your circumstances. Armed with information, you have the power to make a difference.

"Do the best that you can until you know better.
Then, when you know better, do better."

—MAYA ANGELOU
writer, activist, and mother

HOW TO USE THIS BOOK

Because raising kids while juggling life is exhausting, I have designed this book so you don't need to sit down and read it cover to cover. If you are immediately drawn to an area of focus, start there! You can always come back to other sections later. Plus, I've organized the book into digestible "eco-actions" so you can get a lot out of reading one or two pages at a time (because no one knows interruptions like a parent).

While we all have parenthood in common, there is no one-size-fits-all approach to eco-living. I will tell you right now: not *everything* in this book will work for you. We all have different circumstances. So I have written the book to help you find the sustainable swaps, shifts, and habit changes that will work for you and your family.

In part I, *The Basics*, we'll dive into what sustainable living is (and isn't). We'll talk about the perks, debunk myths, and discuss how *saving the world* is not all on you (because, trust me, it's not!). Additionally, we'll answer the common question *"Where do I begin?"* We'll dissect how you and your family can break deeply rooted habits and how to effectively bust burnout. Plus, we'll cover the essentials to build a strong foundation for you and your family to thrive.

In part II, *Eco-Actionist Agenda*, I break down five essential areas of your family's life to uncover practical ways you can make powerful, feasible changes. We'll also discuss what makes you shine and how you can harness those talents to expand your eco-efforts beyond everyday life.

Lastly, in part III's *Eco-Actionist Notebook*, I've compiled all of my green-insider info, including a *31-Day Eco-Family Challenge* (as a starting place if you're feeling stuck); *Your Planet Planner*, a personalized road map to resources in your area; and *The Motherboard*, a resources guide chock full of all of my favorite sustainable shops, brands, and influencers.

The practice of living sustainably honors simplifying, decluttering, consuming less, appreciating more, slowing down, mindfulness, saving money, finding more time for what matters, balance, being joyful, protecting human rights, living in harmony with the earth, and aligning your daily choices with your values. It celebrates wellness, manifests a better future, and gives hope. By the time you are finished reading this book, I hope you feel informed and empowered to make more sustainable choices that are not only better for the planet but transform your life as well.

We are a force of nature, and together we can change the world.

PART I
THE BASICS

SUSTAINABLE LIVING 101

Before you start your eco-journey, let's lay the foundation.

THE BASICS

Taking on sustainability without understanding the basics is like building a house without a proper foundation. It might look pretty for a time, but sooner or later it's likely to come toppling down. With some fundamental eco–inside knowledge, you and your family can establish greener habits and integrate simple, sustainable swaps that will stick.

WHAT IS SUSTAINABLE LIVING?

Sustainable living is a misunderstood term that often conjures up images of hugging trees, eating granola, and depriving oneself of the conveniences of modern society. While I have nothing against any of these things, these stereotypes aren't necessary to live sustainably, nor are they inclusive of all who can and do participate. *Sustainable living* means:

- Regenerating and repairing the earth, ecosystems, and communities through lifestyle choices.
- Living in a way that supports basic human needs and rights without harming the environment and while upholding stable ecological, societal, and economic conditions for future generations.
- An eco-focused lifestyle in which an individual or community strives to reduce their environmental impact and counteract harmful environmental problems, such as climate change, by limiting their greenhouse gas emissions, waste and plastic footprint, and use of natural resources.

In short, sustainable living is about making better choices for the planet and all of the life that exists on it. Doing so doesn't require you to

> "You cannot get through a single day without having an impact on the world around you. What you do makes a difference, and you have to decide what kind of difference you want to make."
>
> **—JANE GOODALL**
> *primatologist, anthropologist, conservationist, and mother*

look a certain way, make a particular amount of money, or be anyone other than the person you are. Each and every one of us has the power to contribute to large-scale change.

So how *do* we make changes? The truth is, there isn't one answer. Our families, situations, and unique talents are all different, so we must find ways in our individual lives to participate through lifestyle choices, daily decisions, and small habit shifts. And the changes each of us makes will have an impact and rewards.

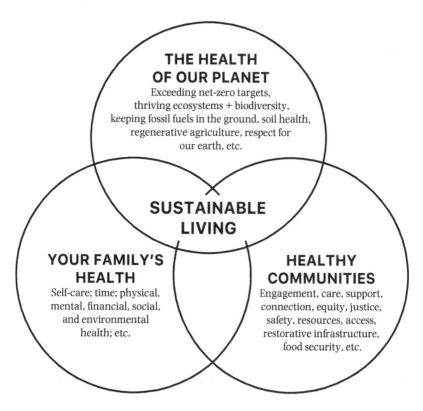

THE HEALTH OF OUR PLANET
Exceeding net-zero targets, thriving ecosystems + biodiversity, keeping fossil fuels in the ground, soil health, regenerative agriculture, respect for our earth, etc.

SUSTAINABLE LIVING

YOUR FAMILY'S HEALTH
Self-care; time; physical, mental, financial, social, and environmental health; etc.

HEALTHY COMMUNITIES
Engagement, care, support, connection, equity, justice, safety, resources, access, restorative infrastructure, food security, etc.

THE PERKS

One element of sustainable living that might surprise you is that it comes with a whole host of personal gains. As you'll soon discover, this deeply rewarding lifestyle is better for your family's health and well-being. Here are some of the top daily benefits of *green* living.

Life, Simplified. Reducing the amount we consume transforms, organizes, and frees us from the grind of constantly trying to obtain (and then having to get rid of) "stuff." It creates room to appreciate what we already have. Living sustainably allows us to shed the chaos and stress that comes with overconsumption while also reducing the burdens we put on ourselves and the earth's resources.

Saves Time. Life with children is busy (and that's an understatement). As much as we say we want to slow down, it often feels impossible to do so. Living sustainably helps us discern and prioritize what matters most and modulate family life to a more sustainable pace.

Saves Money. Consumption is a money pit. As you begin to participate in sustainable living, you will find that you will save money, even if you're already on a tight budget.

Fosters Self-Care. Caring for the planet is also caring for yourself. The health benefits of sustainable living include eating better, getting outside, exercising more, and being mindful. If you experience eco-anxiety, caring for the earth is also a way to improve your mental health.

Builds Community. Community is essential for our well-being and the well-being of our children. As the saying goes, it takes a village to raise a child. Humans need one another to thrive. However, we often become isolated in our hurried lives and forget that we are part of a greater whole. When we engage and establish ourselves in a community that supports caring for each other and the planet, both our individual experiences and the world at large change for the better.

Cultivates Joy. Joy and environmental action may sound like an odd pairing, but they go together like peanut butter and jelly. Considering the environment in your daily decisions takes the mundane to a more meaningful level. Turning out the lights or doing laundry are not generally joy-inducing activities for a family. Still, when we begin to celebrate these everyday actions, we find meaning and purpose in even the smallest of deeds.

Encourages Connection. The environmental crisis is a reminder that we are connected to something greater than ourselves. Making greener choices in our day-to-day lives is restorative, repairing the fractures that have been perpetuated through our culture's thoughtless relationship with the earth and each other. By living sustainably, you also instill these values in your children.

Offers Hope. Leading an eco-lifestyle models to our kids a more sustainable way to live on the planet. Through action, we teach our children that we are all agents of change. Showing the next generation how to make greener choices, we offer hope for a brighter future. Additionally, we give our kids the tools to follow in our footsteps and build upon the foundation we lay.

> "I learned that courage was not the absence of fear,
> but the triumph over it."
>
> **—NELSON MANDELA**
> *activist, politician, Nobel Peace
> Prize recipient, and father*

THE MYTHS

Now that we have a clearer idea of what sustainable living is, let's talk about what sustainable living isn't. When it comes to living an eco-lifestyle, there are many misconceptions. It's vital to debunk these myths because they can create enormous, unnecessary hurdles (and stress) for a budding eco-actionist. The last thing we need is to add *more* to our plates, so let's break down these false narratives.

The Time Myth: *I have to devote a lot of time to living sustainably.* I'll be honest, living sustainably does take a bit of time at first. You may need a moment to orient yourself in the bulk section of your grocery store, to find a new plastic-free toothpaste that you love, or to switch your energy bill over to renewable energy. But once you get the hang of it and set a few systems in place, it becomes second nature.

The Money Myth: *Sustainable living is expensive.* Single-use items like paper towels, dryer sheets, and even packaging cost more money than reusable items. (Yes, you're paying for the cost of packaging.) Disposable products are designed to be used once, then thrown away—only for you to have to spend again to replace them, over and over.

Opting for reusables, which can cost a bit more up front, will save you money over time. Plus, living sustainably at its core is about using what you already have, NOT about going out and buying a bunch of "sustainable stuff." Overconsumption, even of sustainable items, is not sustainable. By reusing and repurposing what you own, you save money and the planet.

DID YOU KNOW?

Sustainable living isn't a new concept. Until recent history, humankind lived in balance with the planet for hundreds of thousands of years. Indigenous peoples still do.

The Recycling Myth: *Sustainable living is all about recycling.* Reducing one's overall footprint is about creating less waste, and that waste includes recycling. While recycling is crucial to limiting what ends up in the landfill, recycling should be a last resort instead of the answer to society's colossal waste addiction. We are currently in a recycling crisis. For decades, the United States was shipping a massive percentage of our recyclables to China to be processed (yikes!). Then, in January 2018, China put a ban in place and is no longer accepting much of our recyclables. So the waste we're tossing in our recycling bin—with the best of intentions—may be ending up in the landfill or mismanaged in yet another country due to our lack of domestic recycling resources. (Double yikes.) The solution is to recycle less and *refuse, reduce*, and *reuse* more!

The Deprivation Myth: *Living sustainably means I have to deprive my family of the things we love.* People often think sustainable living means a minimalistic existence where their kids only play with rocks, sticks, and neutral-colored toys. An eco-lifestyle doesn't mean your family is possession-less or doesn't get to enjoy life's comforts or delights. Sure, if you're trying to live sustainably, you may choose not to buy brand-new plastic toys for your kids. But opting for them secondhand is a way to allow your kids to enjoy some plastic classics like Legos and Magna-Tiles while not supporting the production of new plastic (and keeping perfectly usable toys out of the landfill). Rather than denying yourself or your children, sustainable living is about revising how we make choices so we can have a smaller footprint.

The Whole Household Myth: *If I can't get my whole family on board, I can't do this.* You are only responsible for yourself. While I've had fantasies about making everyone "be green" (and maybe you can relate), that's just not how it works, even in our own homes. It can be frustrating when everyone doesn't take this journey as seriously as you, but that doesn't mean you can't make changes. You choose the foods you eat and the clothes you wear. We will talk more about how to get family members on board in the next chapter, but for now, know you can do this, even if you're going at it alone.

The Individual Action vs. Systemic Change Myth: *My individual actions won't make a difference.* One of the most damaging myths people believe is that their individual actions don't make a difference. While it's true that one person becoming a vegan or riding a bike will not solve the climate crisis alone, the key is that our actions are part of a larger story. As we shift together, our impact is significant—especially living in the US. (The average American's emissions are four times that of the average world citizen!) Becoming conscious of what we put in our shopping carts, how we wash our clothes, and the energy we use to heat our homes can significantly reduce our footprint to a more sustainable level. Caring for the earth is the responsibility of every human on this planet. And while we must actively demand change from corporations and elected officials, we must also call upon ourselves for change and growth. To avoid the catastrophic impacts of a 2°C rise in global temperatures, by 2050 individuals globally must reduce their carbon footprints to 2 tons annually. And to reach this goal, it will take individual, systemic, and government action.

THE BIGGER PICTURE

SYSTEMIC CHANGE AND ~~YOU~~ US

Systemic change and individual action are two sides of the same coin. Take the study that showed that just 100 companies are responsible for 71% of greenhouse gas emissions. Many people have argued that this analysis is

> "We are the ones we have been waiting for."
>
> **—ALICE WALKER**
> *writer, social activist, and mother*

proof that individual action doesn't matter. But what was not included in the media's assessment of that report is that over 90% of those emissions don't happen during production. They occur down the line with us, from infrastructure to consumer habits. (Oh, and not to mention the officials we elect who support environmentally damaging practices.) It's an oversimplification to say that consumer choice alone can solve all of our earth's woes (government and corporate responsibility are essential), but we must steer the conversation away from *systemic change vs. individual action* and understand that BOTH are required for transformation. Pitting one against the other distracts from the necessary work, even leading to inaction.

> "Never doubt that a small group of thoughtful, committed citizens can change the world: indeed, it's the only thing that ever has."
>
> **—MARGARET MEAD**
> *anthropologist and mother*

THE COLLECTIVE FOOTPRINT

As a band of individuals (go, parents!), we have the power to transform the world. A Harvard University study found that it only takes 3.5% of a population engaged in nonviolent civil resistance to achieve radical change. And it isn't just demonstrating in the streets. The study found that in order to instigate change, the movement needs a diverse population of people who can sustain pressure over time, gain support of businesses, and find creative ways to engage beyond just protest.

Together, we can shift social norms and structures when we recognize that many of our mundane, daily choices shape our systems. We can pressure companies and the government by voting at the polls AND with our wallets. We can campaign for curbside composting in our communities, move our money to banks that don't fund fossil fuel expansion, and work to get more planet-friendly foods in our children's school cafeterias. We can talk to friends and neighbors about the changes we are making. Do not let anyone fool you into believing that the collective action of individuals doesn't make a difference. By taking ownership, making changes, and demanding action, transformations can occur.

Individuals, governments, and businesses all need to be part of this movement—but it's also important to remember that it's people, not corporations or governments, who start cultural revolutions. And although

> "The greatest threat to our planet
> is the belief that someone else will save it."
>
> **—ROBERT SWAN**
> *polar explorer, environmental leader, and father*

shifts have been made in recent years to try and get us back on track reducing emissions as a nation (the Inflation Reduction Act is a game changer), it's not enough if individuals don't get on board. Much of the plan that's laid out requires individuals to make different consumer choices. We have to work together to steer this ship in the right direction. Just as we have been reminded in recent years that democracy requires active participation from everyone, so does caring for our earth.

Stronger, Together. The sustainability movement requires us all to do our part. Our differences bring together a diverse set of skills and perspectives that give us the strength to tackle the environmental issues that plague us from a thousand different angles. It's our differences that make us stronger and also hold the capacity to unite us.

Reframe + Rebuild. Wide-scale change is needed for us to build a more sustainable future. But many sustainable systems already exist. However, not everyone who has access to these frameworks is utilizing them. Tapping into any resources available to you is essential for upholding and expanding green infrastructure in your community. If renewable energy is offered in your area, have you switched your energy bill yet? If you have bike lanes on your local roads, how often are you taking advantage of them? While it's important to advocate for greener cities and eco-business practices, we also need to reframe our habits to ensure we're utilizing all that we have at our fingertips.

Support Others. As the saying goes, "A rising tide lifts all boats." Even in our busy lives, identifying ways we can use our advantages to advocate for others and the environmental solutions that would strengthen them is paramount. When supporting individuals and communities, it's valuable to listen to the issues that others are facing so that you can be a true ally (rather than giving others what you think they might need). Get involved by using your voice, abilities, access, time, or money. We are all in this together.

Now is the time for us to rethink, repattern, rebuild, and work together to create the future we want for all of our children.

WHERE TO BEGIN?

The answer: with what you already have.

GREEN MEANS GO

GETTING STARTED: A FOUR-STEP PLAN

Not sure where to start? Let's break this down so you feel activated and supported as you begin your journey into sustainable living. Although every family is different, there are still four basic steps everyone can take to get started.

First, I will help you *define* your eco-anatomy. This includes understanding your footprint, how much you can realistically take on, your local resources, and more. Next, we will talk about the importance of *mindset*. Then you'll learn ways to *sustain* and maintain your new routine. And finally, we'll cover *inclusion*, because there is a place for every human on the planet in this movement.

All right, let's dive in.

01 | DEFINE

A lot of changes need to be made in the world, but that doesn't mean you need to take them all on. Understanding your family's footprint, patterns, and resources will help focus your starting point.

Make a List. Grab a piece of paper and jot down answers to the following: What am I already doing that's sustainable? What eco-habits do I engage in that I'm proud of? What green, ethical businesses do I support? Maybe you can't answer all of these questions, and that's okay. It's just important to note what you're already doing that's a step in the right direction and to use that as a foundation to build upon.

Measure Your Footprint. Sites such as footprintcalculator.org and carbonfootprint.com can help you quickly assess your family's carbon footprint. While it may come as a shock, it will help you get a picture of your current emissions and give you a baseline to reevaluate your footprint in a year to see how far you've come.

Build Your Plan (*psst . . . start small*). Creating a clear and actionable blueprint with your family doesn't need to be stressful. As you fill out your family's eco-actionist agenda on page 35, choose actions that align with your family's lifestyle, resources, and time allowance. Then pick just *one* of those eco-action items to undertake first. This should keep you from feeling like you're trying to do everything at once (and make it less likely you'll burn out or quit). Achievable goals with dedicated persistence will set you up for success.

Look Locally. Spend some time getting to know the *green* resources in your area. Where is your closest thrift store? Do you have a local farmer's market? Is *green* energy an option where you live? Do you have curbside composting or a drop-off point in your community? Answering questions like these will help you ease into your eco-journey. Check out the Planet Planner on page 229 to keep track of your local sustainable resources.

Begin with What You Have. Sustainable living is not about buying a ton of sustainable stuff, nor is it about getting rid of all your possessions. Living sustainably starts precisely where you are, using what you already have. Before you purchase a single eco-product, use up, then phase out any unsustainable, wasteful, or plastic products you have in your home. (One area that immediately comes to mind is the cosmetic graveyard of half-used products you might have lurking in your bathroom.) Trust me; you possess everything you need to begin.

Make It Your Own. Personalize your approach with the tools offered throughout the book. While some families may be prepared to dive in head-first, you may only have time to start by dipping your toes in. Either way, there are a variety of ways to tailor your family's sustainability plan.

- **Your family's eco-actionist agenda:** Use the worksheet on page 35 to design a strategy that taps into all areas of your family's life.
- **Eco-family bite-size challenges:** Woven throughout the book you will find bite-size challenges that you and your family can take on, one at a time.
- **Family fun projects:** From planting a windowsill herb garden to making broth from vegetable scraps, dive into an engaging task with your family using the projects listed throughout the book.

- **31-day eco-family challenge:** If you're feeling motivated to get your sustainability groove on but need some bumper rails to help keep you on track, this step-by-step monthlong challenge will guide you through a series of daily tasks designed to ease you into sustainable living while helping you limit waste, plastic, and emissions as you build new routines.

THE SUSTAINABILITY SCALE: WEIGHING YOUR CHOICES

As you begin your eco-journey, lots of questions will come up. At the start, one that I found myself asking almost daily was, *"Is this choice sustainable or not?"* And frequently I saw that it was not a yes-or-no question. The reality is that sustainability exists on a scale.

As you go through this book, you'll see various sustainability scales presented. Any positive change, no matter how small, is a step in the right direction. Believe me, the *best* choice will not always be clear-cut. But many options are quick and easy to measure. You don't have to get it right every time. It's about doing better, not being flawless. Just go for it, knowing mistakes will happen. Be open to learning along the way. Remember, there isn't just one way to be *green*.

02 | MINDSET

Reframing our thoughts can reshape our world. Being mindful of the stories and narratives we tell ourselves can help us break the toxic cycles of consumerism and comparison while giving us the tools to be kinder to ourselves and allowing us to dream of the future we wish to create. Here are some ways to adopt an eco-actionist mindset.

Shift Your Perspective

Practice gratitude. Adding gratitude to your daily practice is an essential tool to live sustainably while keeping you motivated. Make a list of all of the positive things in your life. It could include relationships, accomplishments, your health, career, the roof over your head, etc. Whatever you feel is meaningful or you're thankful for, write it down. Pausing daily to take stock of all that you have breaks you out of the consumer grind and brings appreciation to the gifts in your life.

> "We don't need a handful of people doing zero waste perfectly. We need millions of people doing it imperfectly."
>
> **—ANNE-MARIE BONNEAU** (Zero-Waste Chef)
> *writer, activist, and mother*

Stop comparing. As you embark on your sustainable lifestyle, use this time to shed outdated thoughts and metrics of what happiness and accomplishments look like, and instead focus on your own path and what brings you nourishment. Remember, you are enough as you are.

Envision it. Fight Armageddon thoughts by imagining the future you hope to create. Forget the doomsday news and take a moment to write down what is possible if we get our act together. By envisioning it, you can start to build it. Your actions today are an embodiment of the tomorrow you wish to build.

The Zero-Guilt Tool Kit

As you shift toward a more earth-friendly routine, you'll find a new stride that streamlines and lightens your life. But things *will* come up that will throw you for a loop, and these stumbles are nothing you should feel bad or guilty about! Here are three rules of compassion you can offer yourself as you begin integrating sustainability into the whirls of your daily schedule.

It's okay to be imperfect. Sustainable living does NOT require perfection. If you aim for perfection, you will always feel like you're failing. We live in a flawed system. Currently, it's next to impossible to exist in our society without generating some emissions or waste, so try not to be hard on yourself (or others). Focus on persistence over perfection.

Don't be an overachiever. Let me remove any pressure: You will NOT be able to do *everything* in this book. It's impossible and unrealistic, and that's okay. Set attainable goals, start small, and do what you can. Then add more when you feel comfortable with the shifts you've mastered. *Everything* should not be the goal. Doing what you can, over a realistic time frame, should be.

Keep it manageable. Even with the knowledge that you can't do everything, it's also important to remember to pace yourself in the areas where you can make changes. While you may feel the urgency to start making habit shifts ASAP, if you bite off more than you can chew, you'll burn out quickly (aka eco-fatigue). Start with one area of your home, like the bathroom or kitchen. Pick one or two habits to shift. Once you've gotten those under your belt, add another. It may take a year before your family has found a week's worth of plant-based recipes everyone can agree on, or your bathroom has evolved into a fully plastic-free zone. Stick with it. In time, meaningful transformations will occur.

MY DAILY DOSE

Set a regular time each morning (when you wake up, brush your teeth, make coffee, etc.) to go through your Daily Dose exercise. You can choose to write in a journal or simply do it in your head. Begin by closing your eyes and take three slow breaths before answering the following:

Today, I am grateful for _____.
My one eco-intention for the day is to _____
_____.

I will _____ (smile, do a mental touchdown dance, etc.) each time I do my eco-action to help reinforce the steps I am taking to make the planet a safer and healthier place for my children and others. One way I will care for myself today is _____
_____.

At the end of the exercise, take a final deep breath before starting your day.

---

03 | SUSTAIN

The majority of our unsustainable tendencies lie in our habits. As you start this journey, be intentional about the patterns and day-to-day regimes you set. Remember, sustainability is an everyday practice, not a destination. Here are three easy ways to begin building a well-rooted *green* routine.

Set a Daily Eco-Intention. Setting a daily eco-intention is a way to ground yourself and keep your plans on track. It could be small, like remembering to bring your reusable tote to the grocery store. Or it could be something larger, like sticking to an eco-family bite-size challenge. Whatever the size of the shift you're working on, giving yourself a moment each day to set your goal will help it stick.

Do What Excites You. Work together as a family to focus actions around everyone's interests. Do your kids love to bake? Focus on plant-based recipes. Are you a bunch of bookworms? Check out books from your library or get them secondhand. Passionate about your job? Focus on integrating climate action at work. Whatever you love, bringing sustainability to your interests will help fuel and sustain you.

Celebrate. Washing clothes in cold water or turning out the lights when you leave the room may not be typical sources of excitement. Yet, pausing and throwing yourself a tiny mental celebration for your earth-friendly deeds will help the action stick while reinforcing that your small steps are connected to something greater. Whether it's an imaginary touchdown dance, throwing mental confetti, or simply a smile, celebrating even the tiniest eco-shifts fuels your brain to keep going.

Bust Burnout

Life happens, and unless you have a regular self-care practice and solid community support around you, burnout can take you down before you know what's happened. Caring for yourself might feel like it should be separate from your sustainability journey, but your physical and mental health are part of the eco-equation. Ultimately, sustainability is building healthy structures and systems for both humanity and the earth.

Just like on a plane, you must put on your oxygen mask before you can help others. Healthy self-care habits are your safety device—and essential tools for this lifestyle. When burnout starts to creep in or you're ready to toss in your eco-friendly towel, the following actions can keep you feeling charged and motivated:

Focus on Self-Care. Sustainable living requires us to care for ourselves. Focus on the basics like eating well, getting enough sleep, meditating, mindfulness, seeing friends, spending time with your partner (if you have one), taking in the awe of nature, reading a book, and exercising. Even if you haven't hit a wall yet, talking to a mental health professional can also be extremely helpful in avoiding burnout. (Therapy rocks, if you haven't tried it.) If your inner voice is screaming that you have too much on your plate and don't have a minute to spare for self-care, then it's even more essential to weave some into your earth-saving routine. (I'd recommend starting with Eco-Action 38 for some TLC.)

> "You have two homes, Earth and your body. Take care of them."
>
> **—UNKNOWN**

Think Collectively. If you're feeling down because your actions seem too tiny in the grand scheme of things, remember the bigger picture. Your individual deeds may appear to be a drop in the bucket, but when you put everyone's efforts together, the bucket overflows. That is the collective footprint. If you need help reconnecting, plug yourself in to your local eco-community. A Gallup global study involving 150 countries found that engaging in the area in which you live is one of the five essential elements of well-being. Collective care can also be a form of self-care.

Go Back to the Basics. If you feel like too much is on your plate, it's time to scale back. Keep doing the sustainable tasks that feel manageable and let go of the ones causing you to feel overwhelmed. It may seem like you are taking two steps back, but pausing to regroup will give you the charge to keep moving forward. Stay focused on the changes you *can* make and what you are doing.

Find an Eco-Buddy. Find someone outside of your household to buddy up with for this adventure. This will keep you activated and accountable and provide a resource to exchange tips and tricks. Plus, it's nice to have someone to vent to about mishaps and frustrations. Sign up to attend workshops and seminars monthly or quarterly together. Make plans to check out your local flea market or set a weekly duo-family date to meet up at the farmer's market.

Let It Go. Be gentle with yourself (and others) along this journey. Try not to look at your "mistakes" as bad. Instead, take them as moments of learning and move forward. Getting fixated on "errors" will keep you stuck in a cycle of guilt, getting you nowhere.

Rebuild Hope. Hope is radical, particularly when the media are biased toward reporting only bad news. When you're feeling hopeless, anxious, or unmotivated, seek out other change makers. Listen to their podcasts, watch their documentaries, read their articles and books, or follow them on social media. Be conscious of surrounding yourself with the voices of people and businesses doing inspirational, positive work. Their actions will remind you of the impact one person can make and that change is possible.

> "Hope is often misunderstood. People think it is simply passive wishful thinking. This is the opposite of real hope, which requires action and engagement."
>
> **—JANE GOODALL**
> *primatologist, anthropologist, conservationist, and mother*

04 | INCLUDE

As part of your sustainability journey, it's essential to make space for others. You may find that family and friends are at different points in their eco-experience—and likely some with no interest at all. Don't let it get you down. There are simple ways to keep others included while still expanding our ideas of how people can find their place in this movement.

Onboarding Family

While you might be eager to jump into sustainable living today, other family members may have trouble adjusting to the idea. Children, who are guided by our choices, are more likely to follow your lead. Even rebellious teens may be inclined to join your efforts, given their generation's significant concern about the environment and their future. In truth, partners tend to be the most challenging to get on board. Time and time again, I hear that a partner is digging in their heels, or at least not ready to make the switch on some unsustainable habits. If this is the case for you, don't fret. Here are some tried and tested tips to get family involved while guiding with compassion.

Lead by Example. If someone in your family started preaching a new lifestyle to you, would you immediately jump on board? Probably not. But when you *show* family members how positive change can occur without turning their lives upside down, they're more likely to adapt.

Avoid Being a Sustainability Shamer. No one is perfect, and there isn't one way to be perfectly *green*. If family members are trying but aren't being sustainable enough for your standards, remember that they're learning and growing too. Celebrate their efforts and good intentions. Keep your criticisms to yourself, and instead model alternative ways to be eco-friendly without disparaging comments. Getting mad, nagging, or lecturing will likely push others away. Inclusion is key. Respect that your partners' and children's choices are theirs to make. Just as yours are yours.

Find a Middle Ground. While you may be ready to give up plastic forever, your partner or children might not be as eager. If they push back, find a compromise like keeping some of their favorite foods that come in plastic on the grocery list. Your family might not want to make every swap or dive in 100%, but you can likely find common ground.

Make It Appealing. Is your partner a coffee lover? Put a reusable coffee filter in the coffee maker as a morning surprise. Are they a movie buff? Watch a *green* documentary together. Do they love meat? Order it from a regenerative, carbon sequestering ranch. Introducing sustainable solutions for their interests or needs can help your partner navigate their way into this new lifestyle.

Focus on You. In the end, you can only control your own choices. Even if everyone isn't willing to make all of the changes you're striving toward, your shifts still have an impact. From what you eat to what you wear, you hold the power to make your own sustainable decisions.

Level the Workload. If you're in a relationship and get stuck with the majority of household tasks or child-rearing responsibilities, asking a partner to step it up sustainably might feel completely unrealistic. If the domestic workload is unbalanced in your home, see Eco-Action 37 for recommendations on where to turn for effective tools to reset the lopsided loads.

For tips on navigating grandparents, see page 118.

CONFESSIONS FROM THE SPOUSE OF A SUSTAINABILITY FANATIC
A Q&A WITH MY HUSBAND

My husband was not an eco-devotee before we began our sustainability journey. Sure, he recycled and understood the importance of not trashing the earth, but he never intended to live a full-on sustainable life. It was solely my eco–life crisis that got him set on this path. I want to offer his perspective on our *green* existence.

Q. *How did you feel when I told you I was going to start living more sustainably and that I hoped we could do it as a family?*
A. It seemed really daunting, like it would be a big undertaking. It felt like it would be unachievable and like we would have to change our whole lives, but I was willing to give it a go.

Q. *Do you feel like that's what happened? And how does it feel now?*

A. That's not what it feels like now, and it hasn't felt overwhelming along the way. Some things were more challenging to shift than others, but now life just feels normal. The more you do it, the easier it gets.

Q. *What are some of the swaps you've made that have felt easy?*

A. My coffee filter (single-use paper to a reusable one), my razor (plastic to refillable single-blade stainless steel), and my toothbrush (plastic to bamboo).

Q. *What felt harder to change?*

A. It took a little while to navigate buying package-free foods from the bulk bins, but it was fine once I figured it out. I actually really enjoy grocery shopping now. It also took me a while to break the habit of using ziplock bags. I have about three that I've been using on rotation for a year now. I just wash and hang-dry them between uses.

Q. *How is it living with someone so enthusiastic about sustainability?*

A. I like that we do it now, and it's nice to think that we're doing our part. I probably wouldn't be quite so active (or have dived in so deep) if it weren't for you, though.

Q. *What advice would you give to someone trying to get their partner to start a sustainable household with them?*

A. Be patient with each other and the process. It doesn't have to happen overnight. It takes time. One thing I learned along the way is you don't have to be doing it 100% perfectly, even though you're striving for that. It's a process.

Talk. Talk. Talk.

Talk to friends and extended family about the shifts you're making. Know your audience, and begin with those who will be receptive and encouraging. (You can get to your climate-denying aunt later down the road.) Keep an open dialogue about the issues facing our planet and the actions you're taking. It may sound small, but talking about the problems and solutions helps promote social change, shifts norms, and influences those around you.

One Size Does Not Fit All

There isn't one way to live sustainably. No two eco-journeys will look the same—even for two families living next door to each other. Factors such as access, income, time, race, physical ability, and health can impact one's capacity to make changes. Understanding your privileges and constraints will help you navigate your journey while also releasing you of any shame or guilt you might feel for not being able to make specific changes. Alternatively, because everyone's situation is different, we must also realize that another family's ability or inability to do certain things cannot be a reflection of what we should or should not be doing. Recognizing that all individuals who are doing this work are on their own paths toward the same goal can help us support one another. That way, we can create space for *all* people to join the movement, assist others along their journey, and avoid marginalization. Everyone's unique place in the world offers a thousand possibilities for meaningful change.

THE ECO-ACTIONIST MANIFESTO

10 standards to strive for

_____

01. PEOPLE ARE PRIMARY

I will center people as part of my environmental journey by prioritizing human rights and the health and safety of myself and others. I will aim to support businesses that elevate those who are underrepresented and do not discriminate or exploit workers' rights.

02. PRIORITIZE THE PLANET

Just as I consider my time and money when making choices, I will also consider my environmental impact before making decisions.

03. PART WITH DAMAGING PATTERNS

I will look at my lifestyle choices and consumer habits to find ways to make sustainable shifts where possible.

04. PROGRESS OVER PERFECTION

I will not try to be perfect. Instead, I will celebrate my progress and successes and recognize that inescapable stumbles will always be part of the journey.

05. PERSISTENCE IS PARAMOUNT

I will approach sustainable living with persistence.

06. PACE YOURSELF

I will pace myself by setting realistic goals. Once I feel comfortable with the changes I have made, I will continue to add more.

07. PATIENCE

I will have patience with myself and others. I won't sustainability-shame individuals but instead will find ways to listen, support, include, and assist them, if requested. There isn't one way to live sustainably, and I will do my best to care for myself and support others in the process.

08. POINT THE WAY

I will lead by example, through words, intentions, and actions, both in my home and in my community. I will strive to hold companies and politicians accountable for their unsustainable acts.

09. POUR LABELS DOWN THE DRAIN

I will not get stuck on labels such as zero waste, vegetarian, vegan, plastic-free, or eco-actionist. I will not let labels stand in the way of making change. I understand that there are no established rules to living sustainably, but I will strive to make positive changes within my capacity.

10. PARTICIPATE WITH MY STRENGTHS

I will use my unique strengths, talents, interests, and abilities to ripple change outside my daily life.

PART II
THE ECO-ACTIONIST
AGENDA

THE ECO-ACTIONIST AGENDA:

Breaking down five essential areas
of your family's life to uncover practical,
powerful ways to heal the world around you.

BENEFITS

FIGHTS
- Climate change
- Plastic
- Pollution
- Waste

SAVES
- Time
- Money
- Wildlife
- Electricity
- Water
- Food
- Forests

REDUCES
- Harmful toxins in your home
- Microplastics
- Stress
- Clutter

SUPPORTS
- Human rights
- Your family's health
- A healthy diet
- Community
- Self-care

CREATE YOUR OWN FAMILY PLAN
A personalized place to begin

___

Develop a sustainable-living road map specifically for your family by selecting *one* eco-action from each of the following Eco-Actionist Agenda categories.

Home
Eco-Action No. _____

Stuff
Eco-Action No. _____

Body
Eco-Action No. _____

Food
Eco-Action No. _____

Community
Eco-Action No. _____

Bonus
Our first Eco-Family Bite-Size Challenge will be:_____

Eco-Family Tips:

✓ Choose actions that make sense for your family and are doable within your family's budget and time constraints.

✓ While the whole family can get involved, assign one family member to take the lead and spearhead each eco-action.

✓ Focus at least two of your selections on high-level climate impact. (Look for *The Climate Crew* seal.)

THE CLIMATE CREW

✓ After deciding on your eco-actions, take on one at a time. It can take anywhere from a few days to a month to feel like you've gotten everything down and are ready to move on to the next action.

✓ This worksheet is just a starting place. You can, of course, choose more than one eco-action per category and mix and match to make it your own.

HOME

UTILITIES

It's time to change your energy and create a more efficient home to fight climate change, preserve resources, and save money.

CLIMATE CRISIS 101

WHAT IS CLIMATE CHANGE?

Climate change is defined as the shift in weather patterns, such as rainfall and average temperatures, over a long period of time. Historically, the term *climate change* has been used to define naturally occurring phenomena, such as cooling and warming periods, which have occurred every 100,000 years or so for at least the last one million years. In the past 650,000 years, scientists can see that this normal phenomenon has occurred seven times. However, the current period of climate change we have entered looks different from anything the Earth has seen before.

A BRIEF SCIENCE LESSON

We've Got Gas. Greenhouse gases occur naturally and create a "blanket" around the Earth, keeping us not too hot and not too cold. However, when fossil fuels are burned, they release additional carbon dioxide into the atmosphere. Other heat-trapping greenhouse gases emitted through human mismanagement include methane, nitrous oxide, and fluorinated gases. These "extra," human-generated greenhouse gases throw things off balance, trapping heat from the sun, which in turn causes the surface temperature of the Earth to rise.

It's Getting Hot in Here. Why is this period of climate change worse than previous occurrences? Currently, the Earth's atmosphere is heating 100 times faster than in prior warming periods, with carbon dioxide increasing more than 250 times faster than it did from natural occurrences during the last period of climate change, 11,700 years ago. Additionally, if you look back at the peaks of atmospheric carbon levels over the last 650,000 years (which scientists can do by studying glacial ice cores and sediment), researchers can see that carbon dioxide in the atmosphere peaked at 300 parts per million (or less). In 1950 we reached that peak. In the 70 years since, we've dramatically exceeded that amount, to over 400 parts per million.

Due to human activity, the planet's average surface temperature has already risen 2.14°F (1.19°C) since the late 1800s. Warming has accelerated in the past 40 years, with the most recent years being the warmest on record. A few degrees might not sound like a lot, but when you compare it to our bodies, you can see how a few degrees can make a big difference. When humans run 2.14°F warmer, we have a 100.7°F fever (and feel like crap). The same is true for the earth. A .5°C increase in global temperatures means the difference between losing all of the world's coral reefs (if we rise 2°C) and being able to save 10–30% of them (if we rise only 1.5°C). And thus, every fraction of a degree counts.

THE TIME TO ACT IS NOW

Emergency Situation. Byproducts of climate change include extreme weather-related disasters, changes in weather patterns, biodiversity loss, warming oceans, melting glaciers, rising sea levels, increased disease, ecosystem collapse, and more—all of which compromise human infrastructure, agriculture, transportation, energy, and our health (essentially our capacity to survive). The bad news? It's already too late to prevent climate change entirely. It's happening.

But don't panic! The good news is that we have not yet hit the point of no return; we can still stop the worst-case scenario, but the clock is ticking. We have a few critical years to shift our direction. NOW is the time to act, before it's too late.

All Hands on Deck. To stop climate change in its tracks, we must reduce our greenhouse gas emissions to net zero. (Net zero is removing greenhouse gases from the atmosphere in amounts equal to those we contribute to the atmosphere.) Scientists internationally agree that by 2030 we must reduce emissions of all seven types of greenhouse gas globally by 45% and reach net zero by 2050 to maintain a habitable planet for future generations. Companies, businesses, and governments can all adopt a net-zero policy. The strategy involves clear infrastructure changes to reduce emissions drastically, counterbalance any emissions that cannot be eliminated, and set science-based targets to reach the goal of net zero by 2050. With the clock ticking, our collective actions, now more than ever, will impact our children's future and that of all human existence.

Where to Focus. Reducing plastics can impact our fight against climate change, but it's not the main driver. The burning of fossil fuels and changes in land use are most responsible for global emissions. These emissions are produced through electricity and heat production (25%), agriculture and forest/land use (24%), transportation (14%), buildings (6%), and industry (21%); a combo of smaller drivers make up the final 10% of the pie. In terms of our daily lives, that means looking at how much we buy, our energy usage—including how we heat and cool our homes—the food we choose to eat, our method of transport, etc. And on a grander scale, it means urging your town or city to adopt a net-zero policy; speaking out about gaining access to renewable energy; petitioning for curbside composting, bike lanes, and electric public transportation in your community; focusing on environmental justice; and so much more. As we build toward a greener future, we must also stay cognizant of protecting biodiversity, ecosystems, and indigenous land as we shift to electric vehicles, put up solar panels, and decrease our reliance on those nasty fossil fuels, as it's all interconnected.

DID YOU KNOW?

Americans make up **5%** of the world's population but consume **16%** of the world's energy.

About **37%** of all carbon dioxide emissions in the United States comes from electricity—making it a major contributor to climate change.

ECO-ACTION NO. 1
Shift Your Energy

Switching your electricity bill to renewable energy is a big way to reduce your family's carbon footprint. Depending upon where you live, it can cost less than you think!

WHAT IS RENEWABLE ENERGY?

Renewable energy (or *green energy*), such as wind, solar, or hydro, is naturally recurring and is not depleted when used. As long as the sun shines, the waves break, and the wind blows, renewable energy cannot run out. Comparatively, fossil fuels like oil, coal, or natural gas come from a limited resource—the remains of decomposing organisms underground. In 2019, the burning of fossil fuels for energy (electricity, heating our homes, driving our cars, flying, shipping goods, etc.) accounted for 73% of total greenhouse gas emissions in the United States.

FLIP THE SWITCH FROM FOSSIL FUELS

In recent years, renewable energy has had a massive surge. At least 50% of Americans now have the option to sign up for green energy, and soon more will too. In cities like San Francisco, the average cost of green energy is about $1.23 more a month. In the coming years, we should see the price of green energy drop below what you're currently paying for fossil fuel–derived energy—and signing up now is one way you can help support the transition. Switch your energy bill today to support the decarbonization of our energy grid! And if you own your home, consider adding solar panels, which are eligible for a federal tax credit until the end of 2032.

ECO-ACTION NO. 2
Be Energy Efficient

Residential energy is responsible for 20% of greenhouse gas emissions in the United States. And the larger your home, the bigger your carbon footprint. Understanding how your family uses energy and what appliances draw the most power will help you adopt energy-saving habits to fight climate change.

KNOW YOUR POWER: CHANGE YOUR HABITS

Upgrade Your Thermostat. Because heating can account for 43% of your home's energy use, becoming a heat-saving hotshot helps the planet and saves you money on your utility bill. Adding an ENERGY STAR smart thermostat to your home adjusts your usage to reflect your family's daily schedule rather than just being on automatically for certain periods of the day, saving money and energy in the long run.

Light It Right. You wouldn't leave the room while the faucet was running. We should be thinking of energy the same way and turn off the lights when we're not using them. Lighting can account for 14% of your energy bill, so in addition to flipping the switch, don't forget to swap out energy-hogging incandescent bulbs for LED ENERGY STAR–certified ones.

DID YOU KNOW?
Our electronic devices use energy when they're not in use. In fact, **75%** of all energy that a device consumes occurs when it's switched off.

Block Vampires. Did you know you that 23% of your electricity bill could be powering electronics and appliances that are turned off or are idle? Nearly half of plugged-in devices draw power even when they're not on. These are called *vampire devices* because they're always sucking energy. According to the *New York Times*, "devices that are 'off' or in standby or sleep mode can use up to the equivalent of 50 large power plants' worth of electricity and cost more than $19 billion in electricity bills every year."

To detect these vampires, check the charger or plug. If it's warm to the touch, even when it isn't in use, it's likely sucking energy. Common culprits are TVs, cable boxes, plugged-in charging devices (after it's charged), game consoles, coffeemakers, printers, DVD players, scanners, and electronics with a standby light or clock.

Simply unplugging devices when they're not in use is a way to stop *phantom power* from occurring. Using a power strip to group devices together is a quick way to halt the power drain. When used correctly, adding smart plugs, like timer switches that can be controlled from your phone, to energy-inefficient appliances and electronics can save you up to 5% on your energy bill.

Ditch the Draft. Are you wasting heat in the winter and cool air in the summer? Typical areas of temperature loss in homes are windows, doors, roofs, walls, and power outlets. If you're a homeowner, there are inexpensive steps you can take to seal and insulate your home that will have money-saving benefits over time. Even an act as simple as closing the damper in your fireplace when it's not in use can reduce your overall energy consumption. (Keeping the damper ajar is the same as having a window open 24/7—and because heat rises, the toasty warm air from your heater goes straight up the chimney.) You can also add weatherstripping to the damper to make it airtight.

ECO-FAMILY TIP
Take Advantage of Rebates. Americans may be eligible for up to $10,000 in climate tax breaks and rebates through the 2022 Inflation Reduction Act. From energy-efficient appliances to solar panels and electric vehicles, if you're looking to upgrade your home while lowering your electricity and heating bill, be sure to tap into those deductions and kickbacks.

ECO–FAMILY BITE–SIZE CHALLENGE

BECOME ENERGY-SAVING EXPERTS

As a family, pick two tasks from each category (six total) to kick off your energy-saving challenge:

GREEN

- ○ Bundle up with a blanket, sweater, or slippers to avoid using the heater.
- ○ For homes with multiple rooms, use an ENERGY STAR space heater to heat just the room you're in instead of heating the whole house.
- ○ Use the elements. During the day, open the curtains and use sunlight instead of switching on the lights. Open windows to cool your home in warmer months instead of relying on AC.
- ○ Turn off lights when you're not in the room.
- ○ Unplug devices not in use.
- ○ Turn off your desktop computer at night.
- ○ Use a lid when boiling water or reheating food on the stove. It saves energy and shortens cook time.

GREENER

- ○ Switch to ENERGY STAR lightbulbs.
- ○ Close your fireplace damper when not in use.
- ○ Use power strips or smart plugs to switch off energy to multiple devices.
- ○ Add window treatments, such as curtains or blinds, to reduce heat loss in the winter and keep rooms shaded and cooler in the summer.
- ○ Use your ceiling fan. Because they can reduce a room's temperature up to four degrees, you can raise the temperature of your air conditioner to use less energy overall.
- ○ Don't run major appliances (heater, AC, washing machine, dryer, etc.) during peak hours to reduce fossil fuel usage and save money on your energy bill. Peak hours vary depending upon where you live, so check with your local energy provider (they tend to be on weekdays from around 4 p.m. to 9 p.m.).

GREENEST

- ○ Switch to *green* energy.
- ○ Install a smart thermostat.
- ○ Audit your home for air leaks and seal or insulate areas of loss.
- ○ When replacing appliances, purchase ENERGY STAR–certified ones.

ECO-ACTION NO. 3
Be a Water Winner

Clean drinking water is crucial to our survival. And yet, with climate change increasing the severity and frequency of drought in the United States and abroad, it's imperative that we use water wisely. We Americans waste more than we realize. *The average American family of four uses 300 gallons of water a day—with approximately 95% of that going down the drain.*

We can save a significant amount of H_2O by becoming conscious of our habits and swapping out inefficient hardware. Reducing water usage isn't as difficult, inconvenient, or costly as it sounds. Your appliances can do a lot of the work for you.

WATER-WISE SWAPS

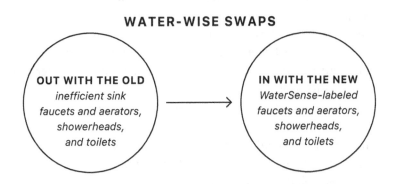

OUT WITH THE OLD
inefficient sink faucets and aerators, showerheads, and toilets

IN WITH THE NEW
WaterSense-labeled faucets and aerators, showerheads, and toilets

	COST SAVINGS	H$_2$0 SAVINGS	PURCHASE COST
WATER-SAVING SHOWERHEAD	**$70 / year** *in energy and water costs*	2,700 gallons / year	**$10+**
SINK AERATOR *renter-friendly swap*	**$250 / lifetime** *in energy and water costs*	700 gallons / year	**$2+**
LOW-FLOW TOILET	**$130 / year** *in water costs*	13,000 gallons / year	**$89+**
ENERGY STAR DISHWASHER	**$40 / year +** **10% energy savings** *and gain 230 hours a year not washing dishes*	5,000 gallons / year	**$400+**

THE WATER-WISE HABIT CHECKLIST

○ **Teach Kids Sink Responsibility.** Remind kids to turn off the faucet while brushing their teeth and lathering up while washing hands.

○ **Toilet Tricks.** If you don't own your home or don't have the budget to replace your toilets to low-flow, fill a glass jar or sealed plastic bottle (with a few rocks in it to weigh it down) with water and place it in your toilet tank. Doing so displaces water and tricks the toilet into using less water for every flush. A family of four can save up to 50 gallons a week. Be sure to test it to make sure the toilet functions correctly or if you need to try a different-size jar.

○ **Stop Doing Dishes.** Doing the dishes by hand is a time drain and takes 27 gallons of water a day compared to the 2.5 gallons it takes an ENERGY STAR dishwasher. Remember to scrape off food (instead of rinsing) before putting dishes in the rack and to run full loads to keep water usage down.

○ **Skip the Bath.** The average five-minute shower uses 10 to 25 gallons of water, while a bath, depending upon the size of your tub, takes 40 to 110 gallons—so choosing to shower is a water- and money-saving win.

○ **Shorter Showers.** Five fewer minutes of shower time could save you 10+ gallons of water.

○ **Recycle Household Water.** Do you need to wait a while for your hot water to show up? Keep a bowl under the faucet to collect running water and use it to water plants.

○ **Fix Leaks.** According to the EPA, 10% of homes have a leak that wastes 90 or more gallons a day.

○ **Head to the Car Wash.** Taking your car to the car wash instead of doing it at home can save up to 50 gallons of water. Plus, it keeps soap, which can be harmful to wildlife, from going down the storm drain.

Also see Eco-Action 13 for water-saving gardening tips.

DID YOU KNOW?

Collectively, American households needlessly waste nearly **1 trillion gallons** from leaks each year—enough water to supply **11 million homes.**

Saving water isn't just about reducing waste; it's about saving energy. Water heating accounts for about **20%** of your home's energy usage.

TRASH + RECYCLING

The solution to ending wasteful habits begins by looking in your trash can.

ECO-ACTION NO. 4

Take a Trash Tally

THREE STEPS TO LESS WASTE

In addition to wasting water and energy, our homes are also large sources of trash. Pausing and taking stock of what actually ends up in your garbage and recycling bins can help you identify areas to start reducing waste and look for sustainable alternatives.

01. Tally. Before taking your bins to the curb this week, grab a pen and make a list of all the trash and recycling your family generated over the past seven days. Are there a lot of take-out containers? How about food packaging? Single-use disposables like plastic wrap and paper towels? Bathroom trash like shampoo bottles, floss, and tampon wrappers? Noticing what's in there will shed light on areas where you're creating the most waste and give you a place to start making changes. And don't forget to get the kids involved!

DID YOU KNOW?

Americans make up just **5%** of the Earth's population but create **50%** of the globe's solid waste.

In the United States, landfills are the **third-largest source** of methane gas. Methane is a greenhouse gas **34 times** more powerful than carbon and a contributor to climate change.

OUR FAMILY TRASH TALLY

Recycling		Compostable/Organic Material	
Item	*Qty*	*Item*	*Qty*

Landfill		Needs a New Home	
Item	*Qty*	*Item*	*Qty*

02. Define. What generated the most trash and recycling? Was it food packaging? Perhaps online shopping boxes? Use the eco-actions listed throughout the book to help you reduce waste in these areas.

03. Continue. Once you feel like you've got your first eco-action down, refer back to your trash tally worksheet and take on the next area on the list. A bonus to reducing your trash and recycling is that you will eventually be able to reduce the size of your curbside cans, saving you money on your monthly waste disposal bill.

ECO-ACTION NO. 5
Stop Recycling (So Much)

Recycling has many benefits. It reduces how much is sent to landfills, conserves natural resources, saves energy, and provides jobs. However, we are currently in a recycling crisis. In total, 91% of all plastic doesn't get recycled, and even when it does, it can only be recycled one to three times before it's trash. So while you may assume that your recyclables are being turned into a new product, there is a good chance they're ending up in the landfill. What's the solution? Reduce and recycle right.

REDUCE YOUR RECYCLING

While recycling is an essential step in limiting what ends up in the landfill, it should be looked at as a last resort. Refusing, reducing, reusing, and composting are critical and often overlooked first steps in curbing how much we toss out. Building on the "five Rs" of zero waste developed by environmentalist and author Bea Johnson, the Sustainability Scale on the next page outlines seven simple measures to limit what you throw away.

THE SUSTAINABILITY SCALE:
How to Reduce Waste Responsibly

Greenest

 Refuse. Say no up front, particularly to single-use items. Doing so can significantly reduce the amount of trash and recycling you generate.

 Reduce. Before purchasing anything (food, clothing, toys, toiletries), ask yourself, "Do I really need this?" If the answer is no, move on.

 Reuse. Reuse items you already own; opt for reusables; and borrow, mend, and repurpose items instead of throwing them out.

 Repair. Repair clothing and household items to avoid tossing anything usable in the trash.

 Rot. Composting is essential to fighting climate change. Food waste is a major contributor, so it's critical to keep it out of the landfill.

 Recycle. Recycling properly will help ensure that items you toss in your recycling bin are actually recycled.

 Rubbish. After following the first six steps, there should be very little in your trash can. It might not be empty, but there should be significantly less than what you are currently sending to the landfill.

Last Resort

RECYCLE RIGHT: END WISHCYCLING

Wishcycling, or wishful recycling, is what happens when someone puts something in the recycling bin with the *hope* it can be recycled. Some commonly wishcycled items include paper towels, pizza boxes, takeout containers, and coffee cups. None of these can be recycled. Wishcycling is a problem because many of the items we throw with hope into our recycling bins contaminate the recycling system, making everything in the container impossible to process (it becomes trash).

The Green Rule:
When in doubt, throw it out.

If you're unsure if something is rubbish or recycling, it's best to throw it in the trash to avoid contaminating the recycling. However, contamination isn't the only issue. Plastic bags, hangers, and electronic cords can break sorting machinery, adding to costs and contributing to the closure of recycling centers. Educating your family on what can be recycled is crucial to keeping sustainable systems up and operating. While capabilities vary depending upon your municipality, here are some basic guidelines.

RECYCLING: DO'S + DON'TS

DO
✓ **Check your local program** to see what is recyclable in your area.
✓ **Sort** your recyclables if required by your municipality.
✓ **Rinse** your recyclables and let them dry thoroughly, so the moisture doesn't contaminate the other recyclables, such as paper, in the bin.
✓ **Break down cardboard boxes.**
✓ **Separate soft plastics** like plastic bags and plastic film packaging. Remember to reuse what you can first. Then, put all soft plastics into a larger plastic shopping bag, so they're contained. Recycle the bundle curbside (if accepted in your area) or drop it off at a collection point (bins can often be found outside major grocery stores).
✓ **Roll your aluminum** into a baseball-sized ball. If it's smaller, the sorting machine won't pick it up. Collect pieces until you have enough to make a fist-sized ball before recycling.

DON'T

✗ **Don't crush your cans.** Check with your local municipality to confirm that it's okay to crush with their system. A flattened can often confuses sorting machines, and they accidentally get separated with paper.

✗ **Don't "wishcycle."** If you don't know where an item goes, it's better to throw it away than risk contaminating your recycling.

✗ **Don't bag it.** Plastic garbage bags are not recyclable. Instead, place recyclables directly in your collection bin.

✗ **Don't recycle wet or food- or grease-stained paper.** It's contaminated and cannot be recycled. It should be composted; otherwise, it's trash.

HOW MANY TIMES CAN IT BE RECYCLED?	
Glass	Infinitely
Plastic	1–3 times
Paper	5–7 times
Metals & Aluminum	Infinitely

ECO-FAMILY TIP

Head to earth911.com to search how to recycle specialty items such as computers, batteries, packing peanuts, and construction materials in your area. Additionally, check with your local Best Buy about their electronic and appliance recycling program.

CLEANING

A healthier planet also means a healthier family. By swapping out harmful cleaning products, you are taking care of yourself, your family, and the earth.

VOLATILE ORGANIC COMPOUNDS 101

WHAT ARE VOCS?

The EPA highlights volatile organic compounds (VOCs) as a major contributor to harmful indoor air quality. VOCs, which can be carcinogenic, evaporate at room temperature from products such as household sprays and cleaners, air fresheners, perfumes, dry-cleaned clothes, furniture, rugs, mattresses, building materials, and paints. You know those "new car" and "fresh carpet" smells? They're off-gassing VOCs. VOCs don't always have a scent, however, so they can be difficult to detect. VOCs can range from "very" to "semivolatile" organic compounds and include formaldehyde, ethanol, acetone, butane, phthalates, fire retardants, and 1,4 dioxane. In addition to creating indoor air pollution, VOCs contribute to smog formation outdoors. Studies have shown that VOC emissions, specifically from consumer and industrial products, in densely populated areas are equal to the ozone pollution levels of fossil fuels. (Say whaaaat? Yes, perfume and cleaning products contribute to air pollution!)

YOUR FAMILY'S HEALTH

VOCs come with a whole host of health issues. Short-term exposure can cause headaches; irritation of the eye, nose, and throat; nausea and vomiting; dizziness; or worsening asthma symptoms. Long-term exposure can lead to cancer, organ damage, and central nervous system damage. Children, especially young children, are particularly vulnerable to health complications associated with VOCs. And because babies and toddlers spend more time on the ground and put objects in their mouth, they tend be exposed to higher levels of VOCs than adults. Studies have found that children exposed to VOCs are more likely to develop eczema, asthma, and hay fever than children who had less exposure. With the average American spending 90% of their time inside, perhaps it's time to rethink what we bring into our homes. (And it probably wouldn't hurt us to get outdoors more, either.)

HOW IS YOUR FAMILY EXPOSED?

Cleaning Supplies. VOCs can be found in spray cleaners, bleach, furniture polish, glass cleaner, air and carpet fresheners, floor cleaner, dishwasher detergent, oven cleaners, toilet bowl cleaners, and more.

Laundry. A University of Washington study found 133 VOCs (averaging 17 per product) in the top-25-selling laundry products, including detergents, fabric softeners, dryer sheets, and stain removers.

Personal Care Products. Smooth and silky shampoo and conditioner, scented body lotion and deodorant, your synthetic perfume—these are just a few examples of how VOCs show up in personal care products. In a 2018 study, researchers tested 42 products, 21 of which made claims of being "green," "organic," or "all-natural." Of those tested, 684 VOCs were found, 207 of which are classified as potentially hazardous under federal regulations. Yet only 5% of the VOCs were listed on the ingredient label.

Clothing. VOCs such as fire retardants and formaldehyde can be found in kids' clothing.

Furniture. Pressed wood (like plywood and particle board), which is often found in build-it-yourself furniture, can off-gas formaldehyde, a known carcinogen.

Plastic Food Storage. Lunch boxes, sippy cups, plastic food packaging, and soft plastic single-use baggies can all contain VOCs. The worst offenders are plastic #1, #3, and #7.

Toys. Pressed wood; plastic; fabric; or painted, lacquered toys can all contain VOCs depending upon how they're manufactured.

Carpets + Rugs. Carpets and rugs tend to off-gas because of their fiber treatments, adhesives, backings, carpet padding, and installation tape and glues.

Paints. While a fresh coat of paint can perk up a room, certain paints can also release harmful VOCs in your living areas.

ECO-ACTION NO. 6
Do a Cleaning Detox

INDOOR AIR POLLUTION

We all want to create a safe home for our children to grow and thrive. However, study after study shows that many of the chemicals found in traditional home cleaning, sanitizing, and disinfecting products are harmful to our families' health and the environment. Note that "the environment" doesn't refer only to outdoor ecosystems; it also refers to the indoor air quality of your home. According to the University of California San Francisco, indoor air pollutant levels are often two to five times worse—and in some cases 100 times worse—than outside air. Children are particularly susceptible to these pollutants, many coming from cleaning supplies.

TAKE A BREATH OF FRESH AIR

Download a clean product finder such as the Environmental Working Group's Healthy Living app to scan a product's bar code and learn more about the environmental and health risks associated with the cleaners you use in your home. Just because a product says it's "green," "organic," or "natural" does not mean it's free of harmful VOCs.

--- DID YOU KNOW? ---

Indoor plants can help improve the air quality inside your home. Ask your local nursery which indoor plants are kid- and pet-safe.

A CLEANER CLEAN TOOL KIT

While there are a number of family-safe cleaning products on the market, homemade cleaning products cost less and are just as effective. Making them can be as easy as adding two ingredients together—resulting in a healthier home.

Baking Soda. Baking soda possesses odor-absorbing and abrasive-cleaning capabilities.

Castile Soap. Castile (pronounced "kas-TEEL") soap is nontoxic and biodegradable and can be used for countless cleaning projects. Look for brands that are palm oil–free (or use sustainably sourced palm oil). If you don't want to buy it in plastic, get it in bar form and use your cheese grater to shave off the soap you need, then add water and go.

Distilled White Vinegar. Vinegar is a cleaning superstar, killing bacteria and cutting through grime, and it costs much less than traditional, toxic, brand-name cleaning products. It can be used diluted with water or full-strength. However, to retain its bacteria-killing properties it must contain at least 5% acetic acid. (Most distilled white vinegars are comprised of 5% acetic acid and 95% water.)

Lemons. Lemons are effective natural cleaners with acidic qualities, antibacterial properties, and a fresh scent.

Salt. Salt can do more than season your food. It's absorbent and a gentle abrasive, making it tough on stains.

For some of my favorite DIY cleaning recipes, head to motheringearthproject.com for a free download.

Note: All cleaning products, including homemade ones, should be stored in a locked cabinet away from children. Even when working with less-toxic products, it's still important to keep your spaces well ventilated when cleaning.

GREEN READS

———

NATURAL HOME CLEANING: OVER 100 WAYS TO CLEAN YOUR HOME NATURALLY
by Fern Green

LOW TOX LIFE
by Alexx Stuart

ECO-ACTION NO. 7
Clean Up Your Kitchen Sink

SCRAP YOUR SPONGE

Did you know that microplastics are shedding off your sponge and going directly into the ocean and possibly even your family's food? It's true. Conventional sponges are made of plastic, as are their scrubby tops, which shed tiny plastic particles. Additionally, sponges that boast odor-eliminating or antibacterial properties are sprayed with pesticides, including triclosan, which has been linked to environmental and health issues such as cancer and skin irritation.

It's time to use plastic- and toxin-free sponge alternatives that are tough on messes but also safe for your family and the planet.

✓ **Swedish Dishcloths.** Swedish dishcloths are super absorbent, can be washed in the dishwasher or washing machine, and last years. Because they dry quickly, they don't harbor bacteria like a wet cloth or sponge (or get stinky). Plus, they're compostable.

✓ **Cellulose Sponges.** Sponges made of cellulose have the same feel as a conventional sponge but are biodegradable and made from wood pulp or plant cellulose. When purchasing, check that it's 100% cellulose (compostable) because it may contain a nylon (aka plastic) filling. Also, be wary of scrubby topped sponges, as some use plastic.

✓ **Bamboo Pot Scraper.** A bamboo pot scraper cleans sticky, hard messes off pans and pots in an instant. (And they don't get gross and funky like the bristly side of sponges when cleaning caked-on food.) They last for years, are made from a renewable resource, and can be composted when they're worn out.

✓ **Dish Brushes.** Wooden dish brushes with natural fiber bristles come in a variety of shapes. You can find them with long and short handles, including ones with long scrubber necks designed for cleaning bottles. Brushes can be cleaned by soaking them for five minutes in distilled white vinegar or boiled in water to revive the bristles. Ones free of plastic or metal can be composted at the end of their lives.

BUY BETTER DISH SOAP

A shocking 65% of conventional dish soaps are rated D or F by the Environmental Working Group. Many contain known carcinogens and neurotoxins such as DEAs; MEAs; TEAs; 1,4 dioxane; dyes; formaldehyde; or phthalates that are linked to eye, nose, throat, and lung irritation, headaches, mood disorders, endocrine disruption, and even cancer. In addition to being bad for our health, many are harmful to the environment.

- ✗ **Don't Be Fooled.** Don't be deceived by soaps that claim to be "natural," "chemical-free," or "made from plants." Commercials with animals cleaned with dish soap after oil spills do not verify nontoxicity, either.
- ✓ **Find Safe Products.** To find safer soaps for your family and the environment, look for certified Safer Choice products on the US Environmental Protection Agency (EPA) website, or scan their bar code on EWG's Healthy Living app.
- ✓ **Try Castile.** Palm oil–free castile soap gets dishes clean but is also gentle on skin and the earth. For "plastic-free," try a dish soap bar. Just rub your sponge, cloth, or dish brush across the top of the soap.

🍃

ECO-ACTION NO. 8
Part Ways with Paper Towels + Napkins

As a nation, we are supporting the clear-cutting of carbon-sink rainforests, biodiversity habitats, and indigenous land in exchange for our single-use tissue products like paper towels. Americans buy more paper towels than all of the other countries in the world combined. And because composting is done sparingly and paper towels cannot be recycled, the majority of them end up in the landfill, emitting methane as they break down. So how does everyone else on the planet manage to wipe their hands and clean up spills and messes without reaching for a single sheet every time? The alternatives are simple, convenient, reusable, and drastically reduce waste.

A Personal Paper Towel Tale: When we first switched away from paper towels, I had a newborn and a toddler. I couldn't imagine life without my go-to paper towels, and I thought this shift would be impossible. We started by taking the roll off the counter and putting it in a drawer. Out of sight, out of mind. Within a few days of removing the paper towels, I never looked back. Over five years later, I can't even remember what I ever used a paper towel for (honestly!). I don't miss them or even think about them when spills or messes happen.

USE BETTER BASICS

Swap Out Your Paper Towel. There are many paper towel alternatives on the market. Different jobs can require different alternatives, so building a varied supply of options can help you meet any type of mess without reaching for a single-use sheet. Here are a few favorites:

- ✓ 100% cellulose sponge
- ✓ Swedish dishcloth
- ✓ Cloth rag
- ✓ Dish towel
- ✓ Cloth napkin
- ✓ Reusable paper towel

Nix Your Paper Napkin. Linen, hemp, or organic cotton napkins are best. Avoid synthetics—they're made of plastic. Cloth napkins can be an investment, but you'll save money over time. Using a freshly cleaned cloth napkin at every meal is unnecessary and wastes water and electricity, so be sure to wash cloth napkins only when needed. To identify whose napkin is whose, use different patterns or colors or a variety of napkin rings, or add a monogram. When your napkin's life has ended, turn the napkin into a rag. When it can no longer be used as a rag, compost it if it's made from 100% natural materials.

NOT READY TO MAKE THE SWITCH?

There are some instances when paper towels are more challenging to avoid than others (like patting raw chicken, or cleaning up pet accidents—especially if you don't have a washer and dryer close by). If you're not ready to give up paper towels or napkins entirely, consider making these smaller swaps to make your single-use habits more sustainable.

Don't Go All In. Keep some paper towels tucked away for the rare occasions when a reusable alternative doesn't fit the bill.

Don't Buy White. Avoid white (bleached) paper products, as the bleaching process is harmful to the environment. Buy brown instead, ideally made from BPA-free recycled paper.

Don't Recycle. Used paper napkins and towels cannot be recycled. They need to go in either compost, if you have access to it, or, sadly, the trash.

🍃

ECO-ACTION NO. 9
Make Laundry Day Sustainable

How we wash our clothing impacts our health and the health of our planet. From climate change to leaching chemicals that affect our bodies and waterways, how and what we use to wash our clothing has an impact.

WASH WISELY

Time It. Skip laundry during peak hours (usually weekdays between 4 p.m. and 9 p.m.) to limit straining the grid. You'll save money on your energy bill as well if you're signed up for a time-based electric plan.

Wash on Cold. An estimated 75% of all the energy your washer uses is to warm up the water. Switching to cold water is not only more sustainable, it can lower your utility bill.

Use an Eco-detergent. Traditional liquid laundry detergent, which usually comes in plastic jugs, often contains toxic and possibly carcinogenic ingredients that are harmful to the environment, animal life, and our health. Make the switch to an eco- and body-friendly detergent, which often comes in paper, metal, or refillable containers. But be wary of greenwashing—many companies falsely market their laundry products as eco-friendly.

Try Oxygen Bleach. Oxygen bleach (sometimes called oxygen brightener) is a safer alternative to chlorine bleach. It can be found plastic-free and is just as effective at keeping clothes bright. Continue to follow care and safety instructions as directed by the manufacturer.

Skip Conventional Stain Removers. Many ingredients used in typical stain removers have been linked to asthma, skin allergies and irritation, and reproductive and developmental toxicity. Additionally, chemicals commonly found in stain removers are hazardous to the planet and do not readily biodegrade. So what's the alternative? Stain remover bars are a fantastic substitute to plastic spray bottles and laundry stain sticks. However, just because a stain remover comes plastic-free does not mean that it's safe for your health. Be sure to look it up on a clean-product finder app.

DRY DELIBERATELY

Hang Dry. The dryer is an energy-hungry appliance (energy = fossil fuels). Simply air-drying your clothes can reduce your household's carbon footprint by nearly 7% annually. Even if you can't do it year-round or for every load, making a shift toward line drying will impact both the environment and your energy bill.

Avoid Dryer Sheets. Single-use dryer sheets are wasteful, made of plastic fibers, and surprisingly toxic. A sustainable and equally effective alternative is the wool dryer ball. It's chemical-free and reduces static cling. Plus, it's made from a renewable resource, can be used thousands of times, and saves you money. Oh, and did I mention they reduce drying time? So if you can't make the shift to line drying, get rid of the dryer sheets, toss in a few wool dryer balls, and you have a win-win solution that is both sustainable and cost-effective.

> ### ECO-FAMILY TIP
> Choosing body-friendly laundry products is of particular importance because of its close contact with our skin. To find clean products, see *The Motherboard* resources guide at the back of the book.

DRY-CLEANING DANGERS

Perchloroethylene (or PERC, for short) is a probable human carcinogen and a known neurotoxin hiding in your closet. PERC is a VOC used by 85% of dry cleaners. The EPA found elevated levels of PERC throughout the homes of people who dry-clean their clothing, particularly in rooms where the dry-cleaned clothing is stored. In addition to being bad for our health, it's terrible for the environment and can leach into our communities, waterways, and ecosystems.

Dry-Clean vs. Dry-Clean Only. Did you know there is a difference? Generally, clothing labeled "Dry-Clean" can be hand-washed at home, while "Dry-Clean Only" requires a professional. When clothing does require a dry cleaner, opt for a "Green Dry Cleaner" that uses either wet cleaning or liquid carbon dioxide cleaning.

🌿

ECO-ACTION NO. 10
Stop Laundry Microplastics

THE MICROPLASTIC MESS

In the production of garments and when washing at home, synthetic fabrics shed microplastics into our waterways. These eventually make their way to our oceans, water supply, and food chain. One load of laundry can shed up to 700,000 microplastic fibers. In terms of volume, a city the size of Berlin (3.5 million people) may be responsible for the equivalent of 540,000 plastic bags' worth of microplastics entering our waterways—every single day. Even just wearing synthetic clothing releases microplastics into the air, polluting our homes and environment.

WAYS TO FEWER MICROPLASTICS

Wash on Cold. Washing clothing in cold water on a gentler setting can reduce microplastic shedding by up to 50%.

Wash Only When Needed. Not all clothing needs to be washed after one wear. Sure, underwear and your teen's smelly socks could all use a good washing after one use. But jeans, sweatshirts, and dresses can often be worn a number of times before needing a wash, limiting the microplastics released during cleaning.

DID YOU KNOW?

Textile shedding accounts for approximately **9%** of microplastics in the ocean.

Get a Microplastic Filter. There are currently three types of filters you can use to help reduce microplastic pollution when washing clothes at home.

- **A bag.** Just place synthetic clothing into a microfiber-trapping bag such as a Guppyfriend, and wash it with other clothing in the machine as usual. One con to the bag is that most Americans have a lot of synthetic clothing, so the bag may not be big enough for the amount of synthetic clothing you own.

- **A ball.** A microplastic ball filter, such as the Cora Ball, is easy to use. Simply toss it into your washing machine with your clothes and wash as usual. For delicate clothing or apparel with tassels or openings such as a wide knit, lace, or crochet, a delicates bag is recommended. One downside to the ball is that it filters out less waste than the other options. However, because it can be used with a full load of synthetic clothing, you're not limited to a midsize bag.

- **A filter.** If you own your washing machine, a microplastic filter, such as the Filtrol™, effectively reduces microplastic pollution by up to 89% per wash. External filters don't require any additional effort once installed (except for remembering to remove the fibers every 10 or so washes). While a bit pricier than the other options, using an external microplastic filter is the most effective of the three options.

Disposing of Collected Microfibers. After several loads, microfibers will have collected in your filter. To dispose of them responsibly, remove the microplastics from the device and place them in a jar. Once the jar is full, screw on the lid (to prevent flyaways) and toss the jar in the trash. They won't be able to do the same environmental harm in the landfill as they would in waterways.

For more on limiting synthetic clothing, see Eco-Action 31.

PALM OIL 101

What Is Palm Oil? Palm oil is a commonly used vegetable oil found in 50% of household items, including laundry detergent; soap; shampoo; toothpaste; lipstick; and foods like crackers, cereal, peanut butter, cookies, pastries, frozen foods, chips, sprinkles, bread, pizza dough, ice cream, and candy.

What's the Problem? Palm oil production contributes to climate change and accounts for 8% of deforestation worldwide. Rainforests and peatlands are destroyed to make way for palm oil plantations. These areas are major carbon sinkholes, meaning they capture and store large amounts of carbon. When they're destroyed, that carbon is released into the atmosphere.

In addition to contributing to climate change, palm oil cultivation is also responsible for biodiversity loss. Rainforests are burned to clear the land for palm oil farms—a catastrophic loss for ecosystems. The expansion of palm oil plantations into these areas has threatened some of the most species-rich regions on earth and is the leading cause of habitat destruction for a number of endangered species.

Palm Oil + People. In addition to the negative environmental impacts, the palm oil industry is also responsible for human rights abuses. Ancestral land has been taken from indigenous people to grow palm oil. Workers and children are often exploited. Additionally, pollution from burning rainforests to make way for palm oil farming has had adverse health effects on locals.

Why Do We Use It? Palm oil is popular because it's inexpensive and can be processed to have no taste, smell, or color, so it is used in many products.

Why Not Use Other Oils? Palm oil is more resource-efficient than other vegetable oils. If manufacturers switched to other oil options—like soy, sunflower, rapeseed (canola), or coconut in their products—it could lead to more significant biodiversity loss because other crops grown for their oils need more land, in some cases 10 times more, to produce the same amount of oil as palm. So, boycotting palm oil is not always the answer.

What's the Answer? Look for products that are certified under the Roundtable on Sustainable Palm Oil (RSPO) Certified Sustainable Palm Oil label. Additionally, choosing unprocessed foods is a step in the right direction.

🌱

ECO-ACTION NO. 11
Get Wise about Palm Oil

Cutting out palm oil entirely might not be realistic, given its wide-ranging presence, but there are ways to reduce it and ensure you're supporting sustainable practices. Here are seven simple steps to make a big dent in your palm oil consumption:

App it.	Many people are unaware of the extensive use of palm oil in their everyday products, but it's not always due to a lack of awareness. There are over 200 names for palm oil derivatives, many of which are difficult to identify. Sometimes palm oil is clearly labeled as just "palm oil" or identified with a similar name like "palm fruit oil," "palm kernel oil," or "palmate," but many name variations are hard to spot on ingredient lists. You do not need to memorize them all. Use an app like PalmSmart to help you identify palm oil in your everyday products.
Walk around it.	Palm oil is generally found in packaged products and food—essentially what makes up the center of the grocery store. If you aim to purchase less packaged stuff and fresher foods, you're more likely to be buying palm oil–free goods.
Certify it.	Look for the RSPO Certified Sustainable Palm Oil label on products.
Unprocess it.	Eating whole, unprocessed local foods means no added palm oil.
Make it.	By making food and your own cosmetics at home, you know what's actually in them.
Voice it.	Use your voice to let companies know you will no longer be buying their products because of their use of unsustainable palm oil.
Share it.	Let friends and family know about the detrimental impacts of palm oil and ways they can engage in making more sustainable choices.

SPACES
INTERIORS + EXTERIORS

From interior design to garden landscaping, considering the elements that you surround yourself with can impact your family's health and the health of the planet.

ECO-ACTION NO. 12
Decode Your Decor

FIGHT WITH FURNISHINGS

No matter your interior makeover project, here are some helpful ways to consider the impact of your decor choices on your family's health and the environment at large.

Plan Ahead. As you start designing your space, consider how your family's needs will change and grow over the years. Buy pieces whose function and purpose can evolve. Before purchasing core pieces, ask yourself if they will still make sense in 10 to 20 years. Sure, you may need to upgrade your child's crib-to-toddler bed for a full-sized one, but are the staple furnishings—dresser, shelves, artwork, and wall color—pieces that can grow with your family? Also, if you are furnishing a nursery, will the furniture you're buying today still work if you're considering having multiple children who will be sharing a room down the road?

Pick Proper Paint. When choosing colors for your next paint job, look for low-to-zero-VOC paint that is also GREENGUARD-certified. Plus, be sure to buy only what you need and donate or properly recycle any remaining paint.

Handpick Healthy Hand-me-downs. Secondhand furniture and rugs are safer from a VOC perspective because they have time to off-gas before entering your home. Secondhand also means that fewer carbon emissions and raw materials are needed to furnish a room. So whether you're buying fast furniture that's been previously loved or high-quality, solid-wood vintage pieces, secondhand is a more sustainable way to decorate.

Buy New, Responsibly. If you'd prefer to buy new furniture, look for high-quality, toxin-free, ethically produced furniture made from sustainable materials. (It gets expensive, so don't be afraid to look for secondhand options first.) Seek out pieces that are GREENGUARD-certified and use natural fabrics that don't contain stain repellents (PFAS) or fire retardants.

Choose Natural Rugs. If purchasing new rugs or carpets, look for ones made from natural materials such as sustainably harvested wool, hemp, jute, organic or recycled cotton, sea grass, or sisal. VOCs in carpets and rugs tend to come from the latex backing, so be sure to find out what material is used. And don't forget to look for a secondhand or sustainably sourced natural rubber pad for your rug too.

For more on VOCs, check out page 53. To learn more about certifications to look for when purchasing furnishings, head to page 237.

FAST FURNITURE 101

It's Trash. Every year, Americans throw away over 12 million tons of furniture and 3.4 million tons of rugs and carpets. Fast furniture is responsible for much of this waste, with its poorly made, inexpensive pieces that capture the latest decor trends. Very little of it can be recycled due to the mixed materials used, so most of it winds up in the landfill within a few years. It wasn't long ago that furniture was built to last generations, but with the disposable culture we now live in, furniture is designed to be used for a few years and then tossed out.

It's Unhealthy. A lot of fast furniture is made from materials known for emitting volatile organic compounds (VOCs) such as formaldehyde. You have likely come into contact with VOCs without even knowing it. They can be odorless or emit that "I'm new" smell. This process is called off-gassing, and VOCs can be present in the air for months or even years after purchase—long after the "new" scent is gone.

Beware of Greenwashing. Many fast-furniture lines tout their sustainability efforts but do little to uphold eco-friendly or ethical business practices. If it says it's *green*, but it's poorly made or comes from a company known for pumping out designs to meet immediate trends, it's likely greenwashed fast furniture.

ECO-FAMILY BITE-SIZE CHALLENGE   NO. 2

SUSTAINABLE STEPPING-STONES
As your teen prepares to fly the nest, help them outfit their new digs in an eco-friendly way. Skip fast furniture. Instead, scour thrift stores, flea markets, and garage sales together for secondhand gems for their dorm or first apartment. It's a fun way to spend time together while teaching them how to care for the planet and themselves.

ECO-ACTION NO. 13
Cultivate a Green Garden

Being sustainable isn't just confined to the four walls of your home. Whether it's a windowsill garden or acres of land, you can promote biodiversity, help pollinators, reduce water use, and replenish the soil in your corner of the world.

PRACTICAL ECO-GARDENING TIPS
Limit Water. If you live in a single-family home, rain barrels are an effective way to cut down on water use in your garden. Just hook them up to your downspout and utilize the rainwater throughout your garden. You can also set up a gray-water system to reuse your home's wastewater. Or keep it simple and collect kitchen water (instead of letting it go down the drain) to repurpose for watering plants.
Plant Natives. Native plants are lower maintenance, usually require less water, and can thrive without the use of fertilizers or pesticides. They also promote biodiversity by providing pollen, nectar, and seeds for local birds and pollinators. Speak with your local nursery to find out more about what plants will do best in your yard.

Use Mulch. Mulch acts as a natural weed barrier and can also help retain moisture in the soil—meaning you won't need to water as often.

Time It Right. Water plants in the morning or evening to reduce daytime evaporation.

Skip Fossil Fuels. Phase out your gasoline-powered mower and leaf blower and use electric instead.

Bee Aware. Honeybees are responsible for 80% of pollination, but since around 1950 the bee population has declined by almost 60%. The loss in bee populations puts US crops at risk. Habitat loss and pesticides play a significant role in their decline, and you can help by planting bee-friendly flowers native to your area in your backyard. Avoid spraying pesticides and herbicides, even ones labeled organic.

Kill Your Lawn. Monoculture lawns are a desolate desert to pollinators like butterflies and bees. Consider removing a section of your lawn to provide essential habitats. If you just can't bear the thought of ripping out any grass, cultivate a mix of turf grasses and low-growing flowering plants to create a lawn environment that is beneficial to backyard play, ecosystem health, and water conservation.

Buy in Bulk. If you have a garden project that requires a lot of soil, try buying it in bulk to avoid potting soil that comes in plastic bags. Some companies will even deliver it to your home.

Focus on Seeds. Seeds carry a history with them, and their story is essential to our future. Right now, four companies own 60% of the global seed market, which is frightening because it limits global food diversity and weakens food security. The seeds you buy matter. Opt for organic or heirloom varieties, and source them from local seed farms, neighborhood seed libraries, or your closest botanical garden, or swap with friends.

Sustainable Seedling Pots. If you're starting your plants from seeds, you can buy compostable seedling trays or make your own with newspaper or toilet paper rolls. If buying starters, they will likely come in plastic. If that's the case, ask the nursery you purchased them from if they will accept the empty trays back. You could also reuse them or offer them on your Buy Nothing group.

Practice Pest Patience. The use of pesticides, even organic and/or homemade ones, can have a harmful effect on soil health and can kill beneficial insects. Try intercropping, alternating crops, herbs, and flowers to confuse pests. Building a garden that attracts beneficial insects and birds that prey on pests is a natural way to avoid having to use harmful measures. Talk to your local nursery or community garden for more tips.

For more on making your own compost, see Eco-Action 57.

FAMILY FUN PROJECT
START AN EDIBLE HERB GARDEN

Herbs are a great place for beginners to start growing food at home, even with limited space. Get the kids involved. The act of growing food cultivates patience, self-esteem, responsibility, and an understanding of and respect for food. Decide collectively what you're going to grow. Then plant seeds together and watch them sprout.

Set up your herb garden on your windowsill or balcony with minimal effort. How wonderful to be able to cut a sprig of fresh thyme or oregano without having to buy a whole bushel of it packed in a plastic clamshell. If you have the space, try planting a few starter vegetables like lettuce or zucchini and see how it goes. If you want to grow more food but don't have the space, consider joining a community garden.

Bonus. If your family is interested in starting a garden at your child's school, head to the Edible Schoolyard Project website for free resources on how to get started.

TRANSPORTATION

How we choose to move through the world doesn't just get us from point A to point B. It also influences the climate.

ECO-ACTION NO. 14
Green Your Daily Drive

LIFE IN THE GREEN LANE

In 2020, transportation accounted for over a quarter of all greenhouse-gas emissions generated by the United States—with passenger cars and light-duty trucks (SUVs and minivans) making up 57% of those emissions. That's more than planes, trains, and boats combined. It's time to rethink how we roll and find ways that work for us individually while reducing our footprints.

Quit Idling. Anytime you are running the car but not driving it, you are emitting carbon emissions (and wasting money). Idling your car for 10 seconds produces more emissions than stopping and restarting it. Personal vehicles alone contribute to about 30 million tons of CO_2 annually, just from idling. If everyone cut out this harmful habit, it would be like taking 5 million cars off the road each year. Of course, there will be times you will need to keep the car on, like during extreme hot and cold weather, but when circumstances allow, turn that engine off when you're hanging out or waiting in your car.

The Green Rule:

Ten seconds or under, it's not a blunder. Any time over, turn off your rover.

--- **DID YOU KNOW?** ---

Over **76%** of Americans drive to work by themselves in their car.

Commute Consciously. Consider taking public transportation, walking, or riding your bike even once a week to keep emissions down. Working from home will help reduce emissions, too (assuming you're practicing wise heating and cooling habits). And if you must drive to school or work, look for a carpool group.

Go Carless *Sometimes*. If being 100% car-free isn't feasible, take smaller steps. Could you try going carless for at least one outing a week to start? From there, try upping your game to see which activities and errands you can do without your vehicle. Certain times of the year may be easier than others; if you can't be car-free year-round, that's okay. Every action adds up. Biking, walking, public transportation, and going carless all are high-impact ways for your family to reduce its footprint, even if it's part-time.

Change Your Ride. If owning a car is a must, think about downsizing to one vehicle or swapping your car out for a hybrid or an electric vehicle. Finding a hybrid or EV used is a double green bonus.

RAISE YOUR VOICE

The Sustainable School Bus. If your district has school buses, they're most likely fueled by diesel, a known carcinogen. Kids who ride inside the bus are most affected, with the health impact comparable to maternal smoking. Advocate for switching your district's fleet to electric buses to spare the air and your children's lungs. The most significant hurdle is the cost. Even though they're less expensive to operate, they're more expensive up front. However, they will save money over time, and the health and earth benefits are worth fighting for.

DID YOU KNOW?

Miami, Florida, made the landmark decision to transition their school bus fleet from diesel to electric. The push was fueled by a middle-school science fair project.

ELECTRIC VECHICLES 101

ELECTRIC VEHICLES: ARE THEY REALLY ECO-FRIENDLY?

After comparing a magnitude of studies, there is an overall consensus: when comparing gas-powered cars to electric vehicles, EVs produce fewer emissions overall than standard gasoline cars when looking at them over their entire life span. But it's not exactly what it seems.

A Case for the Gas-Powered Car. Producing the battery for an electric vehicle comes at an environmental cost. In fact, when you compare an EV to a gas-powered car, there are instances when manufacturing an electric vehicle has a significantly higher overall carbon footprint than a gasoline car. However, this is the only time when the gas-powered car generates fewer emissions. Once the two car types hit the road, it's another story.

Equal Emissions, Until . . . A collaboration between the *Wall Street Journal* and the University of Toledo found that when comparing a gasoline-powered Rav4 with a Tesla Model 3 after 20,600 miles, the two cars generated the same number of emissions when combining their manufacturing and driving footprints. This isn't just true if the EV was charged using 100% clean energy; the assessment is based on a national average of the energy grid, which includes fossil fuels. If the Tesla had been charged using purely green energy, it would have surpassed the Rav4 in being more eco-friendly even sooner.

By the 100,000-mile mark, the overall emissions from the Rav4 were 77% higher than the Tesla. But it's not only the emissions that are greater; it's also the total cost of the car. When you add up the purchase price, maintenance, gas, and resale value of both vehicles, the Rav4 costs more. As the odometer rises, the divide between the cars only grows, the EV coming in even stronger as a clear environmental winner.

It's time to get on board. When you're in the market for your next vehicle, it's time to make the switch. Not just because EVs reduce emissions, but because your gasoline- or diesel-motored car will become obsolete. General Motors plans to stop selling such vehicles by 2035 and Audi by 2033. California has banned the sale of new gas-powered cars after 2035. What will happen to the cost of fuel and combustion engine car resale values in the future as the world phases out its dependence on fossil fuels? Perhaps now is the time to consider making a switch.

EVs Are Not Perfect. While electric vehicles may have a significantly smaller carbon footprint than gasoline-powered cars, they don't come at no cost to the planet or to people. The mining of lithium for EV batteries takes an environmental toll. Scientists are currently working on more eco-friendly and less harmful ways to extract it. Additionally, cobalt is an essential battery ingredient, yet there are human-rights concerns over mining this metal in the Democratic Republic of the Congo. Not to mention that many of the materials needed for EV batteries are on or within 35 miles of Native American reservations.

WHAT CAN YOU DO?

Opting for a secondhand EV is an impactful way to reduce emissions even further and take a more robust environmental and ethical stance. (Until 2032, you can even get a federal tax credit when buying a used EV.) And, by walking, biking, taking public transportation, or going carfree entirely, you're making the greenest choice of all.

STUFF

SLOW THE "STUFF"

Overconsumption is an unsustainable drug for us, the planet, and our children's future. Easing off the excess is an effective way to limit our strain on the earth while also reducing our carbon footprint.

WHAT'S YOUR BUYOLOGY?

Overconsumption is costing us more than we know. . . .

OUR TIME
The more we own, the more time we spend shopping, cleaning, putting things away, looking for stuff, organizing, and getting rid of crap.

OUR MONEY
The average American spends nearly $18,000 a year on nonessentials and carries over $6,500 in credit card debt.

THE PLANET
Overconsumption is one of the main drivers of the climate crisis. A 2015 study found that household consumption, which includes the production and use of all of the stuff we buy and services we utilize, accounts for 60% of global greenhouse emissions—with footprints skewing heavily on wealthier nations such as the United States. You may have heard that the top 10% of the world's wealth is responsible for half of the world's greenhouse gas emissions. But did you know the American middle class falls into that category? A three-person household with an annual income of $57,000 is in the 90th percentile for income worldwide.

So why is it that we are consumed by the impulse to buy? Here are five possible reasons:

- **Retail therapy.** Buying stuff when we're feeling down or like we're not enough. Jealousy and wanting to impress others fall under this category, too, since things are being used fill a void that we see in ourselves.
- **The short-term thrill.** Buying stuff because the act of consuming feels fun, and we enjoy the rush of waiting for a package to arrive or having something new.
- **Bait and click.** Getting hooked by online ads and promotions before we've thought it through.
- **A sense of security.** The false idea that owning in excess means we are safer in the world.
- **It's just so pretty.** Have you ever bought a cute blouse because it's on sale, but it doesn't quite fit right? Yup, sometimes it seems too pretty to pass up.

In a culture where we associate our value with what we can buy, the relationship between our purchases and our self-worth can be complicated. We are bombarded by consumerism from the moment we wake up until we go to sleep. Restraint can be challenging and we can easily become susceptible to quick, unnecessary purchases—even when we have the best intentions. Developing green spending habits can help you fight more by buying less.

Maximize your life, not your possessions.

THE CLIMATE CREW

🌿

ECO-ACTION No. 15
Say Yes to Buying Less

EASE OFF THE EXCESS

In a society already responsible for "too much," buying more is not the answer, even if a product is made sustainably. Here are three ways to help you say yes to buying less.

Use What You Have. The most sustainable option is to use, reuse, wear, and enjoy what you already own.

Choose Connection Over Consumption. When you want to buy something to make you feel better, look for another outlet. (And I don't mean a shopping outlet.) Go for a run, read a good book, get a drink with a friend, spend time with your kids, or plan a date with your partner. Connecting with yourself or someone you care about is much more fulfilling.

Shop Mindfully. Despite attempts to buy less, you will need to make purchases. Following the S.M.A.R.T.I.E. shopping guide below establishes green guardrails around buying necessities.

S.M.A.R.T.I.E. SHOPPING GUIDE	
ASK YOURSELF, *"IS THIS CHOICE NOURISHING OR REPAIRING THE EARTH, PEOPLE, AND COMMUNITIES, OR IS IT HURTING THEM?"*	
Secondhand	Buying items secondhand means no new energy or resources are needed to produce the item, significantly reducing its footprint.
Material	Look for products made from sustainable materials that can be recycled or composted at the end of their life cycle.
Avoid trash	Look for well-made products that will last (ideally for generations) and come in limited packaging.
Reusable	Avoid single-use products. Opt for items that can be used over and over.
Take a moment	Pause and ask yourself if you truly need this item. If ordering online, give yourself one week before clicking "Buy." And keep a list of things you need (and want) so you're less tempted by impulse purchases.
Independent	Purchase from independent, local stores to support your community and individuals instead of large corporations.
Ethical	Look for ethically made goods, meaning that both the company and the ingredients in their products respect people and the planet.

--- **DID YOU KNOW?** ---

The United States makes up just over **4%** of the world's population and yet for decades has used one-third of the world's total material consumption.

ECO–FAMILY BITE–SIZE CHALLENGE

THE "EASE OFF THE EXCESS" EXPERIMENT

Use your spending habits to fight for the future you want by cutting out the excess. Take this one-month challenge to discover ways to make your purchases more intentional and find resources to help you buy less "brand-new."

Get Started. Begin the challenge on the first of the month for a clean start. Prep in advance by checking out the *Green Glossary* at the back of the book for a list of free marketplaces and additional resources that can help you avoid buying brand-new things. Additionally, take a moment to fill out the Planet Planner worksheet on page 229 to create a personal guide of local resources.

Yay	Nay
Don't worry. You can still purchase necessities like food; personal care essentials (hey, we still have to brush our teeth); any medical or health needs, including prescriptions; bills; repairs (a broken pipe cannot wait); essential services; pet basics; etc.	Nonessentials include clothing (assuming you haven't just moved from a nudist colony), makeup, toys, home decor, etc. Instead, use what you already own. If you want a nonessential item, skip buying it brand-new and try getting it secondhand, for free, borrowed from a friend, or as a rental.

One Free Pass. This is optional, but each family member can have one free pass to buy a nonessential during the month. (It helps everyone be more mindful of that one special purchase they make.)

#easeofftheexcess

CLUTTER CHAOS 101

Research shows what every parent already knows: mess = stress. In fact, long-term exposure to clutter can have harmful neurological and biological consequences, including increased stress, anxiety, and sleep loss, while impacting coping mechanisms and ability to focus. But clutter doesn't just add to the strain. It also makes us consume more.

Have you ever stared into the depths of your closet, full of clothes, and felt like you had nothing to wear? Do your kids ever sit in a room bursting with toys and declare, "I'm bored"? I call this phenomenon the *overabundance blues*—when excess stuff leaves us feeling like we have nothing and makes us want to buy more. When items that we love and enjoy become overshadowed by things that we don't use, how can we see through the jumble and behold every-thing we need right in front of us? The answer: consuming less and decluttering our homes responsibly.

> **GREEN ON THE SCREEN**
> ———
> The Story of Stuff (2007)*
> Minimalism (2016)
> *short film

WANT MORE TIME? OWN FEWER THINGS

Work together as a family to:

- ✓ Quit buying stuff you don't need
- ✓ Declutter by creating a household system to sustainably rid your home of unused items
- ✓ Find more in the less
- ✓ Stop comparing yourself to others
- ✓ Collect memories, not things

The results:

- ✓ Less time cleaning, looking for stuff, and putting crap away
- ✓ More time for what matters
- ✓ A calmer home
- ✓ The feeling of "enoughness"
- ✓ A smaller footprint

CUT OUT UNWANTED MESS

Few things in life are more annoying than having to constantly deal with all of the unwanted clutter that makes its way into our homes. Our time is precious, and it gets hijacked by having to tackle it. Here are a few ways to reduce the daily heaps of stuff that seem to just appear in our homes.

Freebies. Say no to random free giveaways and swag. They don't deserve a place in your house, or your time having to get rid of them. Saying no may be easier for you than for your kid. Anticipating tchotchkes ahead of time—postdentist visit, say—and coming up with an alternative like an experience can help mitigate breakdowns for little ones. And just pick your battles. We can't win them all.

Mitigate Junk Mail. Tired of sifting through junk mail? It's time to stop the flow. As the Federal Trade Commission suggests, you can register at DMAchoice.org ($2 fee) to get fewer marketing pieces and catalogs and at optoutprescreen.com to stop credit card and insurance offers. You can also download the PaperKarma app, snap a pic of your unwanted marketing mail, and get less junk in just 6 to 12 weeks (fees apply).

Go Paperless. Switch your billing, banking, and communications from paper to digital.

Request No Extras. When ordering takeout, say no to plastic cutlery, paper napkins, condiments, etc.

Part with Multiples. Avoid keeping (or buying) duplicate items. It reduces your time picking up after your kids and all of the stuff you store. An example would be one fire truck for your kiddo and not an entire fire brigade. (If you have two children who are into fire trucks, then one per child.) Trust me, it's a game changer.

DID YOU KNOW?

The **80–100 million** trees that are chopped down to produce Americans' junk mail every year could sequester **1.7 million** tons of CO_2 annually if left standing.

ECO-ACTION NO. 16
Declutter Sustainably

RID RESPONSIBLY

Unless you do it sustainably, decluttering is messy for the earth. Donation drop-off points are often seen as a simple way to pawn off unwanted items, no matter their condition. This habit has left donation centers overwhelmed, unable to handle or resell all that is left at their doorsteps. So, while donating feels like we're doing something good with our unwanted stuff, a colossal amount of these goods ends up in the landfill. (Thrift stores sell only about 20% of donated clothing.)

When and How to Donate. If you have items in new-to-good condition, they have a much higher chance of being resold. Items that are broken, ripped, stained, smell, or in poor condition are likely going to the landfill. Also, before dropping off unwanted stuff, check what items your local donation center accepts. Otherwise, your things won't be resold and will become trash.

THE SUSTAINABILITY SCALE: HOW TO GET RID OF STUFF ETHICALLY

Ethical Editing. If we can't donate stuff, what can we do with our unwanted goods? Here is your road map. This simple scaled system ensures your clutter finds a new home and limits what ends up being tossed.

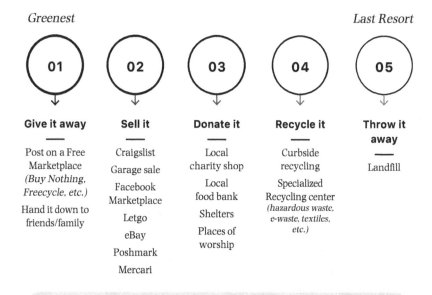

Greenest   *Last Resort*

01	02	03	04	05
Give it away	**Sell it**	**Donate it**	**Recycle it**	**Throw it away**
Post on a Free Marketplace *(Buy Nothing, Freecycle, etc.)*	Craigslist	Local charity shop	Curbside recycling	Landfill
Hand it down to friends/family	Garage sale	Local food bank	Specialized Recycling center *(hazardous waste, e-waste, textiles, etc.)*	
	Facebook Marketplace	Shelters		
	Letgo	Places of worship		
	eBay			
	Poshmark			
	Mercari			

ECO-ACTION NO. 17
Find Your *Free Marketplace*

"SHOP" FOR FREE

Buy Nothing Project is a powerful tool to help you consume fewer "new" things and find what you need secondhand and locally. Think of it as the 2.0 version of your neighborhood thrift store—only free.

What is the Buy Nothing Project? Buy Nothing Project is a worldwide online community that connects people locally. It's a resource for anyone to post items they're ready to part with or ask for things they need. It's often referred to socially as Buy Nothing. Additionally, the term Buy Nothing has also become a generic reference to free online marketplaces, of which there are many. (Like using "Kleenex" for "facial tissue.") Check out *The Motherboard* resources guide at the back of this book for a list of free marketplaces.

How do I join? Join a Buy Nothing group on Facebook or download the Buy Nothing app, which makes getting rid of and acquiring "new" items manageable. Just snap a pic, add a title, and—voila—someone will likely snatch up your stuff quickly.

What can I post? Anything. Outgrown clothing, books, furniture, extra hangers, or odds and ends (including your extensive accumulation of rubber bands). A broken blender might even find a new home. You'd be surprised by what people want.

What can I get? From barely used strollers to empty moving boxes, you can find just about anything you might need (short of a last-minute babysitter).

Is it free? Yes, it's free to join, and everything that's posted is free.

Is there one in my town? Chances are you already have a free marketplace in your area. I have heard from multiple families who live in remote, rural parts of the US who were surprised to learn that they had a group thriving in their region.

HOST A FREE SALE

Want to rid your home of stuff but don't have time to deal with it? Host a Free Sale! Set up the items you want to purge outside your home, like a garage sale. Make a sign: Everything Free. Place all the items out in the morning so you can maximize time for people to take what they need. (Or do it on a day you're decluttering and put things out gradually.) Snap a pic and share your goods on Buy Nothing. As it gets dark, be sure to bring in any leftovers so they aren't ruined by overnight weather and become trash. In the end, you'll have less stuff to find a new home for.

THE CLIMATE CREW

ECO-ACTION NO. 18
Invest in Your Values

DIRTY MONEY

Did you know that your bank can use your money to fund oil and gas pipeline expansion? It's true. When you make a deposit into your bank account, your money doesn't just sit there until you're ready to take it out. Instead, big banks can lend 100% of your deposits to corporations, charging them a high interest rate to fund fossil fuel projects like oil pipelines in addition to other ventures like assault weapon manufacturing. (Many big banks have recently pulled out of funding private prisons due to a swelling of public pressure—see, our voices do matter.)

As of 2019, most megabanks in the US, including JPMorgan Chase (ranked "Worst in the World" by leading advocacy groups), Citi, Bank of America, U.S. Bank, Morgan Stanley, Wells Fargo, and Goldman Sachs continue to finance fossil fuel expansion. Additionally, you may be surprised to find that your 401(K) and stock portfolios could also be invested in oil, gas, and coal projects.

PUT YOUR MONEY WHERE YOUR HEART IS

It's time to invest in change by moving your money away from fossil fuels. When you bank with financial institutions that break entirely from funding fossil fuel projects, you are investing in the future you want.

Let Your Money Talk. Consider switching your bank and investment funds to institutions and portfolios that have divested from funding fossil fuel expansion.

- **Banks + credit unions.** To find the right place to keep your hard-earned cash, head to bankforgood.com or mightydeposits.com
- **Investment funds.** Learn more about divesting from fossil fuels by checking out fossilfreefunds.org to start building a better portfolio. Then talk to your investment adviser or retirement fund manager about the financial pros and cons of moving your money.

Speak out. When you move your accounts away from banks that fund dirty projects, let them know why you are making the switch. Additionally, protest, write letters, hold megabanks accountable on social media, and inform others.

Think beyond your family. If you are in charge of finances for a business, school, or community group, examine if it's right for your institution to move finances into the hands of a financial institution that reflects your organization's values.

GREENWASHING ALERT

Many banks say they are investing in renewable energy or are part of the Net Zero Banking Alliance, but they continue to lend to fossil fuel projects. When researching a bank's sustainability statement, be wary if they stick to small talk and don't bring up the larger issue: the projects they are financially backing.

PLASTIC

Minimize the plastic that shows up in your daily routine.

PLASTICS 101

THE PLASTIC PROBLEM

Plastics get a bad rap for a reason. If you haven't already considered reducing your plastic intake, here are a few reasons why you may want to take the leap.

Climate Crisis. Plastic is human-made from fossil fuels. And while plastic may not be a top contributor to the climate crisis, it still bears some responsibility. It's estimated that 4–8% of the global oil produced each year goes to plastics—and the amount is estimated to increase to 20% by 2050.

Your Family's Health. A 2019 study published in *Environmental Science & Technology* tested 34 everyday products, including coffee cup lids, plastic wrap, freezer bags, and yogurt containers. Seventy-four percent of the plastics tested were toxic to some degree. The study found that toxicity can be found in every type of plastic. (Scary!) Plastics contain harmful chemicals including bisphenols, alkylphenols, perfluorinated compounds (PFAS), brominated flame retardants (BFRs), dioxins, phthalates, UV stabilizers, lead, and cadmium. Studies have found that these chemicals can cause serious health problems such as cancer, metabolic disorders, endocrine disruption, obesity, reduced fertility, neurodevelopment disorders, and more.

Single-Use Madness. Fifty percent of the plastic we use is single-use, meaning that it is used for minutes—sometimes seconds—and then thrown away.

Recycling. Even when you think the plastic you're tossing in your recycling bin will be processed, the fact is that 91% of all plastic doesn't get recycled. The remainder ends up in the landfill or worse, contaminating oceans, killing animal life, and infiltrating our food chain.

Persistent Plastic. Plastic doesn't biodegrade; it just breaks down into tiny particles, known as microplastics (or, when they're even smaller, nanoplastics). Plastic can take hundreds to thousands of years to decompose, and in the meantime it contaminates ecosystems and living organisms, including the human body.

Microplastics. Microplastics are released from plastics breaking down in the environment but can also be shed from our clothing, sofas, curtains, and more. They have been found in the air, drinking water, dust, table salt, beer, seafood (especially mussels), etc. Unknowingly, we eat and breathe them every day; microplastics have even been detected in human blood, lungs, and the placentas of unborn babies. (Nanoplastics may even be able to enter our bodies via our skin through our synthetic clothing.) Additionally, microplastics can act as vectors, carrying hazardous chemicals added to plastics and toxins that they pick up from the environment. We still don't know the full scope of damage by microplastics in humans. A 2019 study published in the journal *Environmental Science & Technology* estimates that humans consume up to 263,000 microplastic particles a year through food, water, and inhalation.

─────────── **DID YOU KNOW?** ───────────
Individuals who get their daily water intake from bottled water consume an additional **90,000** microplastics per year.

THE PLASTIC BREAKDOWN

While we may think of plastic as just plastic, there are many different types, each with its own recycling rules and health risks. However, it's essential to note that while some plastics are considered safer than others, chemicals added to the base plastics to change their color, flexibility, etc., can increase their toxicity levels, making it challenging to assume safety by looking at the plastic number. Studies have shown that there is reason to be cautious with all plastics and to use alternatives when possible.

THIS IS NOT A RECYCLING SYMBOL.

These arrows may look like a recycling emblem, but the symbol does not indicate that a product is recyclable. It simply tells you what type of plastic it is.

Note: Toys can be made from any of these types of plastic.

PET or PETE
(Polyethylene Terephthalate)

• water bottles
• food containers
• wipes

COMMONLY RECYCLED

LOW-HIGH TOXICITY

Heath-related problems are of higher concern when Type 1 plastic is exposed to sunlight or high temperature or is old. For health reasons, it's best to avoid reusing it multiple times for food.

HDPE
(High-Density Polyethylene)

• milk bottles
• shampoo bottles
• laundry detergent jugs

COMMONLY RECYCLED

LOW TOXICITY

PVC or V
(Polyvinyl Chloride or Vinyl)

• garden hose
• inflatable pool
• play mats

PROGRAMS VARY

HIGH TOXICITY

PVC and vinyl are linked to cancer, birth defects, reproductive and developmental disorders, low sperm count, premature puberty, undescended testes, and liver dysfunction.

LDPE
(Low-density Polyethylene)

soft plastics, such as:
• bread bags
• food wraps

PROGRAMS VARY

LOW TOXICITY

PP
(Polypropylene)

• cereal liners
• lunch boxes
• yogurt containers

PROGRAMS VARY

LOW TOXICITY

PS
(Polystyrene)

• styrofoam peanuts
• toys
• plastic cutlery

NOT COMMONLY RECYCLED

HIGH TOXICITY

Styrofoam is a suspected carcinogen and neurotoxin.

Miscellaneous
(Other Plastics)

• baby bottles
• sippy cups
• Tupperware

NOT COMMONLY RECYCLED

LOW-HIGH TOXICITY

Health-related concerns vary depending upon the specific type of plastic.

ECO-ACTION NO. 19
Break Up with Unnecessary Plastic

Plastic is so intrinsic to our daily lives that it seems almost impossible to imagine a world without it. Some plastic is necessary and can be life-saving (hello, car seats and medical supplies). However, the majority of plastic in our daily routine is an unnecessary waste. Here are some easy ways to sidestep pointless plastic to reduce your intake.

DID YOU KNOW?
Fifty percent of all plastics ever produced were manufactured in the last **20 years.**

PARING DOWN POINTLESS PLASTICS

Use the Plastic You Own. From an environmental standpoint, it makes no sense to toss out the plastic you already have just because it's plastic. Care for, reuse, and repurpose it. Only once it's no longer usable should you properly dispose of it and replace it with a plastic-free alternative.

Seek Secondhand. If you need "new" plastic items, see if you can get them secondhand first.

Look for Alternatives. Look for plastic-free packaging when shopping for everyday essentials. For a list of simple plastic-free sustainable swaps, check out page 242; find more on reducing plastic food packaging on page 155.

Choose Plastic-Free Fabrics. Avoid clothing, bedding, furniture, decor, and stuffed animals made from synthetic fabrics (which are plastic). Instead, choose natural fibers like cotton (preferably organic), linen, hemp, and ethically sourced wool.

Avoid Biodegradable Plastic. Biodegradable plastic and compostable plastic are not the same things. See for yourself. . . .

- **Biodegradable Plastic:** Just because a bioplastic is labeled biodegradable doesn't mean it's eco-friendly. It simply means that it can breakdown faster into smaller pieces than conventional plastic. The term biodegradable can be misleading because not all biodegradable plastics are compostable. Unless the product says "compostable" on its label, then the biodegradable plastic should be thrown in the trash. If recycled, it risks contaminating conventional plastic recycling. If littered or composted, it can add harmful toxins or microplastics to the environment.

- **Compostable Plastic:** Compostable plastics are made from vegetable matter like potato or corn starch and are designed to fully break down when placed in a human-controlled environment. Some compostable plastics can be composted in a home composting system (and will be labeled as such), while others require industrial composting, such as compostable bags labeled as "certified compostable." They will not break down properly if littered. And like all compostable items, compostable plastics that are thrown in the landfill can be harmful to the environment, so they should be composted properly instead of being put in the garbage.

GREENWASHING 101

BUYERS BEWARE

Greenwashing is when a company tries to market themselves or their products as *green* without actually making their goods or business practices more sustainable. Why would they do that? Because "eco-friendly" sells. With the sustainability movement gaining momentum, many companies are trying to jump on the eco-bandwagon with false advertising. You can find greenwashing on food products, fashion labels, school supplies, toiletries, product packaging, and more.

HOW TO SPOT IT

Here are some telltale signs that you're being greenwashed:

Misleading words: Words like "natural," "biodegradable," "green," "chemical-free," and "eco-friendly" are often signs that you're being greenwashed. In short, if the product description sounds vague, without details to back its simple eco-friendly language, be wary.

Minimal information on website: Head to the company's website and look for their sustainability section. A company with a strong ethical mission in place will let you know. If their methods seem ambiguous or limited, question it, and choose a company that clearly understands sustainable practices.

Only eco-imagery: Don't be fooled by trees, flowers, green-colored packaging, or minimalist product designs. Companies know what they're doing, and they're out to get your money.

Missing Accredited Certifications: While not all accreditations maintain the same level of criteria, many are reputable and hold companies to a higher standard. Look for certifications like B Corp, Forest Stewardship Council (FSC), Fair Trade Certified™*, Fairtrade*, Fair for Life*, USDA Organic, or an ENERGY STAR seal. When comparing it to a product that is simply labeled as "natural" or "eco-friendly," the certified product is going to be the better bet.

Yes, it's confusing that there are three fair-trade certifications.

ECO-FAMILY TIP

Don't be fooled by packaging and misleading words. Download a green product finder app and scan the bar codes of your favorite foods, cleaning products, and cosmetics next time you're out shopping. You may be surprised to find that many of the products you use are toxic for both your family and the environment. See *The Motherboard* resources guide Tools section for a list of green product finder apps.

ECO-ACTION NO. 20
Switch to Reusables

Breaking up with single-use items means:

1. Shifting away from disposables, no matter the material, and

2. Moving toward reusables made from sustainable materials.

JOIN THE REUSE REVOLUTION

Items designed to be used only once are a problem from start to finish, as they waste resources all the way through their life cycle. And when not correctly disposed of, single-use items are a huge source of pollution. In addition to being better for the planet, switching from disposables to reusables saves you money. See the Bonus Material on page 279 for a guide to Sustainable Swaps. **Avoid This Reusable Eco-Error.** When are reusables not sustainable? When you don't use them. A cotton shopping tote doesn't outperform a single plastic bag from a climate change perspective unless you use that cotton bag 131 times. So be sure to reuse your reusables repeatedly so they fulfill their purpose of lowering your footprint. Additionally, if you have more reusable items than you can use (how many tote bags do you have hanging in your coat closet right now?), find them a new home so they can be used. They're not doing anyone any good sitting there.

ECO–FAMILY BITE–SIZE CHALLENGE — NO. 5

PUT A STOP TO SINGLE-USE EVERYTHING

Could you live without disposable items? Give it a try! Set a challenge for your family to go without single-use items for a week. Even if you're not 100% successful, it can be enlightening to see how many disposable products you encounter, and highlight where to start looking for alternatives. You'll also learn where and when to anticipate disposables—and ways to avoid them.

Refer to Bonus Material for Sustainable Swaps 101 for greener alternatives to single-use items.

PLASTIC MYTHS

MYTH #1. PAPER BAGS ARE BETTER THAN PLASTIC.

Fact. Paper grocery bags are often presented as an eco-alternative to plastic. Yet both are disposable, and each presents a host of problems. From a carbon emissions standpoint, paper bags are worse for the environment than plastic. Plus, it takes 4 times more energy to produce a paper bag than a plastic one. Not to mention they produce 70 times more air pollutants and 50 times more water pollutants than a plastic bag. However, that doesn't mean plastic should get a better "wrap." Plastic bags generate microplastics, kill wildlife, and take 1,000 years to degrade. One hundred sixty thousand new plastic bags are consumed every second, yet less than 1% of plastic bags are recycled. The moral of the story: single-use bags should be avoided.

What Can You Do?

- ✓ **Give bags a second chance.** If you already have a stack of paper or plastic shopping bags at home, reuse them repeatedly until they can't be used any longer. Then recycle them.
- ✓ **Bring a reusable bag.**
- ✓ **Buy recycled.** If you must buy a new bag, purchase one made from recycled materials or upcycled fabric. Their impact is less than a bag made from virgin fibers. Then use it over and over!

MYTH #2. BOTTLED WATER IS BETTER THAN TAP.

Fact. We've been led to believe that bottled water is purer than tap water, but for many Americans this isn't the case.

BOTTLED VS. TAP WATER		
	Bottled	**Tap**
Regulated by:	The FDA	The EPA
Required to test for coliform bacteria . . .	. . . once a week.	. . . at least 100 times a month.
Individuals who get their daily water intake from . . .	. . . bottled water consumed an additional 90,000 microplastics per year.	. . . tap water consumed an additional 4,000 microplastics per year.
PFAS:	Studies have found concerning levels of PFAS in both still and sparkling bottled water. As of this writing, the FDA has set no standards or testing requirements for PFAS in bottled water.	While not eliminated completely, as of 2022 the EPA set forth health advisories to drastically reduce PFAS in tap water.
Cost:	1,000 to 10,000 times more expensive than tap water.	Less expensive.
Taste:	In a blind taste test, two-thirds of participants could not distinguish between tap and bottled water.	
Energy:	Bottled water requires 2,000 times more energy to produce than tap water.	
CO_2:	It takes 2.5 million tons of carbon dioxide a year to produce the plastic for bottled water in the US alone (not to mention the emissions to transport it).	
Water:	1.4 gallons of water is needed to manufacture the plastic used for one bottle.	
Recycling:	Only one in six single-use water bottles gets recycled in the United States.	

What Can You Do?

✓ **Invest in a Refillable Water Bottle.** If all of your family members don't already have a refillable water bottle, now would be a good time to invest in one. It will save you money over very little time. If you don't want to purchase one brand-new, you can pick one up at the secondhand store or through your local Buy Nothing group. If buying brand new, opt for one made from glass or food-grade stainless steel instead of plastic.

✓ **Invest in a Water Filter.** Microplastics and PFAS are often found at higher concentrations in bottled water but are still present in tap water. Also, some households may have higher levels of heavy metals, such as lead, in their water. When you choose the right home water filter, it's a sustainable way to remove close to 100% of microplastics and harmful chemicals. Prices range from $50 for a glass pitcher with a filter to thousands of dollars for a home system that removes microplastics from all of the water in your house. There are also kitchen faucet mounts and under-sink filtration systems. Water filters make water taste better, so if the flavor of your tap water has been a primary driver in your bottled water purchases, a filter may be your answer.

The average American spends $100 on bottled water a year, so money spent on at-home filtration could be recouped within weeks or months. Be sure to research filtration types to be sure it's removing everything you want it to. And change your filter according to the manual instructions to ensure continuous filtration.

DID YOU KNOW?

300 million tons of plastics are generated annually worldwide, **50%** of which is single-use.

A plastic bag is used for an average of just **12 minutes.**

Over **25%** of bottled water is just tap water that's been packaged.

INJUSTICE AT THE TAP

When comparing studies looking at PFAS, microplastics, environmental impact, cost, and taste of tap water vs. bottled, tap is the clear winner. And while many Americans do have access to clean tap water, a striking portion of the population does not. Poor water quality or lack of water access can occur because of incomplete plumbing or violations of clean-water acts—both examples of environmental injustices. Populations or households impacted are more likely to be indigenous or communities of color, live in rural areas, or experience poverty. Education and age are also factors. As we advocate for all to have access to this basic right, we must acknowledge that bottled water may be a necessity for some.

If you're concerned about your tap water, EPA law requires an annual water quality report called the Consumer Confidence Report, which details what's in the water where you live. Examples of how bottled water might be safer than tap water are if you have lead pipes in your home, use a private well for your water that isn't as rigorously tested, or live in an area known for water contamination.

🌿

ECO-ACTION NO. 21
Plastic-Free Pumping + Bottle Feeding

_____ **DID YOU KNOW?** _____
On average, babies fed by plastic bottles consume up
to **1.5 million** particles of microplastics per day.

PLASTIC-FREE BABY BOTTLES

From microplastics to phthalates, BPS, and other harmful chemicals, plastic baby bottles may not be as safe as previously believed. Fortunately, plenty of plastic-free, nontoxic baby bottle options are on the market, with glass and stainless steel being two of the safest, most effective, earth-friendly choices.

Glass Bottles. Glass baby bottles come in two forms: standard glass baby bottles and converted Mason jar bottles. Parents often worry about glass bottles being dropped, but companies have now developed silicone sleeves to help protect the bottles against breakage.

- **Traditional Glass Bottle.** In addition to using them to feed your little one, a benefit of traditional glass bottles is that they can be used with compatible breast pumps, eliminating pumping into a plastic bottle.

- **Converted Mason Jars.** Their advantage is that it can grow with your baby into childhood by switching out the nipple attachment for a sippy cup mouthpiece. You can store, heat, and serve milk all in the same container, and they also work for pumping when you use a pump attachment that connects your breast pump to the Mason jar. Once your child moves to solids, they're also perfect for baby food storage.

Stainless Steel Bottles. When shopping for stainless steel bottles, look for 100% food-grade, 304-grade stainless steel and medical-grade silicone nipples. Also, look for convertible ones so they can last through the preschool years with interchangeable silicone mouthpieces. Made-Safe® has certified some stainless steel baby bottles, which are worth considering. A downside to stainless steel is that it can't be microwaved. It also conducts heat easily, so adding a silicone sleeve can help keep your baby's hands safe with warmed liquids. Some studies have shown that stainless steel can leach nickel and chromium, mainly when they come in contact with acidic liquids, so if that concerns you, glass is the best option.

Note: Medical-grade silicone baby bottles are also a safe option. However, they're essentially trash at the end of their life cycle, so not a top pick.

BREAST MILK STORAGE

Properly storing breast milk is vital and not to be taken lightly. The CDC has clear guidelines for handling, keeping, and thawing pumped breast milk. Opting for glass over plastic to store breast milk is one easy way to eliminate single-use plastic from your daily routine and reduce your baby's exposure. While some breast milk storage bags claim to be phthalate-free, there is still limited information on breast milk bags and microplastics. A study published in the *Journal of Environmental Science and Technology* found that every type of plastic tested displayed toxicity, so avoiding plastics is best when possible.

The good news? Research has shown that glass is a safe option for storing breast milk—even the CDC recommends it. Just ensure the glass containers are clean, food-grade, and have tight-fitting lids.

Mason Jar. Mason jars are food-grade, dishwasher safe, toxin-free, and perfect for breast milk storage. Unlike breast milk storage bags that spill easily (and end up with extra milk stuck in crevasses), the Mason jar reduces milk waste; all you need to do is warm and use the silicone nipple attachment instead of a lid. Plus, they can be used over and over again (saving you money), are easy to label, and stack nicely in the freezer. I recommend buying regular-mouth Mason jars in two sizes, 4 and 8 ounces, so that you can pump, store, and prep bottles in various serving sizes without wasting precious milk or freezer space.

Freezer Tray. Silicone freezer trays are another plastic-free option. They look like plastic ice cube trays but are silicone and come with a lid. Once you fill and freeze a tray with breast milk, you can pop them out and place them in a large Mason jar. (A Mason jar seals more tightly than glass Tupperware.) Then label the lid with the date range of the milk supply. When considering sizes, the 1.5-ounce trays are the best choice. The trays with larger portions create cubes too big to fit in the opening of a baby bottle.

NURSING PADS

Single-use nursing pads are not only single-use waste (six months of breast-feeding equals upward of 400 pads), but they're also a waste of money. Furthermore, disposable nursing pads are uncomfortable with their itchy backsides and lack breathability. The alternative? Washable nursing pads. Here are some things to look for when purchasing:

Material. You want something soft and made from a natural material such as organic cotton or hemp.

Shape. Washable nursing pads come in two shapes: a flat circle and a slight cone shape. Try both to figure out which is more comfortable for your body.

Quantity. Once your milk comes in, you will likely go through a few pairs of nursing pads a day. Even if you have a washer and dryer at home, you probably don't want to do laundry daily with a newborn, so I'd recommend investing in 7 pairs, minimum, to start. After a few months, you will likely wear one pair a day. Consider getting a few different styles to find the ones you like best.

🌱

ECO-ACTION NO. 22
Plastic- and Toxin-Free Dinnerware

PROBLEMATIC PLACE SETTINGS

We all want to feed our children healthy foods. But what about the plates and bowls we're using to serve their meals? Exposure to toxins found in plastic dinnerware can have negative health implications on our growing kids. Harmful chemicals can leak from plastic dinnerware into food when heated—including serving warm food on dishes, microwave use, or when washed and heated in the dishwasher. Acidic foods served on plastic dinnerware do the same. To choose healthier alternatives, you'll want to avoid the following when purchasing new dinnerware.

- BPA & BPS
- Phthalates
- PVC
- PFAS

- Melamine (found in both melamine plastic and bamboo bioplastic)

- Heavy metals such as lead and cadmium

Several nontoxic, plastic-free dinnerware options are available for kids, including glass, stainless steel, and bamboo. They all have their pros and cons, so ultimately it's about finding which one works best for your family. **Getting tough.** Durability is essential, not only for dinnerware to survive that "throw everything on the floor" phase but also for the Earth (and your wallet). And while we can hope that all of your plates will be passed on to another family after your child has outgrown them, there will come a day when they will need to be disposed of. So it's important to consider how they'll be disposed of (recycled, composted, or tossed in the trash). *And remember, getting hand-me-downs from your brother's kids or buying secondhand is always more sustainable than buying anything new.*

THE SAFEST MEALTIME MATERIALS
STAINLESS STEEL

- **Pros:** Studies have found 304-grade stainless steel (also known as 18/8 and 18/10) to be a safe choice for dinnerware. It's a durable material that doesn't run the risk of breaking and can be used for all stages of childhood.

- **Cons:** Stainless steel can be hot or cold to the touch depending on the temperature of the food you serve. There are double-wall options available that keep the outside of the dinnerware at room temperature. Stainless steel cannot go into the microwave, and it's not an option for children who have an allergy or a sensitivity to nickel or chromium. Some studies have shown leaching of these metals, particularly with acidic foods, but it's still widely considered to be one of the safest materials for food preparation and storage.
- **End of life:** Infinitely recyclable.

GLASS

- **Pros:** Duralex dinnerware is durable, inexpensive, nontoxic, classic, and made of tempered glass, which is much stronger than ordinary glass. Glass dinnerware is stackable and dishwasher- and microwave- safe, which are huge bonuses for busy families. Additionally, it can be used by everyone.
- **Cons:** While tempered glass is more durable and doesn't shatter like conventional glassware, it still runs the risk of breaking. Also, be sure to avoid painted glassware, especially vintage pieces, as it may contain lead.
- **End of life:** While most tempered glass is not recyclable, the Duralex brand is, making it a top pick for glass brands.

BAMBOO

- **Pros:** Bamboo is sustainable, eco-friendly, and not easily broken. Its simple "wood" appearance is classic and timeless. Furthermore, it's a sustainable material. Look for bamboo ware that's organic and uses FDA-approved food-grade varnish.
- **Cons:** Bamboo is not microwave- or dishwasher-safe. *Note: Bamboo dinnerware is different from "bamboo-based" ware. Bamboo is brown and looks like wood, whereas bamboo-based dinnerware looks more like (and does contain) plastic.*
- **End of life:** Compostable, unless it comes with silicone interwoven in the design, in which case it's trash.

RUNNERS-UP

PLANT-BASED

- **Pros:** Reusable plant-based dinnerware, not to be confused with bamboo-based, is made from renewable fibers extracted from crops like corn, bamboo, wheat, and sweet potatoes. It's microwave- and dishwasher-safe and can be found free of BPA, PVC, phthalates, lead, cadmium, and mercury. Unlike bamboo-based dinnerware (which looks almost identical), it's free of melamine (plastic).

- **Cons:** Some bioplastics made with polylactic acid (PLA) were shown to contain high toxicity levels in a 2019 study.
- **End of life:** Compostable, often only in industrial facilities.

SILICONE

- **Pros:** It's highly durable, microwavable, and dishwasher safe. Search for brands that offer 100% food-grade silicone with no plastic fillers and are BPA-, BPS-, PVC-, and phthalate-free.
- **Cons:** Kids outgrow silicone dinnerware quickly (most are designed for kids two and under), which means more money and resources. Plus, they stain easily, making them harder to hand down.
- **End of life:** Trash.

ENAMELWARE

- **Pros:** It's dishwasher safe (though better to hand wash), shatterproof, versatile for indoor/outdoor use, and will last for years.
- **Cons:** It isn't as durable for little ones, who are more prone to throw and scratch plates with forks. And, unless you're buying from a highly trusted brand that performs rigorous testing, lead and cadmium leaching is of concern.
- **End of life:** Trash.

WHO DIDN'T MAKE THE CUT?

Melamine. Melamine is a type of plastic that's not recyclable and runs the risk of leaching harmful chemicals into food—particularly when heated or used for hot or acidic foods. The FDA considers it safe to use as long as it's used correctly, so it's up to you if you want to run the risk.

Bamboo-based. Bamboo-based dinnerware, not to be confused with real bamboo, looks like plastic or plant-based dinnerware but generally has melamine (plastic) as its filler. Brands often hide this fact by stating that they use a "food-safe binding resin" and advertising that the dinnerware is biodegradable, which is greenwashing because everything technically biodegrades. Unless the company spells out what plants it uses as its resin or that it's melamine-free, skip it.

ONLINE OVERHAUL

It's not just our physical world that's polluted; it's our virtual world as well. Clean up your online habits by creating sustainable routines for you and the planet.

🌿
ECO-ACTION NO. 23
Green Your Amazon Order

Your week is chock full, and you just realized that you forgot to order [*insert anything you've ever needed in a jam*]. Last-minute Halloween costumes, toilet paper, art supplies for your kid's science fair project that's due on Friday—we've all been there. As busy parents, we have all had those *ahh-I-need-it-now* freak-out moments. Quick and convenient are essential in our hurried lives. Shopping entirely at independent package-free sustainable shops might be an optimal online shopping eco-action, but it's unrealistic to assume that everyone is ready to turn away from the world's largest online retailer, Amazon. If you're not quite prepared to break up with your Prime subscription (yet), here're some ABCs to reduce waste and your overall footprint.

DO THE AMAZON ABCs

Add "Climate Pledge Friendly" to Your Search
Amazon can actually help you to buy products that have a lower environmental footprint. "Climate Pledge Friendly" has its own dedicated online Amazon storefront, which allows you to shop products that have one or more sustainability certification, including Fair Trade, Global Organic Textile Standard (GOTS), ENERGY STAR, the Forest Stewardship Council (FSC), Rainforest Alliance, and Responsible Wool Standard (RWS).

Buy Sustainable Products

If buying brand-new products, consider purchasing reusable items made from sustainable materials over single-use goods. Skip plastic altogether, when possible. Instead of ordering disposable cotton facial makeup-remover rounds, buy reusable, washable organic bamboo ones. Buying reusable, sustainably made products means less waste, less packaging, and fewer delivery trucks on the road because you won't need to replace items every time they run out. And you will save money in the long run.

--- **DID YOU KNOW?** ---

It takes more than 1 billion trees to make the **165 billion packages** shipped in the United States each year.

Choose a Slower Shipping Method

One- to two-day shipping can be a lifesaver at times. However, it's not always necessary. When your order is not urgent, opt for "No Rush Shipping." This reduces your fossil fuel footprint. The faster the delivery, the less efficient the delivery trucks can be in filling their cargo space. If the package doesn't have to be there on a specific day, they can hold it until the truck is full before dropping it at your front door.

Do an "Amazon Delivery Day"

"Amazon Delivery Day" is a free setting on your Amazon Prime account. It allows you to select one or two days a week that you want to receive your Amazon orders. It reduces the number of packages you receive each week by consolidating orders. Setting up your "Amazon Delivery Day" also reduces trips for delivery trucks, thus reducing their carbon footprint. If you need an order quickly, though, you still have the option for quicker delivery.

End "New" Purchases

Amazon sells secondhand items alongside new products. You can search for used items, like toys and books, on the right sidebar when perusing their site. You can also select the "used" box when adding an item to your cart. Amazon will give you a condition description of the item, such as "Used—Like New" or "Used—Very Good." Buying a secondhand product reduces its carbon footprint and strains on natural resources because no new materials or energy were needed to create it.

Frustration-Free Packaging

When you select Amazon's certified "Frustration-Free Packaging," all packaging materials are 100% recyclable and come without excess shipping elements (like those annoying plastic air-filled pillows). Amazon has worked with sellers to eliminate wasteful plastic clamshells, unnecessary cartons, plastic-coated wire ties, etc., from their overall packaging design. It's free to customers and can easily be selected by checking the "Frustration-Free Packaging" box on the sidebar when browsing on Amazon. Not every product comes with this option, but over 1.3 million products do.

Get in New Habits

Before clicking "Buy Now," pause for a day to ask yourself, Do I really need this? If so, *do I have to order it from Amazon?* I know Amazon is easy, quick, and cheap, but those things drive a deeper wedge into many issues like fair wages, plastic pollution, and greenhouse gas emissions. Consider limiting the amount you buy from this powerhouse overall; if it's a must-have, see if you can purchase it locally or through an eco-friendly shop online. It took us three years to cancel our Prime membership, so I relate if the idea of going cold turkey overnight makes you sweat. Doing your Amazon detox slowly will help you minimize withdrawal symptoms and will give you time to find more sustainable shops for your essentials.

SHOP YOUR VALUES ONLINE

Consider Skipping Amazon and Doing This Instead:

- **Choose zero-waste shops.** Choose independent, zero-waste online stores for everyday essentials like plastic-free toiletries and kitchen necessities. Plus, they often ship everything carbon neutral and plastic-free.
- **Buy ethically.** Support businesses that uphold ethical social practices.
- **Make old a "new" habit.** Look online to see if you can find what you need secondhand before trying to buy it new. The online secondhand market is booming, far beyond Amazon, with quality goods from furniture to toys and clothing.
- **Do your research.** Shopping online allows you to look into a company's sustainability mission at the click of a button much more readily than when buying things in person. If the company has an ethical mission in place, they will share all they're doing to make the world a

better place. Beware of greenwashing and look for environmental and social certifications to ensure a company is worthy of your dollars.

- **Keep it in your basket.** Avoid impulse purchases by setting a 7-day rule for all online purchases. Hold goods in your online shopping basket for a week before clicking "Buy Now."
- **Minimize returns.** Returning products is an environmental flop. Ten percent of online returns are donated, thrown away, or burned by retailers. In the United States alone, the amount of trash produced by returned products is equivalent to a year's worth of trash for 5 million people. (Not to mention the 15 million tons of carbon emissions emitted by returns annually.) When you shop online, try to buy only items you're sure you will love and keep to avoid sending products back.
- **Buy big.** If you usually order toothpaste online, order a 10-pack instead of just one each month. It will require less packaging since it won't need to be boxed up 12 times, and will also reduce emissions with just one delivery.

ECO-ACTION NO. 24
Digital Clutter Detox

Overconsumption in our lives doesn't exist only in the physical world; it also includes our digital intake. Detoxing the storm of spam that we are fed electronically can help us lower our footprint, buy less, and keep us on track with our new sustainable lifestyle.

Unsubscribe. A simple step to reduce your carbon footprint (and your sanity) is to clean up your digital space. Because energy is required to power our devices, connect to other devices, and keep information stored on the cloud, a typical email emits about .4g of CO_2e (CO_2e = carbon dioxide equivalent), with large attachment-ridden emails averaging about 50g of CO_2e.

One way to limit the emails that clog your digital world is to unsubscribe from mass marketing. Not just spam from suspicious sources, but all of those marketing emails tipping you off to sales and new products.

Emails from large retailers increase your digital footprint and lure you in to buy unsustainable items. End the madness by hitting "Unsubscribe."

Unfollow. If you're on social media, it's hard not to be tempted by planet-harming trends and products when advertisements and posts constantly bombard you. Fast-fashion brands, in particular, suck us in with their weekly product launches and ever-changing styles. It no longer makes sense to support brands that are not making our world and people's lives better through their business practices. Now's a great time to do a cleanse from the unsustainable companies you follow. Moving forward, choose to follow ethical companies that are doing their part.

DID YOU KNOW?

The average American spends over **14 hours** shopping online each month.

KID CLUTTER

Limit kid clutter. Regain your sanity.

🌿

ECO-ACTION NO. 25
Baby Gear

With so many baby products on the market today, narrowing down what you actually need can be daunting. If you are expecting your first child, you may not be aware of the overwhelming tidal wave of baby and kid stuff that's about to flow through your home. Here are five simple steps to ensure you're setting yourself, your baby, and the earth up for success—but still having fun, cute items. I promise, you can enjoy the process, surrounded by baby sweetness, but without all the clutter.

01. FOCUS ON ESSENTIALS

If you were to purchase every "essential" item that big brands are trying to sell you, you would be drowning in baby stuff. With that said, there are a dozen essentials you will likely want on hand before your baby arrives.

Twelve Baby Basics

- Baby carrier or wrap
- Baby nail scissors
- Car seat
- Safe place for baby to sleep
- Clothes, hat, + socks
- Diapers + wipes
- Glass baby bottles
- Pump + milk storage
- Blanket
- Swaddle
- Burp cloths
- Stroller

Even with this minimal list, there will likely be two or three items your baby will reject and you will need to swap out for another version, model, or size. You can do all of the research in the world to find the "best" baby sleeper with over 1,000 five-star reviews (and three-digit price tags), only to find that your little one refuses to sleep in it. Looking for everything preloved (or renting) is a better option as it allows you to try out different products to see what works best for your child without wasting money or resources.

02. CONSIDER WHAT YOU OWN

Many items parents have been told they "need" are likely things you already own. Could you repurpose your favorite tote or backpack into a diaper bag? How about using an old iPod as a sound machine; washcloths you already have tucked away in the hall closet as burp cloths; or a folded beach blanket for a changing station? Sometimes planning for your baby's arrival just means thinking outside the box. And if your repurposed items don't work out, that's fine. (Remember, not all of your brand-new items will be hits, either.) But going for the sustainable option first is better for the earth and your wallet.

03. GO WITH PRELOVED

Begin with Hand-Me-Downs. Ask friends and family to pass down staple items like clothing, baby equipment, books, and toys. It's not such a big ask. As a mom of two, I can tell you that many parents are very eager to reduce their clutter and give items away that their children have either outgrown or outloved. And in turn, when your baby has outgrown things, continue the cycle by offering your family's baby clothing and equipment to new parents.

Shop Secondhand. Preloved items will always be more sustainable than buying brand-new ones, even if that new item is eco-friendly. The long-term impact of buying new clothing and equipment is also much more significant with baby items because your growing child won't be able to use or wear things for more than a few months.

Rent It. There are several companies out there that rent high-quality, attractive baby equipment and clothing. You can include rental items on your baby registry so friends and family can gift the rentals to you. In addition to being better for the environment, it also saves space by not needing to store items months before you actually need them and allows you to try out items. It's a game changer to exchange rental items your baby doesn't like for other options that might suit you or your baby better.

04. FILL IN WITH NEW ECO-ITEMS

Get Items that Grow and Multitask. Look for items that can grow with your baby, such as a convertible high chair that your child can use from birth to age seven. It will save you time researching options at every stage of growth and reduce your environmental impact by sticking with one piece of equipment for years rather than having to upgrade every few months. Additionally, mobile items, multipurpose equipment, or gear that can be used both at home and on the go are valuable choices.

Go Eco. If you can't get an item secondhand, register for goods that are sustainably made from responsible materials such as GOTS organic cotton, hemp, linen, felt, FSC-certified wood, natural rubber, and stainless steel, and which are free of harmful chemicals including BPA, phthalates, pesticides, PVC, formaldehyde, and toxic dyes and perfumes.

05. THINK LONG-TERM

Set up a 529 Plan. To limit physical gifts, consider adding a link on your registry to a college savings account, also known as a 529 plan, for your child.

Hold Off. If you don't receive everything on your registry, pause your purchasing. Getting to know your child first and yourself as a new parent can be priceless before buying too many things. It may be tempting to buy 10 adorable organic cotton infant onesies, but you may come to find that your baby is 9 pounds at birth and will never wear them. Or that those snaps on the bottom of the onesie are nearly impossible in the dark at 3 a.m., and now you're kicking yourself for buying so many. Pacifiers are another item we assume babies will need, but not all babies are keen on them. Maybe get one to see if your baby is into it—there is so much that depends upon who your child is, and you won't know until they arrive.

🍃
ECO-ACTION NO. 26
Trim the Toys

By the age of 13 most American children own 117 toys, but on average kids only play with a maximum of 10 toys regularly. Six out of 10 parents feel overwhelmed by the number of toys in their house. And not only are we purchasing toys at an alarming rate ($4,300 worth before kids become teens), there is also a trash issue. Most toys are destined for the landfill. Seventy-five percent of families get rid of 3 to 14 toys each year. Plus, studies have shown that too many toys can inhibit your child's cognitive and neurological development. And just as familiarity with toys can lead to boredom and disinterest, so does overabundance. (Just another example of the *overabundance blues*.) Opting for *green* playtime is essential for your child's well-being and to ensure the Earth's health for their future.

DID YOU KNOW?

American kids consume **40%** of the world's toys but make up just **3.1%** of the global population of children.

MAKE PLAY SUSTAINABLE

Create a Toy Rotation. Set up a toy shelf and only put out 5 to 10 toys. (Remember, research has shown children only play with 10 at a time, tops). Every few days or once a week, swap out some of the lesser-played-with toys for others that you have stored away—using what you own but limiting how much you put out. Children also get overwhelmed with clutter, so offering them a small but meaningful selection of toys can help your child to immerse themselves in more imaginative play. It also helps them focus while sparking excitement about what they have in front of them.

Use What You Have. You do not need to buy a new set of plastic-free toys to make playtime more eco-friendly. As long as the toys you have are safe for your child to use, there is no need to get rid of unsustainable toys if they're still part of your child's play.

Set up a Toy Exchange with a Friend. Has your child already done their puzzle 100 times and lost interest? Set up a toy exchange with another family and trade anything from games to trucks. Set a date to swap back, and likely your child will have newfound excitement after having space from some of their toys.

Buy Secondhand. Join a Buy Nothing Group to get "new" toys or search for secondhand toys online using resources like eBay, Poshmark, Toycycle, or Mercari. If bringing plastic toys into your child's play, try to look for secondhand first. A secondhand toy can spark as much joy as a "new" one!

Quality over Quantity. Choose heirloom, plastic-free toys that are built to last generations. Be more selective about which toys come into your home, and buy fewer overall. Choose open-ended toys like solid wood blocks, silk scarves, and eco–art supplies, which spark the imagination and can be used in a myriad of ways.

Support Sustainable Toy Brands. If you must buy new, purchase toys made from eco-friendly materials such as sustainably harvested wood, natural rubber, or organic cotton. If they're made in the USA, even better. Be sure to look for ethical employee and business practices.

Build with Nature. Get outside. Use branches to build a fort, rocks, and leaves to make mandalas, or do a nature scavenger hunt at your local park.

Rent. Sign up to rent baby toys, Legos, and more. Be careful to note the difference between toy subscriptions, where they send a new toy every month, and toy rentals, where your child gets a toy every month and then you send it back when they're done.

Limit Packaging. Look for new toys with less packaging, particularly plastic.

Get Recharged. If you have battery-powered toys, buy rechargeable batteries instead of disposable ones. This limits resources and waste while keeping kids happy (because a recharge is much quicker than waiting for their parents to run to the store to buy more).

> **ECO-FAMILY TIP**
> For eco-friendly beach toys, head to the thrift store and buy muffin tins, measuring cups, and mixing bowls and spoons instead of new plastic sand toys.

🍃

ECO-ACTION NO. 27
Back-to-School Eco-Essentials

Most school supplies are destined for the garbage the moment they are produced. They're designed to last one school year (if that) and are tossed out when summer begins—only to be repurchased again at the start of the following school year. While not exactly single-use, they have a short life span, with most products being made of plastic or mixed materials that can't be recycled. This type of waste has become normalized, and in the long run comes at an expense to both you and the Earth. Being mindful of the impact school supplies have on the planet is a natural teaching point for kids too.

SUSTAINABLE SCHOOL SUPPLY TIPS

Use What You Have. Before buying anything, look at what your child already has to avoid buying duplicates. Don't purchase "eco-friendly" supplies to replace perfectly good ones you already own. Only when they can no longer be used should you look for sustainably made replacements.

Buy Supplies Wisely. Look for supplies made from recycled materials (recycled paper, recycled fabrics, etc.) that can also be recycled or composted at the end of their life.

YAY	NAY
✓ Recycled, BPA-free paper	✗ Virgin paper
✓ Plastic-free recyclable or compostable supplies	✗ Plastic supplies
✓ Unpainted pencils, refillable pens, wax markers, and natural rubber erasers	✗ Coated pencils, single-use pens, and toxic or scented markers
✓ Sturdy cardboard binders and 100% recyclable binder dividers and notebooks	✗ Glitter and toxic or scented craft supplies and glue (VOCs)
✓ Stainless steel pencil tin	✗ Vinyl binders, pencil cases, and paper clips
✓ Kraft, washi, or masking tape	✗ Spiral-bound notebooks
	✗ Plastic tape

─────── **DID YOU KNOW?** ───────

The outer paint coating on pencils is plastic. That means microplastics are released when sharpening (or chewing on the end).

Buy Secondhand Books. If eBooks aren't an option or preferred, purchase secondhand textbooks instead of buying them brand-new.

Buy Quality + Timeless Items. Buying a high-quality backpack that will last years will save money and resources. Instead of chasing trends like trucks or unicorns, purchase something more timeless (like a single color) that your child can use for years. To decorate a backpack, opt for pins or patches that can be removed when curiosities shift. Look for natural, uncoated fabrics such as organic cotton canvas; avoid bags made of PVC or vinyl (think shiny or smelly plastic).

ECO-FAMILY TIP

Don't forget to look for secondhand sports gear and equipment for your young athletes.

CELEBRATIONS + GIFTS

Make meaningful memories that express care for the Earth and each other.

🌿

ECO-ACTION NO. 28
Green Your Celebrations

ECO-ENTERTAINING

Holidays, birthdays, graduations, and more—through these special occasions we pause to mark time, build memories, uphold traditions, and commemorate transitions. In short, celebrating is vital to the human spirit. Yet, with the forces of consumerism and social media, these important events often get muddled—adding pressures to buy more to make your celebration "picture perfect." You can still have a visually stunning party, but by shifting the focus to the experience and the essence of what we are celebrating (life, love, and each other), we can bring deeper meaning to our holidays and milestones while still caring for each other and the planet.

THE PARTY

Servingware. Get a set of secondhand dishes, cutlery, and glassware that can be used for larger parties and holidays throughout the year to avoid disposables at every event.

Provide the Proper Bins. Set out labeled recycling and compost bins for attendees to toss beverage containers and food waste.

Food + Drinks. Try to serve package-free food. Offer cut-up fruits and veggies. Make hummus and opt for a baguette instead of crackers, which usually come packaged in plastic. Buy organic or regenerative foods, if possible.

Keep it easy. You can even go to a local deli and have them fill your containers. If making food, adjust your recipes according to head count. (It's so easy to wind up with excess food.) Consider making your celebration meat-free (or at least cut out the beef.) Use a drink dispenser or large glass bottles that people can pour instead of drinks in individual containers. And don't forget to say "cheers" with sustainable, local wine and beer.

Plan for Leftovers. If storing leftovers, do it plastic-free. Whether you use a reusable Tupperware container, Mason jar, beeswax wrap, or dishcloth, think ahead about how you plan to store your leftovers. And if it's a big feast, don't be shy about asking guests to bring a Tupperware to carry home leftovers too.

Borrow. Opt to borrow or rent linens instead of using disposable single-use tablecloths or buying cloth ones brand-new.

Dress the Part. The most sustainable clothing you can wear is what is already in your closet. The next best option is to buy secondhand. If you're looking for something specific and can't find it preloved, opt to rent your attire instead.

THE DECOR

Reuse It. Reuse the decor you already own from year to year. Make your decorations part of your time-honored traditions,

Make It. Get crafty with the kids and upcycle recyclables to make festive decorations for any holiday. Look to nature to decorate. Think sticks and yarn for Halloween spiderwebs or local foliage and flowers to create drool-worthy tablescapes.

Buy It. Look for preloved items online and at your local thrift store if you need "new" pieces to round out your holiday flair.

Light It. From birthday cakes to menorahs, candles are part of many festivities. Look for ones free of unsustainable palm oil, lead wicks, paraffin, and phthalates—better for your health and the environment.

'TIS THE SEASON *TO CONSUME*

In the weeks between Thanksgiving and New Year, Americans produce 25% more trash than any other time of year. No matter what holidays you celebrate, consider folding in mindful traditions that can still bring joy and momentous memories—without the waste. By becoming more attentive to how we mark these festivities, we can shed some of the pressure by rooting ourselves deeper in the true meaning of what we are celebrating while also being conscious of our impact. Here are a few simple ways to host you holidays with intention:

Order Eco-Holiday Cards made from 100% post-consumer recycled paper. Avoid cards with glossy, glitter (oh, hi there, microplastics), shiny, or gold-foiled coatings. None of these can be recycled. If you're ready to go paperfree, consider sending an electronic card.

Wrap It Right. Holiday gift wrap is a significant source of the season's waste. For more tips and tricks on shifting your wrapping habits, see Eco-Action 29.

Deck the Halls. Make your own decorations. Get the kids involved! Use pinecones and foliage to decorate the table, mantel, and wreath for the front door. If you already have a garage full of decor, use it; skip buying anything new.

Swap Your Holiday Lights. If you're replacing old strands of holiday lights or need to buy new ones, go with safer, energy-saving LED.

Gobble, Gobble. If a turkey is part of your holiday festivities, put the bones, any vegetable scraps, and water in a pot to make soup stock. Freeze it for future use or make turkey soup with the stock in the morning. If you can forgo the bird, opt for lots of tasty side dishes instead—because isn't it all about the stuffing and mashed potatoes, really?

🍃

ECO-ACTION NO. 29
Rethink Gifts

GIFTS GONE WILD

In the United States alone, more than $16 billion is wasted on presents that are deemed "unwanted" every year, with the average person spending $71 a year on gifts that recipients have reported they didn't want. Returned gifts also come at an expense. From the greenhouse gases spewed on their way back to their retailer, they leave a trail of emissions in their wake. Many returned gifts—5.8 billion pounds to be exact—go straight from retailers to landfills. (That's right. Returned presents don't necessarily get put back on the shelves or restocked for online resale.)

KIDS' BIRTHDAYS
WASTE–FREE FROM A TO Z

Ask guests to write a letter to your child that will be saved and opened on their 18th birthday—in lieu of toys

~~Balloons~~

Cloth tablecloth* instead of single-use

Digital invites

Experiences over stuff

Find ways to use what you have for party entertainment. Kick around a soccer ball at the park. Play musical chairs. Decorate cupcakes. Build forts and rocket ships with shipping boxes. Set up a dress-up station or get your groove on with a dance party.

Go easy on the food. Kids play more than they eat. It's easy to go overboard and end up with food waste.

Homemade sweets reduce packaging waste. Also, brownies, cookies, and cupcakes can be served without plates and utensils—unlike cake—meaning less waste and less cleanup.

Instead of plastic food packaging, order pizza and then compost the boxes afterward.

Juice + water: Pour drinks from a pitcher instead of buying individual water bottles or juice boxes.

Kindly ask for plastic-free gifts, no gifts, or for $2 from each guest so your child can pick out one gift.

Look to nature. Climb trees. Do a nature scavenger hunt. Go for a hike. Play at the beach. Do a group bike ride.

Metal* or bamboo** cutlery

No straws

Offer bins for guests to toss recycling and compost—even if the party isn't at your home.

Prepare for leftovers. Make space in your fridge in advance and be sure to plan for a way to transport extra food home if the party is out and about.

Quit giving party favors. If you feel you must, offer a treat to-go or something usable like a minipot with seeds they can plant.

Reusable plates* (or do compostable ones if not at home)

Stay close to come (or host at home).

Timeless decorations can be used from year to year. It limits single-use waste and makes the decor part of your yearly traditions.

Upcycle items you already own, like strands of holiday lights or old glass jars as drinkware and vases.

Vegetarian, plant-based foods. Sliced fruits and veggies and peanut butter and jelly wedges are always a hit.

Washable cups* (or compostable ones) over plastic.

"X" out disposables and plastic from the day.

Yay! Don't forget to celebrate your eco-shifts—give yourself a pat on the back.

Zero waste does not mean zero joy, memories, traditions, or excitement. It simply means taking the environment into account when planning your celebration.

* buy secondhand or borrow
** buy compostable

Whether you're the giver or recipient, unwanted gifts are a waste of money, resources, and time. With the Earth in peril and our homes bursting with stuff, it's about time we clean up our gifting habits.

GIVE BETTER

There are many ways to give sustainably while sparking joy without turning to plastic or going against your values. Here are some ways to gift better:

Ask + Listen. We all love the element of surprise, but guessing what a recipient wants means we can miss our target. Go ahead and outright ask people what they want or need. If you're uncomfortable, don't ask but listen (and keep a top-secret list on your phone). Make a note if your partner keeps complaining about their defective BBQ tongs. When it comes time to give a gift, they'll wonder how you knew exactly what they wanted.

Give Consumables. Gifts that can be consumed are always a win. Whether a bottle of wine, Fair Trade chocolate, infused olive oil, or a canister of loose-leaf tea, look for organic and local when possible. But "consumable" doesn't need to mean "edible"; it can also be a practical, usable gift such as a beautiful bar of soap.

Gift Experiences. Carpe diem! Give the gift of dinner at the recipient's favorite restaurant, a class (either online or in person), a museum membership, a national parks pass, or money for a child's college savings account.

Go Green. Look for gifts made from eco-friendly materials such as organic cotton, linen, hemp, bamboo, sustainably sourced wood, or recycled plastic. Don't forget to support sustainable and ethical brands. Reusable products such as produce bags, a French press, beeswax wraps, or a travel straw set make great stocking stuffers and host gifts.

Give Yourself. Gift your skills by teaching your areas of expertise to those who want to learn: give piano lessons, yoga instruction, a cooking class, or a photography lesson if you have the know-how. Remind friends and loved ones how important it is to pamper themselves by making them bath salts or body scrub. DIY children's gifts can also be a big hit. Think homemade play dough, sock puppets, or a trunk of vintage costumes you've found or made. And who doesn't love homemade treats like cookies, jam, or bread? Always a winner.

Gift Vintage. Peruse your local flea market for unique, one-of-a-kind gifts. One year my mom gifted me a pair of sterling silver vintage candlesticks, and now they grace our dinner table every night.

Give a Donation. Donating money in the recipient's name to a cause they care about is a thoughtful gift that can mean a lot to the right person.

Skip Monogramming. If your recipient doesn't like a gift, it's next to impossible for them to donate or give it away if it's personalized with their name or initials.

GET BETTER

Talk to Friends and Relatives. Fill them in on the sustainable journey you're embarking on and why sustainable gift exchanges are important to your family.

Create a Wish List. Ask your kids and partner to keep a running *want list* throughout the year. Don't just wait for birthdays and holidays to add to it. Keeping it updated regularly helps everyone keep tabs on items they need or have been eyeing while also reducing the panic of creating a last-minute list of not-so-relevant items. This way, if Grandma, who lives across the country, wants to send a midsummer surprise, she will have better direction on what to give. Be conscious of what you ask for by including local shops, responsibly made products, and plastic-free items. Everyone appreciates the time saved from trying to guess the perfect gift. Ask others what they want as well to normalize the conversation of sharing what's on each other's wish list.

WRAP BETTER

Repurpose and Reuse. Avoid buying any new gift wrap by reusing gift bags. If you prefer the wrapped look, reuse brown paper bags, newspapers, magazine pages, your child's artwork, wall calendars, or old maps. In many towns, wrapping paper cannot be recycled (yikes!). No matter where you live, avoid gift wrap that contains foil, glitter, or plastics. It cannot be recycled anywhere.

Think Outside the Box. Use a tea towel, bandanna, or square piece of cloth to wrap a gift. (Google search *furoshiki*, the Japanese art of fabric gift wrapping.)

Avoid the Tape Trap. Scotch tape is plastic and isn't recyclable. Opt for colorful and festive 100% paper (aka washi) tape instead. It's pretty, biodegradable, and made out of renewable resources. It also looks super cute on packages as a ribbon alternative.

Tie It Up. Ribbon cannot be recycled and is trash unless you reuse it. If you don't have any saved from prior gifts, use jute or baker's twine, which can be composted (or reused).

Ship Sustainably. If shipping gifts, use paper shipping tape instead of plastic tape. Reuse old boxes and mailers—you can even stop by your local grocery store or hardware store to pick up a discarded box from their stockroom. Plan ahead and choose the slowest form of shipping to reduce carbon emissions.

GRANDPARENT GIFT MANIA

Grandparents love to shower their grandchildren with presents. An AARP survey found that 86% of grandparents buy gifts for their grand-kids. With an annual average total spend of about $2,500 per child, presents are the number one category (by far) in their fund allocations. The toy industry earns $28 billion annually, with grandparents making up $7 billion of that total. And though their gifts are well-intentioned, this overboard buying can be overwhelming for kids and parents alike.

Encourage connection over consumption. Remind the grandparents that they're loved and encourage other ways to strengthen their bond with their grandchildren. If they're far away, set up a weekly Zoom call or propose letter writing to keep them feeling involved. Set up a toy mailbox in your home as a unique portal to grandparents, where your kids can collect artwork for them (which you can then mail together) and you, in turn, can place letters they've sent to their grandkids. When visiting, if they show up at your home with a gift, graciously take it at the door. Put the focus on the person, not the present, by celebrating that "Grandma is here!" and only bring the gift out once they have had time to enjoy each other's company. If they live locally, encourage quality time with regular weekly dates.

Set clear boundaries. Request no-plastic gifts year-round. Before birthdays and holidays, send your children's gift wish list to grandparents so they can buy presents that your kids will love and use. If the unnecessary, plastic, or unsolicited gifts continue, kindly let them know that your home has surpassed its capacity and that the presents will be given to children in need.

Create memorable moments. Ask grandparents to gift experiences instead of things. Suggest they contribute to swimming lessons, dance classes, or a college fund instead of physical gifts. A museum membership is also a fun gift that keeps on giving. Take lots of photos and invite them to come along to the event they're supporting.

BODY

CLOTHING

Green is the new black. Build a sustainable and ethical wardrobe by adopting better purchasing practices and adequately caring for what you already own—all without sacrificing your personal style.

FAST FACTS

Climate Change

According to the United Nations, the fashion industry contributes 8–10% of global carbon emissions due to its long supply chains and energy-intensive production. That's more than aviation and maritime shipping combined.

Water Waste	Buy Secondhand
Nearly 20% of global wastewater is produced by the fashion industry.	Approximately 1,800 gallons of water are required to make one new pair of jeans.

Living Wages	It's Gendered; Women . . .
Fashion Checker, a campaign created by the Clean Clothes Campaign and funded by the European Union, found that 93% of brands surveyed were not paying garment workers a living wage.	• Make up 80% of garment workers • Are consistently paid less than their male counterparts • Are targets of abuse and assault When you support clothing brands that uphold fair and ethical workplace standards, you are also supporting women's rights.

THE FATE OF FASHION 101

ARE YOUR CLOTHES TRASH?

It's nice to think that our donated clothing is ending up in someone else's closet, but only about 20% of secondhand clothing is resold. And, once that 20% has run its course, even that's likely headed for the trash. According to the Environmental Protection Agency, 84% of our clothing ends up in landfills or incinerators, with only about 14% being recycled and the remainder being exported overseas. In addition to taking longer to break down, textiles that end up in the landfill emit methane gas during decomposition, a greenhouse gas that is up to 34 times more potent than carbon.

According to the EPA, in 2018 alone over 2.2 million tons of clothing and footwear were incinerated. Furthermore, to dispose of unsold clothing, fashion brands burn it, contributing to climate change, releasing microplastics into the air, and creating air pollutants harmful to human health. We are starting to see a new trend toward the production of recycled synthetic fabrics. However, the percentage of clothing that's recycled is still relatively small.

BREAKING DOWN THE BREAKDOWN

It takes the following number of years for your clothes to break down:

Natural Fabrics
- **Cotton:** 1 week to 5 months
- **Linen:** 2 weeks
- **Wool:** 1 to 5 years

Synthetic Fabrics
- **Polyester, spandex, nylon, etc:** 20 to 200 years

ECO-ACTION NO. 30
Wear Your Values

Growing kids, your expanding baby bump, worn-out clothes, fluctuating weight—all of our closets need a refresh from time to time. But it doesn't need to come at a cost to the earth or individual style. Shopping responsibly helps us build a beautifully curated closet filled with pieces we love and want to wear while reducing our overall footprint.

> "Buy less, choose well, make it last."
>
> **—VIVIENNE WESTWOOD**
> *fashion designer and mother*

Wear What You Own. The most sustainable option is to wear what's already in your closet. No matter the material, brand, or production methods used, wearing what you already own is always more sustainable than buying something new.

Buy Less. Buying fewer clothes can have a far-reaching impact. In 2018 alone, the average American bought 68 articles of clothing, and most people don't keep their clothes for long. People in the United States throw out a whopping 70 pounds of clothes annually, totaling 5% of landfill space. But it isn't just the Earth that's overwhelmed by our bursting wardrobes; it's us, too. Americans experience "wardrobe panic" (the feeling of having nothing to wear) at least 36 times a year, while 28% of the clothing in our closets has either never been worn or hasn't been touched in the past 12 months. Being selective, mindful, and sparing when purchasing clothes is a sustainable way to create a wardrobe full of loved pieces you actually want to put on.

Buy Secondhand. Even when sustainably produced, brand-new clothing comes with a footprint. Buying secondhand reduces an article of clothing's carbon and water footprint by 73%. It also limits strains on resources, such as water and energy, because no new materials were needed to create the garment. Additionally, it keeps wearable clothing out of the landfill or from being incinerated.

Buy Ethically. If purchasing new clothing, buy high-quality, responsibly made pieces that will last. Most ethical brands will detail their commitment to their workers and the environment on their website. Ethical clothing generally costs more because the planet and people are being treated with dignity, but not all expensive clothing is made ethically. From unsafe working conditions to unfair wages, people across the globe are living in poverty and risking their lives to bring us our clothing here in the US. From industrial chemicals added to your clothing, harming workers and local ecosystems, to environmental pollution, what your clothes are made from, and how, matters. If ethical clothing is not in your budget, opt for secondhand—it's better for the planet anyway.

Stop Buying Fast Fashion. Fast fashion is a phenomenon of mass retailers designing, manufacturing, and selling inexpensive clothing to meet the latest trends. Instead of launching a new line each season, the average fast-fashion company has 52-microseasons that generate excessive textile waste, waterway pollution, and carbon emissions. These clothes are often poorly made and thrown out after a short life span. This business model is exploitative and comes with an enormous environmental and humanitarian impact. Workers are mistreated, particularly women. Many fast-fashion brands engage in greenwashing to hide their offenses, but it's impossible to sustainably and ethically produce a T-shirt for $8, even if they say it's green. Cost isn't always an indicator, but looking at the price tag can help you spot a fast-fashion brand.

Rid Responsibly. Cleanse your closet of clothing that you don't wear anymore. Offer what you can through your local free marketplace or by hosting a Swap 'n' Social for friends (see page 214). For old clothing, handbags, socks, etc., that cannot be worn or repurposed, order a Take Back Bag at fordays.com or through Retold Recycling. Donate bras in wearable condition to I Support the Girls, Free the Girls, or The Bra Recyclers. To support women in your community, check with your local women's shelter to see if bra donations are accepted. Old undies and unwearable bras can be recycled through Knicky. (They're recycled into insulation and carpet padding.) Gently worn shoes can be sent to Soles4Souls, or recycle any brand of unwearable shoes through Nike's Reuse-A-Shoe program.

Once you're done purging your closet, you will also be free of that "I don't have anything to wear" feeling (aka the *overabundance blues*), because all of the clothing in your closet will be items you wear and love.

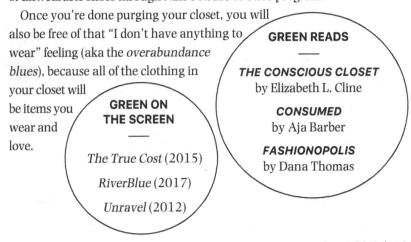

GREEN READS
—

THE CONSCIOUS CLOSET
by Elizabeth L. Cline

CONSUMED
by Aja Barber

FASHIONOPOLIS
by Dana Thomas

GREEN ON THE SCREEN
—

The True Cost (2015)

RiverBlue (2017)

Unravel (2012)

THE S.E.E.M. FASHION CHECKLIST

Not all fashion is as green as it S.E.E.M.s. Whether you or your partner
are shopping for kids' clothing or buying for yourself, here is a
simple checklist to ensure you're making the most sustainable choice.

SECONDHAND	Can I get this secondhand, rent it, or borrow it?
ESSENTIAL	Is this necessary? Do I already have something similar? Do I truly need it? Will I wear this a minimum of 30 times? Does it go with my existing wardrobe?
ETHICAL	Is the company sustainable and are they socially responsible? Is their brand transparent about their business model and ethics policies? Were the people who made this garment paid a living wage across the supply chain?
MATERIAL	If it's not secondhand, is it made of a sustainable material? Is it well made? What kind of dyes were used? Does it need to be dry-cleaned? How can this material be disposed of at the end of its life?

NO. 6

ECO–FAMILY BITE–SIZE CHALLENGE

NIX NEW CLOTHES

Starting on the first of the month, challenge your family to buy no brand-
new clothing for the entire month. See if you can buy what you need
secondhand, borrow it from a friend, or rent it. At the end of the month,
have a family meeting to see what everyone learned and discuss how to
implement those lessons to buy fewer brand-new things moving forward.

#nixnewclothes

ECO-ACTION NO. 31
Skip Plastic Fabrics

THE PLASTIC PUT-ON

Did you know that you're probably wearing plastic right now? Polyester, acrylic, nylon, spandex, and other synthetic fibers are all forms of plastic and make up 60% of all clothing worldwide. I'm talking about yoga pants, fuzzy fleece pullovers, athletic wear, etc. Synthetic materials are petroleum-based (made from oil). Around 70 million barrels of oil are used to make polyester fibers a year. Not to mention that a shirt made of polyester has twice the carbon footprint of one made of cotton. Almost all fabrics come from one or a combination of the following sources:

PLANT
cotton, linen, jute, bamboo, hemp

TREE
rayon, viscose, modal, lyocell

ANIMAL
leather, wool, silk, fur, cashmere

OIL
polyester, nylon, acrylic, spandex (sneaky plastic)

BUY BETTER MATERIALS

Be Conscious about Fabrics. Choose to buy plant- or tree-based fabrics instead of synthetics. Look for fabrics made from recycled materials, as it helps close the textile loop and reduces clothing ending up in the landfill. Choose organic wool or cashmere over leather and fur when buying animal-based fabrics. If choosing bamboo, you should know that a toxic chemical process is often used to turn the bamboo into the soft, silky fabric rayon—thus having adverse environmental consequences despite being made from an eco-friendly material. Instead, look for clothing made from lyocell (also known by its brand name, TENCEL® Lyocell) for a more sustainably manufactured fabric with a similar feel.

Buy High Quality. Buying well-made pieces that will last means replacing clothes less often. "Quality" doesn't have to be expensive. You can find impeccably made secondhand clothing that costs less than buying poorly made clothing brand-new—and it will last a lifetime.

Vegan Does Not Mean Eco-Friendly. Vegan leather (once referred to as "pleather") is generally made from PVC and polyurethane (chemical derivatives of petroleum). In short, vegan leather is toxic, plastic, and best avoided. Yet some brands are innovating plant-based leathers made from pineapples, apples, mushrooms, corn, cork, or even kelp. While these advancements are a step in the right direction, they may still be produced with some plastic or potentially require more resources, such as water, to make than plastic-based leather. Solutions are complicated, but advances in plant-based leathers are a better path toward sustainable leather alternatives than pleather. Be wary when buying vegan leather, no matter if a fast-fashion or luxury brand produces it, and do your research to ensure sustainable practices. Companies that are making strides will be transparent about their process.

Avoid "New" Synthetics. Love your yoga pants but not the environmental impact of wearing plastic? There is a loophole: buy them made from recycled materials (green-ish) or secondhand (greenest). You'll be reusing what already exists in the world.

Go Organic. Cotton is notorious for heavy water and pesticide use. Organic cotton, however, uses no pesticides, less water, no GMO seeds, and less energy, which is better for our bodies and the planet. When shopping for cotton, look for an organic GOTS certification label on the product.

UNDERSTANDING ORGANIC FIBERS

When clothing is labeled organic, it means that some or all of the fibers used to make that piece of clothing were grown without the use of chemically formulated, human-made fertilizers, pesticides, or herbicides. There are three tiers of organic:

- **100% Organic.** *Made using only organic materials, including the thread*
- **Organic.** *Made with 95% organic materials*
- **Made with Organic Ingredients.** *Contains 70–95% organic materials*

Choosing organic fabrics is far superior to clothing made from conventionally produced fibers. However, the "organic" label addresses only the crops used in making the fabric, not what happens during manufacturing. So while it may be organic, you don't know if toxic dyes or chemical finishes have been used. Choosing organic is a step in the right direction, but there are even better options.

Go with GOTS. To ensure that you invest in environmentally and socially responsible products, look for the Global Organic Textile Standard (GOTS) certification on clothing labels, bedding, home textiles, and even personal hygiene products. This certification is the world's leading authority on organic fibers. It guarantees the highest standards from the field throughout the entire supply chain, including strict social criteria and banning the use of toxic chemicals such as formaldehyde and heavy metals. GOTS has three levels of certification: "*GOTS Organic*" (95% organic fibers); "*GOTS*" (70–95% organic fibers); and "*GOTS Made with (X%) Organic*," with "*GOTS Organic*" being the most rigorous of the three certification standards.

GREEN READS
—

MENDING MATTERS and *MAKE THRIFT MEND*
by Katrina Rodabaugh

SEWING FOR KIDS
by Alexa Ward

ECO-ACTION NO. 32
Care for What You Own

Mending and repairing your clothes and accessories is a way to fight against our disposable, throwaway culture. Adding a patch or improving a boot sole doesn't just keep clothing out of the landfill; it means you're not buying an entirely new piece of clothing to replace what can be fixed. We need to reframe our cyclical habit of consumption and disposal to one of repairing, mending, and fixing. Taking care of what we have is one big step toward creating a less wasteful life.

Keep a "Fix It" Bag. Keep a bag in your closet, and over time pop in any clothing that needs to be repaired. When the bag is full, deal with it in one go instead of a dozen one-offs.

Repair It Yourself. Mending holes and sewing on patches are pretty rudimentary. (I took one sewing class in kindergarten and have never used a sewing machine, and I can do it.) There are some outstanding books and online tutorials to help get you started. If sewing isn't in your family's skill set, iron-on or peel-and-stick patches are an adorable, effective way to repair kids' clothing and gear without breaking out the needle and thread.

Find a Professional. If you can't mend something yourself, find someone who can. Become familiar with local repair shops. Tailors, cobblers, leather repair shops—frequenting these businesses extends the life of clothing.

Buy a Fabric Shaver. A fabric shaver is a basic, inexpensive device to add to your sustainability arsenal. It removes pilling from sweaters and clothing, bringing them back to nearly new condition and extending the life of your wardrobe.

PHYSICAL + MENTAL HEALTH

Taking care of our bodies, both physically and mentally, is an essential element of environmental action.

HIDDEN HARMFULS 101

THE HEALTH OF OUR KIDS

Kid's clothing, baby equipment, playroom furniture, crib mattresses, diaper cream, bubble bath—we often assume items such as these are safe because they're made specifically for kids. However, many products contain harmful chemicals and materials that shouldn't be making their way into our lives, no matter a person's age. While exposure to small amounts of one of these chemicals may not cause harm, it's the lifelong cocktail of toxic exposure that's of concern. Testing for toxicity generally happens one chemical at a time, not for the hundreds of toxins and their combined impact. The best defense is to limit exposure in your family's everyday environment. Here is a quick guide to common hidden harmfuls and how they impact your family's health.

Bisphenols. Bisphenol A (or BPA) is a chemical used in the manufacture of polycarbonate plastics. When used in food and beverage containers or dinnerware, it can leach into what we're consuming. It can also be found in toys. In addition to impacting child behavior, studies have shown possible links to brain and prostate gland development in fetuses, infants, and children. Research also shows possible connections to reproductive health, increased blood pressure, type 2 diabetes, and cardiovascular disease.

Although plastic baby bottles containing BPA were banned in 2012, studies have shown that even BPA-free plastic can leach harmful chemicals, such as BPS and BPF. These chemicals can have similar adverse health effects to BPA. Even low doses have been shown to be toxic. While the impacts of BPA are well documented, the impacts of BPS and BPF are less known. Current studies are finding links between exposure and hormone disruption, behavioral issues, preterm birth, and obesity in children.

Avoid bisphenols by steering clear of plastic when possible. Use plastic-free water and baby bottles. Choose fresh foods, free of packaging. Use glass, ceramic, or stainless steel for storing food, and avoid using plastic when storing, heating, or serving warmed foods.

Endocrine Disrupters. Endocrine disrupters are chemicals or compounds that mimic or mess with the body's hormones, known as the endocrine system. They're linked with adverse reproductive issues, developmental malformations, immune and nervous system problems, and an increased risk of cancer. According to the FDA, fetuses and children are at higher risk for significant and long-term health effects. Endocrine disrupters can be found in everyday products such as plastics, furniture with flame retardants, personal care products, pesticides and fungicides on our food, and bleached white paper products. In addition to humans, endocrine disrupters also impact wildlife.

Avoid endocrine disrupters by limiting plastic products—particularly food packaging and toys. Skip processed food and bottled water. Don't mix warm foods and plastic. Eat organic foods or wash conventional produce well to try and remove chemicals. Reduce pests in your home through pesticide-free methods. Choose essential oils over synthetic fragrances. And look for goods, including personal care products, that are free of phthalates and parabens.

Fire Retardants. Flame retardants are chemicals often added to furniture or fabrics to prevent or slow fire. They're commonly found in mattresses, car seats, furniture, toys, play tents and tunnels, and some children's pajamas. Flame retardants have been linked to cancer and reproductive, hormone, immune, and neurological problems, including decreased IQ, hyperactivity, and impaired memory and learning. Children are at three to five times higher risk of exposure when compared to adults living in the same home—with 97% of Americans having measurable amounts of organohalogen flame retardants in their blood. Flame retardants also pose an environmental risk, lingering for years and polluting waterways and organisms.

Avoid fire retardants by choosing products and furniture that have no added flame retardants. Regularly remove dust by washing toys and keeping floors and surfaces clean using a HEPA filter vacuum. In certain products, flame retardants are mandatory by law, as in car seats. In those instances, look for products that use Merino wool fabric or do not contain Tris and other brominated or halogenated flame retardants.

Formaldehyde. Formaldehyde is a probable human carcinogen and pollutes indoor air when off-gassing from products. It is commonly found in sealants (glues) and paints used in composite wood or upholstered furniture, curtains, flooring, gas stoves, and toys (including some dolls and stuffed animals, toys painted with acrylics, or those made from particleboards or plywood). It can also be found in laundry and dish detergents, body wash, and shampoo, among other products. Exposure has been linked to cancer, skin irritation, and breathing difficulties.

Avoid formaldehyde by opening windows at home regularly. Purchase products that use solid wood, stainless steel, 100% certified organic fabric, and water-based paints in their construction. Because off gassing can last for years, buying secondhand home furnishings helps limit formaldehyde contact.

Synthetic Fragrance. Synthetically fragranced products, such as personal care products, air fresheners, soap, scented laundry detergent, and cleaning supplies, can be harmful to human health. The majority of over 4,000 chemicals used to scent products are unregulated. And yet, one product can contain dozens of chemicals hidden behind the word "fragrance" or "parfum" in its label. Considered the *new secondhand smoke*, the chemicals behind these fragrances have been linked to hormone disruption, cancer, allergic reactions, and developmental and reproductive toxicity. "Natural" scents, such as lavender, can be produced synthetically, making it confusing for consumers to determine if the product is made with a synthetic fragrance or an essential oil. Many fragrances are petroleum- or coal-based (fossil fuels) and contain harmful phthalates. The 2018 Breast Cancer Prevention Partners report

"Right to Know" found that of the 140 products they tested, the most hazardous of all was a children's shampoo. Even "unscented" (not to be confused with "fragrance-free") products can have synthetic fragrances added to mask or neutralize unwanted chemical scents. Reduced use also limits air and water pollution.

Avoid synthetic fragrances by looking specifically for the term "fragrance-free" on products but also double-check the ingredient list for words like "fragrance," "perfume," "parfum," or "cologne."

Parabens. Parabens are a group of chemicals often found in personal care products including shampoo, lotion, toothpaste, sunscreen, and makeup. They're an artificial preservative used to lengthen the shelf life of ingredients that would otherwise mold or be prone to harmful bacteria growth. When we use them on our bodies, they disrupt our hormones—with possible harm to reproductive organs, fertility, and birth outcomes—and increase the risk of cancer and skin irritation. Currently, the FDA has no unique rules that apply to preservatives in cosmetics. Additionally, parabens have been detected in rivers, drinking water, and reservoirs. At present, the general risk that these chemicals pose to the environment in unknown. However, low levels of parabens, such as butylparaben in sunscreen, are known to kill coral reefs.

Avoid parabens by looking for products labeled paraben-free or USDA certified organic. Avoid products that include "ethyl," "butyl," "methyl," "propyl," or the word "fragrance" in the ingredient label. Opt for products made without high water content, such as bar soap, instead of bottled products. Avoid preservatives by choosing fresh foods or products made in small batches. And choose reef-safe sunscreen.

PFAS. PFAS, which stands for per- and polyfluoroalkyl substances, are a class of human-made chemicals that are added to consumer goods to help make them water-, oil-, or stain-resistant. Known as "forever chemicals" due to their indestructible nature, they're toxic, even with low-level exposure. PFAS are a hormone disrupter and have been linked to adverse immune outcomes in children, neurodevelopment, dyslipidemia, and cancer. A study by the Centers for Disease Control and *Prevention*'s National Health and Nutrition Examination Survey found PFAS in the blood of 97% of the 1682 Americans who participated. Another study, which tested 2,000 cord blood samples from pregnant women, found PFAS in 90% of participants.

Unfortunately, PFAS are found nearly everywhere, with drinking water being a prominent source, as well as our food, air, soil, and many products in our homes. Common culprits include stain-resistant furniture upholstery and carpets, clothing, grease-resistant food packaging like microwave popcorn bags and takeout containers, cleaning products, personal care products, mattress protectors, dust, and nonstick cookware (hello, Teflon). High levels are also often found in outdoor and athletic apparel, rain gear, and period underwear. In the environment, they negatively impact the health of animals and can persist long-term in groundwater and oceans—contaminating marine food chains and fresh drinking water.

Avoid PFAS by choosing fabrics without water-, stain-, or oil-resistant coatings or look for PFAS-free labels. Remove dust regularly from surfaces in your home. Avoid bottled water and instead use a water filter in your home that has been third-party proven to remove PFAS from drinking water. Bring your own plastic-free container for takeout or restaurant leftovers. Skip using Teflon and use ceramic, cast-iron, or carbon-steel cookware instead. Additionally, avoid water-resistant makeup and use the Environmental Working Group search tool to ensure your personal care products are safe.

Phthalates. Phthalates are a class of chemicals added to plastics to make them soft and flexible and are also used to add fragrance to products. Common children's products that contain phthalates include toys, baby bottles, teething rings, baby mattresses, and personal care products. Additionally, phthalate particulates can be found in indoor air and dust. Heating plastics in the microwave also increases exposure. Like BPA, phthalates are an endocrine disrupter, and some are known carcinogens. Risks include asthma; allergies; eczema; adverse effects on fetal, infant, and child development; obesity; and cancer.

Avoid phthalates by steering clear of plastic—particularly with the #3, #6, or #7 label. Quit heating food in plastic or using plastic dinnerware for warm foods. Eat less packaged food and meat, which have shown high levels of phthalates. Use a HEPA filter vacuum in your home and dust regularly. Skip fragranced goods. And look for products that are labeled "phthalate free."

Plastics + Microplastics. See pages 86–90 for more on plastics and pages 62 and 256 to learn about microplastics.

PVC and Vinyl. Polyvinyl chloride (PVC or vinyl), also known as plastic #3, has been linked to cancer, asthma, reproductive disorders, obesity, and learning and developmental issues. PVC can contain harmful chemicals including PFAS, mercury, lead, and phthalates. Even PVC labeled "phthalate-free" can still contain other harmful, toxic additives. While some PVC may be considered less toxic, toxic-free PVC isn't really a thing. Common children's products containing PVC include toys like plastic baby dolls and rubber duckies, raincoats, inflatable pools, play mats, shower curtains, changing pads, waterproof mattress covers, product packaging, flooring, school supplies, backpacks, and lunch boxes. In addition to being harmful to human health, PVC is also dangerous to the environment through water, air, and soil contamination and ozone depletion.

Some PVC is next to impossible to bypass (like your pipes), but many choices are still possible by avoiding toys and products with the #3 plastic symbol. If reflooring your home, avoid vinyl. Choose plastic-free school supplies, and say no to vinyl shower curtains, wallpaper, blinds, plastic wrap, and soft plastics with a strong odor upon unpacking.

Toxic Dyes. Toxic dyes are used in the majority of clothing manufacturing. Some but not all of AZO dyes, which make up over half of commercial dye used, are known carcinogens and can cause tumors in garment workers and skin allergies in consumers. AZO is notorious in the fashion world but can also be found in cosmetics, plastics, printing, food, toys, arts and crafts materials, and more. Formaldehyde and heavy metals, such as lead and cadmium, are also part of the textile dyeing and finishing process. While natural dyes are not toxic, the binding chemicals (mordants) used can be. From an environmental standpoint, conventional dyes require a mind-boggling amount of water, and the wastewater is commonly dumped into waterways in some countries, polluting ecosystems and drinking water with toxic chemicals, dye, heavy metals, and microfibers.

Avoid toxic dyes by buying less or secondhand, which will have the biggest impact on fashion pollution. If buying new, focus on trustworthy brands who are committed to testing for toxins in their fabrics. Also look for certifications like GOTS, OEKO-TEX® STANDARD 100, and Cradle to Cradle. And be sure to wash clothing before wearing. Also see Eco-Action 31 for more on fabrics.

ECO-ACTION NO. 33
Choose Clean Cosmetics

From formaldehyde to lead, what's lurking in your cosmetics? Lotion, body wash, shampoo, lipstick—many of these goods claim to be "clinically proven" or "natural," but the fact is, this industry is shockingly unregulated. It clearly states on the FDA website that "under the law, cosmetic products and ingredients do not need FDA premarket approval, with the exception of color additives."

Due to lax legislation that has essentially gone unchanged since 1938, many of these products put you and your family at higher risk for allergies, respiratory diseases, endocrine disruption–related disorders, and cancer—as well as adding environmental toxins to water, soil, wildlife, and the air.

DID YOU KNOW?

On average, American women are exposed to **168 chemical ingredients** in their personal care products daily.

Dangerous, deceitful, and unchecked, our bathroom cabinets and makeup bags are like the Wild West. Unfortunately, the burden is on us, the consumers, to ensure that the products we are using are safe for our bodies, our children, and the planet. From the ingredients to the people who make the products, here are four primary factors to help you make the best personal-care choices for you and your family.

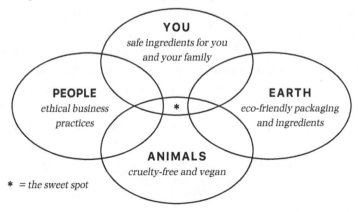

YOU
safe ingredients for you
and your family

PEOPLE
ethical business
practices

EARTH
eco-friendly packaging
and ingredients

*

ANIMALS
cruelty-free and vegan

* = the sweet spot

YOU

Safe Ingredients. Scan products or research specific ingredients through the EWG's Healthy Living or Think Dirty app. MADESAFE® is another useful resource to find products with safe ingredients.

Organic. Pesticides? Yuck. Choose products with organic ingredients. See page 169 for more on the importance of organic.

PEOPLE

Support Ethical Businesses. Buy products from companies that uphold fair wages and safe work conditions. Additionally, look for Fair Trade and B Corp certifications.

EARTH

Sustainable Packaging. Choose products that come in plastic-free packaging that's recyclable or compostable, such as paper, glass, or metal. Many toiletries and makeup can now be found in refillable packaging as well.

Palm-oil–free. Opt for products that are free of palm oil or contain certified sustainable palm oil. See page 63 to learn more.

ANIMALS

Cruelty-free. Look for the Leaping Bunny certification to ensure the product was not tested on animals.

Vegan. Authorized products that do not contain animal-based ingredients will carry the Certified Vegan logo.

DID YOU KNOW?

Microbeads are a microplastic. Microbeads are small spherical pieces of plastic found in many products, including toothpaste, facial scrubs, body wash, soaps, and household cleaning agents. Many of them are designed to go down the drain, polluting ecosystems and wildlife. They also pose a problem for humans, with harsh properties that cause microabrasions and can lead to skin, gum, and eye infections. Because of their size, they can get embedded between teeth and gums or under the eyelid, leading to scratched corneas. If accidentally ingested, they can cause internal bleeding and ulcers and block the digestive tract. No, thank you.

ECO-ACTION NO. 34
Embrace Period Power

Traditional tampons and pads contain a whole host of yucky stuff that's harmful to both you and the planet. The most common toxins that show up in these products include dioxins and furans (from bleaching), pesticide residue (from nonorganic cotton), plastics, paraffin and polyethylene (for smoother removal), and fragrances (VOCs). These chemicals have been linked to cancer, endocrine disruption, reproductive toxicity, and allergies.

Due to their makeup, conventional pads and tampons are destined for the landfill. Throughout one menstruating person's lifetime, between five thousand and fifteen thousand tampons and pads will be used, costing the planet and as much as $18,000 per person. Periods aren't the problem; it's the products. But there are effective, affordable solutions.

JOIN THE RED TIDE REVOLUTION

Organic Cotton Pads and Tampons. While they're not reusable, organic cotton pads and tampons are a good step in the right direction. Look for unbleached products (or bleached without chlorine) that are fragrance-free and use plastic-free packaging and applicators.

Menstrual Cup. The menstrual cup's popularity lies in the fact that it's reusable and can be worn for up to 12 hours before emptying and rinsing. While they're trash at the end of their life span, the cups can last 5 to 10 years with regular monthly use, meaning you will need only about 7 total in your lifetime. Be sure the one you choose is made from 100% medical-grade silicone and is preferably dye-free.

Period Undies. Period panties can be worn during light to moderately heavy flow, with some of the more absorbent options holding up to 5 tampons' worth of blood but without the wet, heavy feeling of a pad. In addition to being worn on their own, they pair well with a menstrual cup or tampons if you're prone to leaks. One pair lasts 2 to 5 years and can be worn for up to 24 hours before needing to be rinsed and then washed on laundry day. Period undies are popular with teens just starting their period because they look and feel exactly like regular underwear. Organic cotton is a better material for your body and the planet than synthetic alternatives. Also, confirm that undies are free of plastic, nanomaterials (which can usually be identified when the product claims to be "antibacterial" or "antimicrobial"), and PFAS.

Washable Pads and Liners. Similar to period panties, washable pads and liners are reusable. They're less expensive than period underwear and conveniently can be worn with undies you already own. Look for similar product details when shopping for washable pads and liners as listed for period undies.

🍃

ECO-ACTION NO. 35
Say Good-Bye to Toilet "Paper"

Americans flush 15 million trees down the toilet every year. But it's not just the lost trees (or plastic packaging) that are the issue. Conventional toilet paper contains harsh chemicals such as bleach, formaldehyde, and dioxins. Not exactly what you want coming into contact with your family's sensitive bits, not to mention the water and energy needed to produce your plush virgin paper rolls. And while you may be shaking your head wondering what an alternative could be, there is a significant market for sustainable options that are soft and safe for your most delicate areas.

CHANGE HOW YOU ROLL

Recycled. According to the National Resource Defense Council, if every American household replaced just one toilet paper roll of virgin fiber a year with a roll made from 100% recycled paper, we could save over one million trees. When purchasing, look for 100% recycled-paper toilet paper that's BPA-free.

Bamboo. Bamboo is a renewable resource that can be harvested in 3 months, while a tree can take 20+ years. It's plush, soft, and will have you hooked after one use. Just remember to look for chlorine-free, FSC-certified brands.

Bidet. With easy-to-install, inexpensive attachments now on the market, bidets are making a comeback. They use an eighth of the water that conventional toilet paper uses. Go with the cold-water option since heating the water increases energy usage. One exception: if you live in a drought-ridden area, toilet paper will put less strain on your local water supply.

> **ECO-FAMILY TIP**
> Set up an eco–toilet paper subscription to be delivered to your house. That way, when your kid uses the last roll without telling anyone, you're not forced to buy tree-based TP that comes wrapped in plastic from the corner store in a rush.

Head to the National Resource Defense Council's website and check out their "Issue with Tissue Scorecard" to see how your toilet paper squares up.

ECO-ACTION NO. 36
Reduce, Reuse, Rediaper

> **DID YOU KNOW?**
> Conventional disposable diapers produce **60 times** more trash than cloth and require **20 times** more raw materials, such as crude oil and wood pulp, to produce.

CONVENTIONAL DIAPER, WIPES, AND CREAM CONCERNS

Diapers. Conventional disposable diapers often contain hazardous chemicals that can impact your baby's health, including phthalates, pesticides, VOCs, and other harmful substances linked to cancer, impaired reproductive development, endocrine disruption, and skin irritation. The Consumer Product Safety Commission requires only that diapers be tested for lead but otherwise does not require manufacturers to test their materials or products for safety. (Shocking!)

Baby Wipes. Conventional baby wipes also come with a whole host of toxic ingredients, including phthalates, fragrances, and preservatives (such as formaldehyde, which was detected in 24% of 51 popular, positively reviewed wipes). They've also been linked to cancer, neurotoxicity, endocrine disruption, and more. Plus, baby wipes are often made of conventional cotton, polypropylene (plastic), or polyester (also plastic) or a combination of all three, and linked to environmental pollution and possible exposure to pesticides and leaching of chemicals onto babies' skin.

Diaper Cream. Standard diaper cream contains petroleum (yes, fossil fuels), phthalates (there are those darn endocrine disrupters again), parabens, sodium borate, and 1,4-dioxane (a known carcinogen linked to cancer).

PLANETARY PROBLEMS

In addition to being harmful to children, disposable diapers are also damaging to the environment. Did you know one disposable diaper takes 500 years to decompose in a landfill? As Americans, we are obsessed with single-use diapers, and the numbers show it. Ninety-six percent of American babies wear disposable diapers, with the average American baby using around 2,500 diapers in just their first year. In China, only 6% of babies wear disposable diapers. In India, 2%.

Additionally, disposable diapers generate 7.6 billion pounds of waste annually in the US alone—and are the third-largest consumer item in landfills. And it's not just the waste that makes them unsustainable. It takes one cup of crude oil to make one disposable diaper. Plus, they contain plastic, and the manufacturing process is highly pollutive. Their production requires raw materials, energy, and water and generates a significant amount of wastewater. All in all, they're a harmful single-use item from beginning to end.

I want to be clear: all of this shouldn't make you feel guilty about diapering your child. You did not create this system. But if you're able and interested in changing your baby's diapering routine, shifting to cloth or compostable diapers, using eco-wipes, and switching to safe diaper cream can make a difference.

CLOTH DIAPERS

Cloth diapers often conjure mental images of a large piece of cloth, a giant safety pin, AND a big mess. But the truth is, they have come a long way. Nowadays they look more like regular disposable diapers and are easy to use. There are numerous brands on the market, some of which are more sustainable than others.

When purchasing brand-new, look for GOTS Organic cotton linings and preferably natural, breathable materials such as wool, organic cotton, or hemp for the outer layer. Look for options that are not dyed and are free of phthalates, parabens, pesticides, bisphenols, flame-retardant chemicals, and PFAS. While not as eco-friendly or potentially as healthy for your child, microfleece inner layers and synthetic outer layers are good at wicking liquids, so it's up to you to decide which is the best option for your family.

All cloth diapers are composed of two parts: an inner lining and an outer shell that can be put together in a variety of ways (sewn, snapped, Velcroed, etc.). Here's a quick guide to six common cloth diaper types.

A QUICK GUIDE TO CLOTH DIAPERS	
All-in-One	All-in-ones are made up of two parts: an absorbent center and waterproof outer layer, which are sewn together into one diaper. They're quick and easy to take on and off (like a disposable diaper) because there is no folding, stuffing, or prep needed. Since all of the parts are sewn together, the whole diaper must be washed after each diaper change. *Most expensive*
All-in-Two	In an all-in-two diaper, the outer layer and absorbent insert are separate pieces that need to be attached together, creating one small extra step from the all-in-one. Depending upon the brand (and the size of the mess), you may be able to get away with reusing the outer layer a few times before needing to wash it. All-in-twos are versatile because you can adjust the absorbency and often mix-and-match outer and inner layer brands.
Hybrid	Hybrid diapers are the halfway point between disposables and cloth diapers: a washable, waterproof outer layer and a disposable inner layer.

Fitted	Fitted cloth diapers have a fitted inner layer, which looks like a standard diaper, and a diaper cover that goes over the inner layer. Because the insert is fitted, there is less of a chance of mess than with other cloth diaper options, making them great for overnight. The inner layer can be washed separately, which cuts down on laundry and cost, making them a less expensive option than all-in-ones.
Pocket	The outer waterproof portion of the pocket diaper has a pocket to hold a waterproof insert which can be adjusted according to absorbency needs (day vs. night). The con is that you need to wash the entire diaper (inner layer and outer shell) at every washing.
Prefold/Flat + Covers	This type is what you think of your grandmother using and is the most complicated of the cloth diapering methods. The "flat" (which needs to be folded) or "prefold" (which is already folded) is an absorbent layer that gets paired with a diaper cover. The bonus is that only the insert needs to be washed at diaper changes, cutting down on laundry and cost. *Least expensive

*At the time of research for this book, no studies had been published on PFAS and cloth diapers. Until there is a study to back it, it's safer to assume that the synthetic, moisture-wicking materials used in cloth diapers may contain PFAS.

Washing and Care. If you can handle washing your clothes, cloth diapers require the same amount of care. Follow the washing instructions from the brand you've chosen. When purchasing, triple-check the drying instructions, since certain styles must be hung to dry (which may or may not be an issue for you). Between washings, dirty diapers (and cloth wipes) can be stored in a wet bag or washable pail liner for easy, smell-free convenience.

ECO-FAMILY TIP
Have two wet bags on hand so you can wash the dirty bag when you wash the diapers and have the second available for any diaper changes while the laundry is running.

Quantity. Depending on which brand and type of cloth diaper you go with, some options, such as the all-in-one cloth diapers, grow with your baby, which means you won't have to buy a lot of new sizes as your baby grows. This chart provides a good quantity starting point:

Birth to 6 months	20 to 24 diapers
6 to 12 months	15 to 18 diapers
1 to 2+ years	12 to 15 diapers
Near potty training	5 to 8 cloth diapers

Note: You can begin with fewer but be prepared to do laundry daily.

Cost. Cloth diapers are an investment up front but can save you hundreds of dollars in the long run. Over two years of wearing cloth diapers, including the cost of water to wash them, the total cost is about $700 to $800. Disposable diapers would cost well over $2,000 over the same period, and all that money goes directly to the landfill. Cloth diapers can also be resold or reused for later siblings, saving even more.

COMPOSTABLE DIAPERS

Compostable diapers, not to be confused with greenwashed "biodegradable diapers," are safer for the planet and your baby than conventional disposable diapers. While traditional diapers tend to contain harmful chemicals, most compostable diapers are free of these substances. Furthermore, they're durable, absorbent, and soft on babies' skin. While they're safe to compost at home (without poop), not everyone has access to a home composting system. Fret not. There are also diaper composting services that pick up soiled nappies and drop off new packs each week or offer mail-in options. However, it's essential to note that industrial citywide composting or community compost collection points will generally not accept compostable diapers. And buying compostable diapers, then throwing them in the trash negates their purpose, so be sure to dispose of them correctly.

Remember, sustainability doesn't have to be all or nothing—and that goes for diapers too. You can use compostable diapers for the first six months or at night only and then switch to cloth or go 50/50. Whatever the compromise, opting for cloth even half of the time helps. If you decide in the end that cloth diapers don't work for your child, be sure to pass them on to a family who will use them.

ECO-WIPES AND CREAM

Cloth. Cloth wipes clean messy bums better than conventional wipes. Plus, their thick, absorbent fabric also keeps your hands cleaner. Soft cut-up T-shirts and flannels work well. Alternatively, you can buy premade ones. To prevent irritation and effectively remove and clean off residues, moistening the wipes with a solution is essential. You can buy or easily make a wipe spray yourself. (Water alone isn't enough and can lead to ouchie skin.) After use, simply toss the soiled cloth in a wet bag, designed for this exact purpose, with any cloth diapers until laundry day.

Compostable. Single-use, compostable wipes (not to be confused with flushable or biodegradable wipes) are gentle, effective, and come without the toxic ingredients in traditional disposable wipes. Like compostable diapers, compostable wipes can be composted at home or through a compostable diaper collection service. They are generally not accepted by curbside citywide composting.

Diaper Cream. If you're striving to avoid plastic and fossil fuels, opt for plastic- and petroleum-free diaper cream. There are several brands out there that come in glass or metal jars. You can even make diaper cream if you're up for it. If you're using cloth diapers, be sure to check your cloth diaper brand's recommended diaper creams list, since some diaper creams (such as Aquaphor and Desitin) don't always wash out of cloth diapers.

NOT READY FOR REUSABLES ON THE CHANGING TABLE?

If this is beyond your comfort zone (or what you have access to), here are some changes you can still make:

- Use eco-diapers and wipes made from sustainable materials.
- Swap out disposable swim diapers for a washable swim diaper.
- Switch the plastic bag liner in your diaper pail to a washable one.
- No matter how you diaper (cloth, compostable, or disposable), flush your child's poop down the toilet. It shouldn't go into the landfill.

ECO-ACTION NO. 37
Gratifying Green Self-Care

SELF-CARE IS NOT SELFISH

We cannot care for others (the planet included) until we care for ourselves. It's a basic principle, and yet, as parents, it can feel hard to apply in real life. Lack of time, exhaustion, guilt, and putting ourselves on the back burner keeps us from doing what's fundamental: taking care of ourselves. Most of the time, this isn't our fault—we live in a system that doesn't support families (e.g., no national paid parental leave after the birth, adoption, or fostering of a child; no free-to-low cost childcare; no public preschool; no family-friendly work schedules; etc.).

A large portion of unpacking our loads will come from working with your partner(s) (if you have one) to ensure the domestic workload and parenting tasks are balanced. If you have not yet read Eve Rodsky's book *Fair Play*, I highly recommend it for leveling the responsibilities at home.

While it may sound easier said than done to do so, creating boundaries and claiming time to fill your cup is imperative. (Going to the grocery store alone doesn't count.) Mark off time on the family calendar for yourself. When we take care of our basic needs, we also model and normalize these essential behaviors to our children.

OVERINDULGENCE ≠ SELF-CARE

We often think of overindulgence as a form of self-care, but don't confuse the two. Quick fixes and instant gratification like retail therapy are not the answer. The effects are short-lived and do not get at the root of what you're trying to find comfort from. This doesn't mean you need to deprive or never pamper yourself. It's about looking for ways to nurture ourselves and our relationships in a way that fosters deep-seated, long-term, restorative repair.

NOURISH YOUR WHOLE BEING

Self-care can be done alone or in a community and includes nourishing your whole being—body, mind, and spirit—daily. Here is a simple way to set a daily intention to help keep you on track.

Today I will care for by body by _____,
my mind by _____, and my spirit by
_____.

GREEN SELF-CARE PRACTICES
MIND. BODY. SPIRIT.

- Drinking enough water
- Exercising
- Eating healthy foods
- Sleeping
- Dancing
- Stretching
- Making a DIY face mask
- Getting a massage
- Wearing sunscreen
- Listening to what your body needs
- Reading
- Taking a class
- Detoxing from the virtual world
- Journaling
- Trying something new
- Attending a lecture
- Doing a puzzle
- Watching something funny
- Talking to someone about what's bothering you
- Meditating
- Practicing gratitude
- Sitting in the sunlight
- Breath work
- Listening to music
- Spending time outside
- Walking with or calling a friend
- Setting boundaries
- Planting something
- Creating art
- Giving yourself a 20-second hug

Taking care of ourselves is essential—not only for our sanity
but in our fight to save the planet.

ECO-ACTION NO. 38
Ease Eco-Anxiety

FROM HELPLESS TO HOPEFUL

If you are feeling anxiety about the state of the planet, you are not alone. Eco-anxiety is remarkably common, yet it does not affect everyone to the same extent. Small steps, like limiting media consumption, can be helpful. But often, feelings of fear or being overwhelmed require more to ease the angst. Here are a few ways to help limit feelings of hopelessness:

- Turn anxiety into action with realistic life changes.
- Find your people. Connect with others through volunteering and advocating to build your eco-community.
- Spend time in nature.
- Take a digital detox.
- Focus on self-care: mind, body, and spirit.
- Find a mental health professional or support group. See *The Motherboard* at the back of the book for resources

GREEN READS

—

THE CLIMATE OPTIMIST HANDBOOK
by Anne Therese Gennari

COPING TIPS FOR KIDS

Increasingly, young people are showing signs of eco-anxiety too. In a worldwide study of 10,000 teens and young adults aged 16 to 25, nearly 60% of respondents said they felt "very worried" or "extremely worried" about climate change, and 45% said these feelings impacted their daily lives. Only 5% said they were not worried at all. These young people have every reason to feel afraid; their future is on the line.

So how can we help teens feel more secure about the world they're inheriting? Firstly, we can model what is possible for a brighter future by making changes in our own lives as parents. Secondly, we can empower them to be leaders while supporting them in building sustainable lives of their own. **Listen.** Of the 81% of young people who have talked to someone about climate change, nearly half said they were dismissed or ignored. We must hear and validate our children's questions, feelings, and concerns, even if we don't have all the answers.

Reassure. As much as possible, limit doomsday news. Remind them that it's not too late and that their fight to save the planet will make a difference.

Point out all of the solutions that exist, such as renewable energy and habitat rehabilitation, in addition to all those out there who are working toward a better future. Reiterate that their voice matters, that they're powerful and influential; their passion can be used as fuel to impart change. Use this book as a road map for tangible ways for them to begin mobilizing.

Encourage Action. A fundamental way to feel empowered and fight fear is to act. Cheer your teens on as they get involved in making a difference at home, at school, and in the community.

Get Them Help. Don't hesitate to reach out to a mental health professional for additional support.

THE
CLIMATE
CREW

ECO-ACTION NO. 39
Take a Break

TRAVEL SUSTAINABLY

From sand to snow, vacations are times we build precious memories, catch up with loved ones, and unwind. Getting away from it all and taking it easy is undoubtedly important for our mental health. And yet, in a world that's increasingly more accessible through air travel, jumping on a plane for an overnight trip or long weekend away has become the norm—60% of Americans fly one or more times a year. When looking at the average American's annual carbon footprint, air travel can account for an oversized slice of the pie, even if you fly only once each year. Taking one round-trip domestic flight can produce more CO_2 than the average person emits annually in many parts of the world. Even as aircraft become more fuel-efficient, demand is increasing and causing emissions to skyrocket.

While some air travel might feel unavoidable, consider ways to balance getting in some much needed R&R while minimizing your footprint. Don't underestimate how rewarding and meaningful a vacation can be when you consider your trip's environmental and social impact.

——————————— **DID YOU KNOW?** ———————————
American travelers are responsible for a **quarter**
of worldwide passenger flight emissions.

SET A GREEN ITINERARY

Planning. As you dream about your next vacation, consider taking a road trip close to home. If you must fly, see if you can find a way to stay in your destination city a while so you can see and do more, reducing frequent short trips that pack a heavy carbon footprint. Research spots off the beaten path to avoid contributing to the damages of mass tourism (overpriced housing for locals, loss of culture, costly food for locals, congestion, pollution, etc.). And skip the cruise ship altogether, as they have a larger carbon footprint per passenger than if you flew to your destination.

Flying. With family and friends scattered across the globe (and work travel forcing us onto planes), avoiding air travel can feel impossible. Google Flights now shows the carbon emissions of each flight to help you make more informed decisions. The simple act of flying direct can significantly slash carbon emission. (About 25% of the flight's emissions come from takeoff and landing alone.) And you should feel good about flying coach; your footprint can be as much as nine times less than flying first-class.

While not entirely negating your flying footprint, you can buy carbon offsets, which aim to balance your emissions by investing in projects that reduce and sequester carbon. The cost varies depending upon how far you're traveling, but it's often around $10 a person. If the organization you support with your offset is a 501(c)(3) nonprofit, your offset could be tax-deductible.

Driving. When your tires are correctly inflated, you can improve your gas mileage by up to 3%. If you can avoid hauling cargo on your roof, do so. It can reduce fuel economy by a whopping 10–25% when driving at freeway speeds. Use cruise control when possible, and avoid idling at rest stops. If renting a car in your destination city, choose an EV or hybrid. And if it's possible to travel to your destination by bus or train, do it!

Staying. Choose locally owned boutique hotels (double bonus if they're eco-friendly) rather than supporting large corporate chains. Rent a vacation home with a kitchen to help you reduce food waste by storing package-free snacks, reheating leftovers, etc. Alternatively, stay at a sustainable hotel that upholds the same eco-standards as you.

PACK AND PREP INTENTIONALLY

Clothing. It's always tempting to buy new outfits before a trip. Instead, use what you have and fill in any gaps with secondhand pieces. And remember to pack lightly; the heavier your luggage, the more fuel you use. Consider renting any children's gear you may need at your travel destination. Don't forget those plastic-free toiletries. And if you're headed to the beach, pack coral reef–safe sunscreen. (The fish will thank you.)

Munchies. When on a road trip, pack homemade sandwiches and bulk bin snacks at home to avoid generating lots of trash at fast food joints. And if everyone is still hungry, stop at restaurants (with real forks and knives) instead of "dine 'n' dash" spots. Bring along a zero-waste kit (see page 164); it will come in handy to avoid disposable cutlery and carry leftovers when on the go.

Get Your Home Ready. Before leaving for your trip, run through this checklist to ensure your home and pretravel habits hit all of their eco-marks.

PREDEPARTURE CHECKLIST

- ○ Unplug devices and electronics not in use.
- ○ Turn off lights or put specific lights on a timer for added security while away.
- ○ Reset your thermostat (summer: 80°–85°F / winter: 60°F) or put it on vacation mode. If you live in an area where frozen pipes could occur, set the thermostat a bit higher, and be conscious of pets if they're home alone.
- ○ Lower the temperature on your water heater, set to vacation mode, or turn it off.
- ○ Eat perishables in the days leading up to your trip. Take what you can with you and freeze the rest that would otherwise go to waste.
- ○ Double a recipe the week before you leave and freeze the second portion so you have dinner waiting when you get home and can avoid trash-filled takeout.

RELAX AND ENJOY

Get Around. Once you've arrived at your destination, consider renting bikes, walking, or taking public transportation to explore. Research tipping customs (and pay people fairly).

Support. Many communities worldwide rely on tourism for their livelihoods, so use your time away to respect and learn about other cultures and ecosystems while supporting local economies and the environment.

Skip corporations and chains. Instead eat and shop at locally owned businesses. Think about getting involved on your trip through volunteering and supporting the community in its resilience to climate change.

Rest. Hang your *Do Not Disturb* sign on the door to avoid unnecessary laundering of linens. Turn off lights, limit water usage, and turn off heat or AC when you're out.

Eat. If you're at a vacation rental, stock up your kitchen by shopping at the community co-op bulk bin grocery store or farmer's market. Add sustainability to the menu by eating local, plant-based, organic foods.

ECO-ACTION NO. 40
Enjoy Sustainble Sex

GET IT ON . . . SUSTAINABLY

With eco-living, sustainable practices can also be applied between the sheets. From family planning to Earth- and body-safe products, being green has never felt so good.

Contraceptives. If you are trying to get pregnant, be sure to speak with your healthcare professional to get the care you need. If you want to delay or avoid pregnancy, remember to use whatever birth control method is best for you. Although waste might be on your mind, don't worry if some contraceptives, such as condoms or birth control pill packaging, create more waste than, say, an IUD (or more permanent methods such as tubal ligation or a vasectomy). What's most important is finding the most suitable option for your body and family planning needs.

Lingerie. If lingerie makes you feel sexy, look for companies that use sustainable materials such as organic cotton, bamboo, deadstock, or recycled fabrics that are not dyed or processed using harmful chemicals. As with everything you buy brand-new, look for third-party certifications, such as Fairtrade or B Corp, to ensure ethical workplace practices. Additionally, many eco-brands use compostable packaging and ship plastic-free, which is an added win.

Toys. Many sex toys are made from toxic materials, which is frightening given where they go. Look for phthalate-free accessories (phthalates have been linked to cancer and infertility). Additionally, skip the disposable AAA batteries and look for rechargeable or solar-powered toys.

Lubrication. Most lubes on the market are petroleum-based or use toxic chemicals, which can cause both short- and long-term health issues, including reproductive problems and cancer. Read the label and look for natural, organic, water- or plant-based ingredients. Ensure your product is also free of phthalates, sugars, glycerin, and petroleum by scanning the product's bar code on EWG's Healthy Living app. Because your skin can absorb chemicals up to eight times faster than if you'd ingested it orally, consider the "eat it" rule: *if you wouldn't be comfortable swallowing what's on the ingredient list, skip it.* Avoid scented, warming, and flavored lubricants as well.

Note: Before using a new lube, do a patch test on your arm and research its compatibility with bedding, condoms, and sex toys.

FOOD

THE POWER OF FOOD 101

FOOD FOR THOUGHT

Did you know we can regenerate the earth and heal our bodies and communities with food? From the ecosystem in which it's grown to the people who produce it, the choices we make when purchasing food impact everything from soil health and the climate crisis to the livelihood of individuals. In short, the source of our food matters.

Becoming mindful of consuming more plant-based foods, choosing sustainably grown foods, and reducing food waste are three fundamental steps you and your family can take to fight climate change. In fact, from a climate perspective, these three steps are far more critical than what material your food is packaged in. Still, there are many things to consider when it comes to sustainable eating, such as ecosystem impact; land use; water use; air, soil, and water quality; and, of course, human impact. All of these issues are considerations when making more eco-friendly choices around what we're feeding our families.

FOOD EQUITY

Not everyone can be selective about food. For some, eating three meals a day is a challenge. Many communities are resource-deprived—living in "food deserts" full of highly processed, nutritionally void foods with no access to basic produce, let alone sustainably grown fruits and vegetables. If you are in a situation where you cannot be selective about food, I want to remind you that there is still a place for you in this movement. It's not about doing it all. It's about doing what you can, given your circumstances.

For information on advocating for food equity, see page 216.

THE SUSTAINABILITY SCALE:
How to Eat Sustainably

01

A Great Start
- Limit packaging
- Local and in-season
- Organic
- Ethically grown food

02

Finding Your Eco-Groove
- Eat more plants
- Reduce food waste

03

Kick-ass Impact
- Compost
- Support regenerative farms
- Choose less, better, or no meat/animal-based foods
- Advocate for food equity

FOOD PACKAGING

Simple steps and habit shifts can limit the avalanche of food packaging that flows into and out of our homes.

───────────

🌿

ECO-ACTION NO. 41
Limit Packaged Foods

Moving away from packaged foods, particularly those that come in plastic, may sound daunting, but I promise it's achievable and can be done stress-free. The big tip: you don't have to do it all at once (or be perfect). Finish up the packaged food you already have at home before trying to replace it with package-free options.

─────────────── **DID YOU KNOW?** ───────────────

Processed foods tend to be packaged foods. For every **10%** of your diet that comes from ultraprocessed foods, your risk of death increases **12%**. Moving away from processed foods is not only good for the environment, it's also better for your family's health.

According to the Environmental Protection Agency, containers and packaging make up over **28%** of what we dispose of annually.

FOUR STEPS TO LESS FOOD PACKAGING

01. Buy Naked Produce. Skip produce that comes packaged and buy it "naked." You can bring your own produce bags to fill or just put fruits and veggies directly in your cart bagless. If you don't have access to package-free produce at your grocery store, look for a farmer's market in your area.

02. Look for Alternative Packaging. If you're worried your family might revolt against going package-free, just know that you may not need to break up with as many foods as you think. You can frequently find sustainable alternative packaging like peanut butter in glass jars rather than plastic or snacks you've been buying packaged—like pretzels, nuts, and dried fruit—in the bulk bin section. You and your family might even find new foods that you love equally or more than packaged foods. Some guidelines for making sustainable packaging choices when package-free isn't an option:

INSTEAD OF . . .	LOOK FOR . . .
Plastic jars	Glass jars, cans, or in bulk
Processed bread packaged in plastic	A fresh bread loaf *Using a reusable bread bag*
Candy bars in plastic wrappers	Chocolate bars in paper + aluminum
Tea bags	Loose-leaf tea
Single-use coffee filters	Reusable coffee filters or French press
Beverages in plastic	Beverages in glass or aluminum

Buy Large. Buying bigger means less packaging. However, that's only true when the food isn't subdivided into small packages within the oversized outer container. For example, 12 mini bags of trail mix that come individually packaged and grouped in one larger plastic bag is much more packaging (and much less food) than buying the biggest single package of trail mix possible. It may take an extra 30 seconds to individually portion the trail mix out at home, but we're talking seconds. And it will keep your packaging waste down.

Bulk Bin Shop. Some conventional grocery stores have a bulk bin section, while other stores, such as co-ops, specialize in a wide variety of package-free foods and products. Bulk departments tend to contain foods like dry ingredients (like flours, sugars, salts, and pastas) to pantry staples (dry beans, snacks, nuts, coffee, etc.). If their selection is robust, you may even find inedible bulk goods like shampoo, soap, laundry detergent, and even dog food. Bulk bin grocery shopping is a great way to reduce packaging waste because you can bring your own jars and containers and refill them repeatedly. However, some items can be more expensive in bulk, so pay attention to prices if on a budget.

ECO–FAMILY BITE–SIZE CHALLENGE   NO. 7

SET A 3/4 GOAL

Depending upon where you live, you'll find differing levels of ease (or effort) in reducing food-related packaging. Grocery shopping 100% package-free (or at least plastic-free) can sound inconceivable, especially at the start, no matter where you live. Setting a goal can help you make shifts without feeling like you're undertaking a task beyond your ability.

The Goal. Strive to keep 75% of your shopping cart plastic- and/or package-free.

Ease Into It. Before you try this, assess your grocery haul after your next trip to the supermarket. Then set your first goal to reduce packaging from what you've just purchased. It's unrealistic to think you can go completely packaging-free overnight.

Before You Start:
- Search online to see if there is a grocery store with a bulk bin section in your community. Go check it out and bring along a few containers for purchases of some new foods to try at home.
- Eat what you already own to make room for your new package-free or sustainably packaged purchases.
- Give yourself time. It may take 6–12 months to convert your pantry and refrigerator to mostly plastic-free foods.

BULK BIN SHOPPING 101

What Do I Bring to a Bulk-bin Grocery Store? When bulk bin shopping, you'll want to bring along a few reusable essentials to help keep waste down. The first few times, it may take a moment to get yourself organized. But after a couple of trips, it will be second nature. Here's a checklist:

- ○ **Empty jars or containers (5–10).** Save glass jars that would have typically been recycled, such as empty, cleaned jam or pasta sauce jars. You can buy glass jars onsite if you want to, but that isn't necessary if you can reuse something you already have on hand.
- ○ **Reusable produce bags (4–5).** You can buy cloth produce bags but also reuse produce bags (over and over) that you obtained during your last grocery trip. Or get the kids involved and make some from scrap fabric or old sheets if you have time.
- ○ **Tote bags (2–3).** You will want to bring a couple of tote bags to take home groceries. Or you can reuse paper or plastic bags from your last trip to the supermarket.

How Do I Bulk-bin Shop? Take the following steps:

- Weigh your jar or container at a weighing station at the store. Then, notate the container's weight (known as the tare) on a sticker they provide.
- Fill up your container with whatever item you're purchasing (rice, raisins, peanut butter, lotion, soap, etc.) and notate the bulk bin item number on the sticker with the tare weight.
- At checkout, the cashier will weigh the filled container and subtract the tare weight you've notated (so you don't pay for the weight of the container, just what's inside it).

How Do I Store Bulk Foods at Home? Once you've brought your bulk goods home, keep them in their jars. Not only do glass jars look pretty, but they're also excellent at keeping out unwanted pests and don't leak toxins like plastic. Wide-mouth jars are best for storing items like flour and sugar because you can easily scoop a measuring cup into them. And don't forget to label by writing directly on the glass or lid with a wax pencil, or use compostable washi or masking tape and a marker. Avoid plastic labels if possible.

No Bulk-bin Section? If you don't have a grocery store with a bulk bin section in your area, don't fret. There are affordable online shops that will send you all of your pantry staples in reusable packaging that can be sent back and refilled. See *The Motherboard* resources guide in the back for a list.

ECO-ACTION NO. 42
Store Food without Plastic

Old habits and false advertising have led us to believe that plastic and single-use items are quick, convenient, and essential for storing food properly. Whether in the freezer, fridge, pantry, or on the go, plastic and disposable wraps and bags do not need to be part of the equation. In truth, there are many other practical, reusable, and cost-effective ways to store food that work just as well (if not better), do not generate waste, and are better for your family's health.

Finish First. Use what you already own before buying anything new. So if you have plastic Tupperware and plastic wrap, use it. Only once the containers are broken and the wrap is finished should you replace them with eco-alternatives.

Reuse and Upcycle. Don't buy brand-new pieces if you can repurpose, upcycle, or find what you need preloved.

Don't Buy It All. I guarantee you do not need everything on the list below.

Pass It On. If you try something and don't like it or are concerned about continuing to use the plastic you own, offer it up on your local free marketplace to ensure it finds a new home.

FOOD CONTAINERS	
Glass Jars	Jars can be used in the freezer or fridge or for storing dried foods, bulk goods, leftovers, and cut produce. You can repurpose empty food jars or buy new Bell or Mason jars. These brands are great because of their wide mouths and tight seal, and their thick glass can withstand defrosting and expansion when freezing without easily breaking.

Glass Containers	Many glass containers are freezer-, dishwasher-, microwave-, and oven-safe and come with a variety of lid options.
Stainless Steel Containers	Stainless steel containers are durable and great for storing food or on-the-go. You can find airtight, leakproof options that are also great for freezing food. Some versions are even oven-safe (without the lid).
Baskets and Crates	A ceramic basket or colander is an effective way to store berries. Natural baskets and wooden crates are good ways to store produce on the counter or in the pantry.
Glass Baking Dish	Baking and casserole dishes with a glass or ceramic lid are perfect for storing food instead of covering with plastic wrap.

FOOD COVERS	
Dish Towel	Cover a bowl with a dish towel and use a rubber band to secure it. It's an inexpensive and effective way to cover food without turning to plastic wrap.
Silicone Covers	Silicone covers come in various sizes and shapes, including options to cover bowls, cans, and cut produce.
Beeswax Wraps	Beeswax wraps are reusable and typically last a year if properly cared for. When you hold one around a bowl or plate, the warmth of your hands seals it in place. You can also fold them to wrap up sandwiches or make a pouch for snacks.
A Plate	For leftovers: Simply place a plate on top of a bowl that needs to be covered. For melons: Cut a melon in half. Place the melon on top of the plate, cut side down.

FOOD BAGS	
Silicone Bag	Look for sealable silicone bags that are dishwasher-, oven-, freezer-, and microwave-safe. They can be used for storing chopped produce, soup, dry goods, snacks on the go, popping popcorn, and more. Plus, they come in a variety of sizes.
Breathable Bag	A cloth or mesh bag (organic cotton, hemp, jute, or recycled plastic) or a repurposed cotton pillowcase are all examples of breathable bags. Bags can be used when buying foods in bulk or loose produce. They're also useful for storing produce, bread, or dry goods.

ECO-ACTION NO. 43
Nosh on Low-Waste Snacks

Kids' snacks, food packaging, and unhealthy choices go hand in hand. While there are some healthy packaged options out there, the less packaged it is, generally the healthier choice it is. Fruits and vegetables are the original package-free snack, but many other options are big wins with kids. Here are some kid favorites:

PACKAGE-FREE SNACKS KIDS LOVE

EASY PEASY
- Bulk trail mix
- Bulk raisins
- Bulk chocolate chips
- Bulk pretzels
- Bulk dried fruit
- Bananas and peanut butter (bulk or from a glass jar)
- Ants on a log
- Cut fruit
- Cut vegetables
- Yogurt (that comes in a glass jar)

MAKE WITH THE KIDDOS
- Smoothies
- Popcorn (made from bulk kernels)
- Homemade kale chips
- Homemade bagel chips
- Homemade hummus and veggies
- Homemade banana bread
- Homemade popsicles
- Homemade (or bulk) granola
- Homemade muffins
- Homemade whole wheat waffles dipped in yogurt

ECO-ACTION NO. 44
Choose Better Takeout

Takeout dinners can be a lifesaver for any parent, but a lot of packaging waste is generated in the process. (Not to mention dangerous PFAS—"forever chemicals"—lurking in grease-resistant takeout containers.) In addition to bringing your own bag, here are some simple ways to make takeout less wasteful.

Choose Minimally Packaged Meals. Some food types require less packaging than others or use plastic-free containers that can be recycled or composted, such as:

- Burritos: wrapped in aluminum (rinse and recycle)
- Kabobs: wrapped in paper* (compostable)
- Pizza: cardboard box* (compostable)

Choose Better Packaging. If you have access to composting, choose restaurants that serve their takeout in compostable paper-based to-go ware instead of plastic clamshells, bioplastics, or Styrofoam. Few cities have restaurants or services that offer reusable, returnable takeout containers, but if yours does, take advantage of it. If a restaurant will allow you to bring your own container for them to fill, go for it! It never hurts to ask.

Skip Extras. Request that no plastic cutlery, paper napkins, and condiments, etc., be included with your meal.

food- or grease-stained paper is not recyclable

———————————————— **DID YOU KNOW?** ————————————————

Black plastic containers and packaging commonly end up in the landfill even if you put them in the recycling bin. That's because black plastic cannot be sorted using the Near Infra-Red (NIR) technology widely used at recycling centers. As a result, it becomes trash.

In 2016 alone, **561 billion** food-service disposable items were used in the US—**75%** of which came from takeout.

✿

ECO-ACTION NO. 45
Keep Outings Low-Waste

Busy schedules and hungry kiddos are a recipe for meltdowns and single-use waste. We all know that grabbing food quickly while on the go is essential at times. And while it may seem faster to reach for a packaged granola bar to throw in your bag, planning ahead in different ways can create quick routines that will help reduce waste and are also stress-free and convenient.

Prep Snack Packs. Every parent knows that packing snacks is essential. Instead of reaching for packaged foods before leaving the house, scoop bulk snacks such as raisins, cashews, walnuts, and pretzels into reusable, kid-friendly containers. Prepare in advance—it takes less than two minutes to make enough for an entire week. Then store your premade "snack packs" in the pantry. Fruit is also an easy snack on the run.

Carry a Zero-Waste Kit. A zero-waste kit has everything you need to help you and your family limit using single-use items while you're out. You can keep one in your car, purse, child's backpack, or diaper bag—whatever works for you. After your utensils have been used, have your child lick them clean and wrap them in your cloth napkin to keep your pouch from getting soiled until you can wash everything for the next time you're out.

Bring a Container. Bring a container with you when dining out instead of getting a single-use container to carry inevitable kid leftovers home. If that seems like too much to remember, store a few to-go containers in your car for such occasions. Plus, bringing your own limits your family's exposure to PFAS too.

Don't Skip Dessert. Reducing packaging waste does not mean depriving yourself of things you love. It often means just approaching them differently. When heading out for ice cream, ask for a cone instead of a cup and spoon (or bring your own bowl and spoon). If you want to really be *green* about it, order sorbet or, where available, vegan ice cream. Trying to reduce waste doesn't mean you have to skip life's pleasures.

Pack It Out. Plastic happens, even when you do your best to avoid it. If find yourself with a plastic fork or water bottle, hold on to it until you can recycle it. So often, plastic gets tossed in the closest trash can, but it's just as easy to throw it in your bag and wait until you see a recycling bin. The same is also true for compostable elements, like orange peels or paper napkins, that can be brought home to compost.

FAMILY FUN PROJECT
DIY ZERO-WASTE KIT

What Is It? A zero-waste kit is a handy pouch with reusable utensils in it. Its purpose is to help you avoid having to use disposable plastic cutlery and napkins when you're out and about.

What You'll Need
- Any type of pouch that will fit everything listed below
- A reusable knife, fork, spoon
- A cloth napkin
- Optional:
  - Reusable straw
  - Chopsticks
  - Food container, silicone snack bag, or foldable tote

How to Assemble. You can spend nothing to very little to create your zero-waste kit. Reuse an old pencil case or cosmetic bag for the pouch. If you have any extra cutlery rattling around in your silverware drawer, throw that in or head to the thrift store and pick some up for less than a dollar. Or just wash and reuse any extra plastic cutlery you have stashed. If you don't have cloth napkins, use a bandanna or old burp cloth from your child's baby days. The kit takes a few minutes to throw together and can be used and reused for years to come.

ECO-ACTION NO. 46
Pack a Trash-Free School Lunch

Packing a trash-free lunch means your child does not need to visit the trash can or recycling bin at the end of their meal—meaning no plastic snack baggies, single-use juice boxes, or plastic utensils. Every element used to support their meal is reusable, and anything left over would be inedible compostable food waste, such as a banana peel.

If you don't have kid-friendly food containers (or need to add to your collection), secondhand stores and Buy Nothing groups are great places to start. If purchasing new, look for plastic-free options. And don't forget to LABEL every container. Here's a quick checklist of what to include:

HOW TO PACK A TRASH-FREE LUNCH	
INSTEAD OF . . .	TRY THIS . . .
Single-use utensils	Washable utensils
Paper napkins or paper towels	Cloth napkin
Plastic snack bags	Reusable snack bag or container
Aluminum foil, Styrofoam, plastic bags or wrap	Large food-grade stainless steel food container with dividers and a hot-food thermos
Single-use cartons or cans	Refillable water bottle
Single-use pouches	Reusable squeeze pouch
Throwaway lunch sack	Reusable lunch box made of sustainable or recycled materials

WHAT'S YOUR SOURCE?

Local. In-season. People. Ingredients.
These all impact our bodies, communities,
and the environment. Being mindful about
where and how your food is grown can
transform the world.

ECO-ACTION NO. 47
Buy Local and In-Season Produce

DID YOU KNOW?

Conventional food distribution generates **5 to 17 times** more
carbon emissions than foods grown locally or regionally.

Air-freighting food generates **50 times** more CO_2 than sea shipping.

In 2016, more than **50%** of fruit and over **30%** of vegetables
were imported to the United States.

Depending on who you talk to, locally grown food is defined as food grown
within a 100-to-400-mile radius of your home and typically not produced
on a large, commercial farm. On average, an American's food travels 1,500
miles from farm to plate. The fossil fuels burned to transport food long
distances on cargo boats, freight trucks, trains, and planes results in additional greenhouse gases emitted, with air-freighted foods having the highest transport-related emissions. Highly perishable foods such as asparagus,
berries, green beans, and fresh fish are commonly flown in, which makes it
important to buy them when they're in-season and locally sourced.

LOCAL AND IN-SEASON: BETTER FOR US

In addition to being better for the environment, eating locally and in-season benefits your family and community too.

Supports Your Local Economy. Buying local foods puts money back into the hands of the people who work and live there. When purchasing food at traditional food outlets, such as the grocery store, a farmer typically receives just 16 cents for every dollar of food sold, but when you buy food at the farmer's market, a farmer takes home 90 cents for each dollar spent.

Promotes Healthy Farming Practices. In a 2015 survey, 81% of farmers who were selling at farmer's markets said they integrate soil health activities, such as the use of cover crops, limited tillage, and/or on-site composting. These practices not only support soil health, they also reduce carbon emissions.

Supports Local Food Security. To build climate resilience, it's essential to support your local food supply and limit our reliance on foods coming from afar.

Nurtures Community. Buying food from the farmer's market sparks conversations and friendships—enabling you to further connect to your community and the people who grow your food.

Nutrient-Dense. As soon as produce is picked, it starts to lose nutrients. Fruits and vegetables brought in on ships and rail are typically picked before they're ripe in order to avoid early spoilage when traveling long distances. They're then "artificially ripened" with chemicals and gases when they arrive. Not only does this practice make the produce less nutritious, it also leaves out-of-season foods tasting bland. By eating locally and in-season, you give your family tasty, nutrient-dense foods picked at their peak.

It Costs Less. If you're looking for a way to save money and eat a healthy diet, buying produce that is in season is also usually less expensive. A grapefruit, for example, will cost twice as much in summer when it's out of season than it does in the winter when it's in season. More is available during its local growing season, which drives down the price.

Encourages Crop Diversification. Buying an assortment of foods grown locally supports a diversity of crops grown in your area, which reduces the dangers of an area (or even a nation) being dependent upon one variety of produce.

IS LOCAL ALWAYS BETTER?

From a climate change perspective, the type of food you eat is more important than where it's grown. When looking at the total greenhouse-gas emissions generated from food production, transportation is responsible for only a small percentage of food's carbon footprint. So if choosing between a vegetable imported from Mexico or a conventional cut of beef from a nearby farm, the imported vegetable will be a better choice from an emissions standpoint. However, if you can choose between a vegetable grown locally or one grown far away, pick the local, in-season option, as it will have a much smaller footprint. Again, there is a lot to consider when it comes to food—greenhouse gases are just one piece of the picture.

FARMER'S MARKET 101

Shopping at your local farmer's market is a beautiful opportunity to eat locally grown foods and invest in your community. Farmer's markets are open to the public and allow food producers to sell directly to consumers instead of going through a third party like a grocery store. Cutting out wholesalers means more money goes straight to local farms. While many only operate during certain seasons, some regions have a farmer's market year-round.

If you have never shopped at a farmer's market before, your first time can feel intimidating. With so many stalls and vendors selling produce at various costs, finding the best deal, most sustainably grown, and best-tasting produce can be overwhelming. Here are some "do's" and "don'ts" to make your farmer's market outings more sustainable.

> **ECO-FAMILY TIP**
> Don't have a farmer's market in your area? Sign up for a CSA (Community Supported Agriculture) box, where local farmers drop off produce at your doorstep.

DO	DON'T
Walk, ride your bike, or take public transport.	Don't drive if you can get there a more sustainable way.
Bring cash, good walking shoes, and a hat for sunny days.	Don't expect an ATM onsite.
Bring a market tote to carry home all of your goodies.	Don't ask for a single-use plastic or a paper bag to carry purchases. They aren't generally provided and are not a sustainable choice.
Sample the produce that vendors offer.	Unless food is offered as a sample, don't snack on produce until you've purchased it.
Bring your own produce bags.	Don't use single-use plastic produce bags.
Bring jars and containers to fill with berries and soft fruits so they don't get crushed. Give berry baskets back to vendors for them to reuse.	Don't take plastic berry baskets home with you. Oftentimes, vendors will not take them back once they've left their stalls.
Bring a container and your own utensils for lunch at the market.	Don't use single-use utensils or plates.
Look for organic certification on the vendor's signs. If you cannot afford organic produce or do not have organic farming in your area, ask the vendors how they engage in sustainable practices at their farms.	Don't miss out on talking to vendors. You can learn so much about what's in season, how it's grown, how to prepare it, and how to properly store it just by asking!
Let your kids dance to the live music, and sample everything.	Don't leave the kids at home. The farmer's market can be a great place for kids to experience new foods.

ECO-ACTION NO. 48
Eat Organic

INTRO TO ORGANIC

What Is It? Organic, organic, organic—what does it mean and why is it important? Organic farming is an agricultural system that does not use GMOs (genetically modified organisms) or human-made chemicals such as pesticides, herbicides, antibiotics, growth hormones, or fertilizers when growing crops or raising livestock. Organic farming practices reduce pollution and soil erosion, conserve water, increase soil fertility, and use less energy. Also, organic foods don't contain pesticides, which is better for your family's health and the health of our ecosystems.

DID YOU KNOW?

Studies have shown switching to an organic diet decreases pesticide levels in children and adults.

Is Organic Sustainable? Some studies suggest that organic farming may be worse from a global warming standpoint than traditional farming because of lower food yields coming from land of equally sized conventional farms, but there are more elements to consider, such as pesticide use, soil health, and reduced pollution. Furthermore, when we pair organic farming with the essential collective practices of reducing food waste and eating a plant-based diet, less land space is needed.

Your Family's Health. While organic produce contains the same nutrient content as conventionally grown foods, studies have shown potentially harmful effects from increased pesticide exposure. Pesticides in foods have been linked with ADHD and Alzheimer's disease. In 2020, *Consumer Reports* released a five-year data analysis from the Department of Agriculture which found higher pesticide levels detected in foods than were deemed safe by *Consumer Reports*. Not only is choosing organic essential to your family's health, it's also crucial to protecting farm workers and those who live in agricultural areas because of their increased exposure to pesticides. Scientists still don't know the full impact that pesticides have on humans through everyday food consumption, but opting for organic produce when you can helps limit risk.

CAN'T AFFORD IT? START HERE!

Certain foods routinely contain higher pesticide residue than others. Even after washing, scrubbing, and peeling foods, pesticides can persist. According to the Environmental Working Group, these 12 have the highest contamination levels. If looking for a place to start buying organic foods, avoiding these heavy hitters would be a great place to begin.

EWG's Dirty Dozen

- Strawberries
- Spinach
- Kale, collard, and mustard greens
- Nectarines
- Apples
- Grapes
- Bell and hot peppers

- Cherries
- Peaches
- Pears
- Celery
- Tomatoes
  (Raisins, while not fresh produce, contain some of the highest levels of pesticide residues.)

BUGGING OUT

A 2019 *Biological Conservation* report found that 40% of insect species are in threat of extinction. Primary drivers of their waning numbers include habitat loss due to intensive agriculture and urbanization, synthetic-pesticide use, fertilizer use, and climate change. Why should we care? Insects are pollinators, spread seeds, and are essential for soil health. We need them to survive. Plus, they balance our planet by helping control the population size of other organisms while being food for many animals. The aforementioned report also articulates that the plummeting number of insects threatens a "catastrophic collapse of nature's ecosystems," including human food supply. Eating organic foods, supporting sustainable food systems, and adding pollinator plants to your garden are simple ways you can help support their survival.

🌿

ECO-ACTION NO. 49
Diversify Your Plate

BITE INTO BIODIVERSITY

Every life form, including humankind, is dependent upon the functions of other organisms to survive. Through our agricultural practices, humans are negatively impacting the world's biodiversity and threatening the existence of all life across the globe, including our own.

biodiversity [bio-di-ver-si-ty]

1. The variety of life within an ecosystem.

It isn't just the act of clearing forests for farmland, using pesticides, and polluting waterways that impact biodiversity. It's also the types of crops that our industrial agricultural system chooses to grow. Seventy-five percent of the world's food comes from just 12 plants and 5 animal species. When looking at daily calories, over 40% come from just three foods: wheat, rice, and corn. This a dangerous "game" to play. Just take the Irish potato famine in the 1840s. Slightly warmer, wetter weather in 1845 created conditions for a fungus-like organism called blight to thrive—destroying the majority of the lumper potato crop, which had become the primary food source for the country. One in eight Irish people died from starvation, and nearly a million were forced to leave as refugees.

To avoid repeating devastating mistakes of the past, a diverse food supply is essential as we head into accelerating climate change. If history has taught us anything, it's that low genetic variation can be disastrous when it comes to food security. More variation means there are higher odds that some varieties will fare better than others through hard times, leaving us with food on our plates—protecting our food systems, our cultures, and our livelihoods. Becoming aware of the issue is the first step—then try these things.

Eat Diverse Foods. Diversifying what you eat doesn't necessarily mean trying new cuisines. It can also mean eating different varieties of foods you already love. Take apples. Of the 15,000 apple varieties that once existed in the United States, only 20% currently remain. Maybe your family love Gala and Granny Smith apples, but trying other varieties helps support biodiversity in farming.

Support Local Farms. Buying produce from your local farmer's market allows you to speak directly with the farmer to learn more about their biodiversity practices. Talk to them about their produce varieties. Sample and buy new ones that you like.

Skip GMO. Genetically modified foods reduce genetic diversity in the environment.

Vote with Your Wallet. Check products for labels like Fair Trade, FSC (Forest Stewardship Council), Rainforest Alliance Certified, and Certified Sustainable Palm Oil. These certifications support healthy biodiversity practices around the globe.

Get Involved Locally. You can support biodiversity in your community. Grow native plants in your yard. Help your kids and pets stick to trails when hiking. Protect open spaces. Donate or volunteer with local habitat restoration.

─────────────── **DID YOU KNOW?** ───────────────
The planet is at the start of its sixth mass extinction. What sets this event apart from the five historic extinctions is that it is the result of a species—us. Shrinking biodiversity of animals, plants, and ecosystems is due to habitat destruction, pollution, the introduction of invasive species, overhunting, and human-caused climate change.

ECO-FAMILY BITE-SIZE CHALLENGE   NO. 8

GET STARTED: FOOD SOURCE SOLUTIONS

As a family, pick three of the following tasks to kick off your challenge to add more locally grown, in-season, diverse produce to your daily diet:

- ○ Focus on the Dirty Dozen list as a place to start buying organic.
- ○ Visit your local farmer's market with your family weekly.
- ○ Avoid foods out of season and not grown locally. Buy or download a seasonal produce calendar for your region and post it someplace you can refer to it regularly.
- ○ Buy produce varieties, such as a diverse assortment of apples, broccoli, or carrots. You may find them at the grocery store, but a farmer's market is a great place to look (and talk with vendors about options).
- ○ Look for certifications that help support biodiversity, such as Fair Trade, FSC (Forest Stewardship Council), Rainforest Alliance Certified, and RSPO Certified Sustainable Palm Oil.
- ○ To avoid palm oil, strive to buy most of your food around the grocery store's perimeter, avoiding packaged food that's generally sold in middle aisles. Download the PalmSmart app and scan bar codes when grocery shopping to find which products have palm oil lurking in them. Inform friends about the detrimental impact of palm oil and how they can avoid it. (See page 63 for more.)

THE CLIMATE DIET

Bite into meaningful climate action
by reexamining what you eat.

PLANT-BASED EATING 101

PLANTS FOR A BETTER WORLD

You have the power to fight climate change three times a day by turning your family's attention to what they're putting on their plates. Conventional animal agriculture is responsible for 41% of deforestation worldwide and is a leading cause of biodiversity loss and water and air pollution. Because livestock emissions are responsible for one-third of human-generated carbon emissions, a source second only to fossil fuels, consuming a plant-based diet is a simple way to start reducing your family's footprint at home.

> ———— **DID YOU KNOW?** ————
> Livestock emissions are responsible for **one-third** of human generated carbon emissions, a source second only to fossil fuels.

A PLANT–BASED DIET: WHAT'S THAT?

A plant-based diet focuses on foods that come primarily from plants. While I know that may sound very self-explanatory, there's a catch. Meat eaters, vegetarians, and vegans can all eat a plant-based diet. What it boils down to is ensuring that the majority of your diet comes from plants. So whether you choose to eat meat and/or animal-based products in moderation or plan to become a full-fledged vegan, you too can hop on the plant-based bandwagon by enjoying an array of fruits, vegetables, grains, legumes (like beans and lentils), mushrooms, nuts, seeds, healthy oils, herbs, spices, and fermented foods.

PLANT-BASED MYTHS

Before diving into the eco-action, let's break down some false narratives.

✗ **Myth:** I will be bored out of my mind (and constantly hungry) eating just plants.

✓ **Fact:** I promise you that neither is true. A plant-based diet can be full of incredibly flavorful and exciting foods that are also high in fiber, leaving you feeling full and satiated.

✗ **Myth:** Plant-based foods are always healthy.

✓ **Fact:** A plant-based diet can be very nutrient-dense. It has the power to boost your immune system, reduce inflammation, lower diabetes risk, increase heart health, lower cancer risk, help you maintain a healthy weight, lower cholesterol, and protect the brain. Plants are rich in vitamins, minerals, fiber, and other nutrients vital to maintaining good health. Plants don't have added sugars or sodium and rarely contain saturated fats. So how could they be unhealthy? It depends on how the food is prepared. Healthy plant-based foods would not include sugary fruit juices, processed bread, sugary cereals, and fried vegetables such as French fries and potato chips.

✗ **Myth:** I won't be able to get enough protein.

✓ **Fact:** While protein is an essential part of a person's diet, you may actually be getting more than you need. The World Health Organization suggests 10–15% of an adult's diet come from protein—around 46 to 56 grams depending upon one's weight. Most Americans eat about 100 grams of protein a day, around twice the recommended amount.

✗ **Myth:** A plant-based diet is more expensive than a traditional meat-based diet.

✓ **Fact:** The truth is a plant-based diet can cost much less. Meat, dairy, and eggs are expensive. Countless plant-based foods are not only more cost-effective than animal-based foods, they're also a whole lot cheaper than treating an illness due to a poor diet. While fresh produce can sometimes be expensive, buying unprocessed plant-based foods that are canned, dried, or even frozen are all cost-effective options you might not have considered. Here are some nutrient-dense plant-based foods you can buy on a budget.

PLANT-BASED ON A BUDGET				
Brown rice	Oats	Whole wheat or multigrain pasta	Stove-top popcorn	Whole wheat bread
Corn tortillas	Canned or dried beans	Canned or dried lentils	Tofu	Tea
Peanut butter, peanuts + seeds	Edamame	Jar or canned marinara sauce	Canned tomatoes	Canned pumpkin
Bananas	Apples	Oranges	Pears	Melons
Lemons + limes	Onions	Zucchini + squash	Broccoli	Carrots
Cabbage	Kale	Garlic	Russet or sweet potatoes	Beets

✗ **Myth:** Eating a plant-based diet won't make a difference.

✓ **Fact:** It's true that your family becoming vegetarian or vegan will not shift climate change alone, no matter how many tofu burgers you eat. However, your actions do not exist in a bubble. By purchasing food from regenerative farms, you support the growth of businesses engaged in climate action, and you're signaling to grocery stores to carry more of these types of products. When talking to friends and family about the importance of plant-based eating, you shift the paradigm around you. So while your family's weekly vegetarian chili dinner might not save the world by itself, you're embodying climate solutions, shifting the cultural landscape, and passing these ideals on to your children.

✗ **Myth:** I have to give up meat entirely.

✓ **Fact:** Becoming a vegan for ethical reasons is something to consider. But from a climate standpoint, how the animal is raised and how often you choose to eat it makes a huge difference. While conventional livestock production is one of the main sources of greenhouse gas emissions, livestock that's raised on a regenerative farm can actually help sequester carbon. See Eco-Action 51 to learn more about regenerative farming.

🌿

ECO-ACTION NO. 50
Eat More Plants + Less Meat

THE
CLIMATE
CREW

Eating more plants and less meat is better for our health and the wellness of the planet. But with busy days, work, and trying to find a moment to ourselves, most parents find that starting a new cooking routine feels daunting. Here are ways to shift toward more sustainable meals.

PLANT-BASED EATING FOR BEGINNERS

Get Inspired. Head to the library with your kids and check out plant-based cookbooks. Pop onto social media to follow plant-based chefs and find drool-worthy meal ideas. Start a plant-based recipe share with friends. If you have a partner, take turns preparing new plant-based dishes.

Start with Meatless Mondays. Make it a goal to eat meat-free on Mondays. If you're a heavy meat-eating family, this is an excellent place to start.

The Green Rule:

Less Meat + Better or No Meat = A Healthier Planet

Limit Meat throughout the Week. Ready to take plant-based eating a step further? Cut out meat at breakfast and/or lunch 7 days a week. If you're willing to eliminate beef and lamb entirely, you can reduce your food's carbon footprint by 24%.

Add One Plant to Every Meal. Add one more fruit or veggie at mealtime by chopping up summer strawberries to sprinkle over your granola, adding a handful of winter squash to your soup, or including guacamole and fresh salsa in your bean and brown rice burrito.

Eat Whole Foods. Whole foods (foods that are minimally processed) are more nutrient-dense and require fewer resources to manufacture and package. Applesauce, for example, is often sweetened and made without the peel, making it higher in sugar, less fibrous, and lower in antioxidants than a whole apple.

Slowly Add New-to-you Plant Proteins. Plant proteins don't bite (a little plant-based humor for you), so there is nothing to fear. However, it takes effort to find new recipes and ingredients and learn how to cook them. Don't burden yourself by taking on more than you can handle. Take it slow—add one new plant protein a month.

Focus on Snack Time. Another simple way to start eating fewer animal-based products is to focus your efforts between meals. If there is one thing that is certain, kids love to snack. Keeping midmorning and afternoon noshing plant-based can be stress-free and leave kiddos well fed. Here are some simple shifts you can make to create a snack time that is less harmful to the environment but still keeps the kids happy.

GREEN READS

———

PLANT-POWERED FAMILIES
by Dreena Burton

THE PLANT-BASED BABY & TODDLER
by Whitney English and
Alexandra Caspero

PLANT-BASED ON A BUDGET
by Toni Okamoto

THE PLANT-BASED DIET FOR BEGINNERS
by Gabriel Miller

THE PLANT-BASED SNACK SHIFT	
Instead of . . .	**Try this . . .**
Cheese and crackers	Hummus or nut/seed butter and crackers
Sliced deli meat	Edamame
Cheesy nachos	Guacamole and chips
Chicken nuggets	Veggie nuggets
Beef jerky	Trail mix
Quesadilla	Hummus and veggie pinwheel
String cheese	Celery and peanut butter
Cookies	Vegan cookies or energy balls

PLANT-BASED MEAL IDEAS

BREAKFAST

- Steel cut oatmeal with coconut milk, chia seeds, flax seeds, fruit, and crushed nuts
- Granola with oat milk, bananas, flax seeds, and chia seeds
- Sprouted grains toast with peanut butter and fruit
- Whole wheat waffles with chia seeds, flax seeds, and fruit
- Smoothie with plant-based milk, chia seeds, and berries

LUNCH

- Avocado whole wheat toast with chickpea mash and nutritional yeast
- Classic peanut (or seed) butter and jelly sandwich on sprouted bread with sliced banana and sprinkled chia seeds
- Whole wheat penne pasta with marinara, white beans, roasted veggies, and nutritional yeast
- Whole wheat tortilla rolls with avocado and chickpea mash
- Wild rice salad with sliced grapes and dried cranberries
- Veggie nugget dippers with ketchup or honey mustard sauce

DINNER

- Vegan chili
- Veggie, bean, and rice bowl
- Rice, bean, and avocado burrito
- Veggie and tofu fried rice
- Bean burger with homemade sweet potato fries
- Spaghetti and meatless bolognese sauce

DESSERT

- Blended frozen banana "ice cream"
- Fresh berries dipped in brown sugar
- Cinnamon baked pears
- Chocolate chip stuffed raspberries
- Vegan ice cream

ECO-FAMILY TIP

Forget Labels. If you've been contemplating becoming a vegetarian but are not ready to give up chicken-apple sausage, eat the sausage and eliminate meat everywhere else in your diet. The same is true for anyone thinking about becoming a vegan. If you love honey more than life itself, don't give it up! Don't let one food stand in the way of eliminating other animal-based products in your life. Please, oh please, don't let labels like "vegan" or "vegetarian" hold you back from making change. There are no rules, but there must be action.

INTRO TO PLANT PROTEINS

Legumes	
1 cup cooked lentils	17.9g protein
1 cup split peas	16.3g protein
1 cup cooked pinto beans	15.4g protein
1 cup cooked black beans	15.2g protein
1 cup cooked chickpeas	14.5g protein
1 cup cooked kidney beans	13.4g protein
1 cup cooked green peas	8.6g protein

Milks and Eggs	
1 cup pea milk	8g protein
1 cup soy milk	6.9g protein
1 plant-based egg	3–5g protein

Nutritional Yeast	
¼ cup nutritional yeast	8g protein

Nuts and Nut Butter	
½ cup shelled peanuts	17.3g protein
½ cup shelled almonds	15.1g protein
½ cup shelled pistachios	12.4g protein
½ cup chopped pecans	10g protein
½ cup chopped walnuts	8.9g protein
2 Tbsp. smooth peanut butter	7g protein
2 Tbsp. smooth almond butter	6.7g protein

Fruits and Vegetables	
1 cup cooked spinach	5.3g protein
1 ear yellow sweet corn	5g protein
1 cup asparagus	4.3g protein
1 avocado	4g protein
1 cup cooked broccoli	3.7g protein
1 cup chopped apricots	2.2g protein
1 cup cooked Brussels sprouts	2g protein
1 cup blackberries	2g protein
1 cup peach slices	1.4g protein
1 cup peeled grapefruit wedges	1.4g protein
1 cup diced cantaloupe	1.3g protein
1 medium-sized banana	1.3g protein

Seeds	
½ cup shelled pumpkin seeds	21.2g protein
½ cup shelled sunflower seeds	12.3g protein
3 Tbsp. hemp seeds	9g protein
2 Tbsp. sunflower seed butter	5.6g protein
2 Tbsp. chia seeds	4.7g protein

Seitan (pronounced SAY-tan)	
200 calorie serving (187oz.) seitan	33.4g protein

Soy Products	
1 cup firm tofu	43.5g protein
1 cup boiled soybeans (edamame)	31.1g protein
100g cooked tempeh	19.9g protein

Spirulina	
1 Tbsp. spirulina	4g protein

Grains	
1 cup groats	20g protein
1 cup buckwheat flour	16g protein
1 cup cooked spelt	10.7g protein
1 cup cooked teff	9.8g protein
1 cup (246g) cooked amaranth	9.3g protein
1 cup (185g) cooked quinoa	8.1g protein
1 cup muesli	7.3g protein
1 cup cooked wild rice	6.5g protein
1 cup cooked oatmeal	5.9 protein
1 cup soba noodles	5.8g protein
1 slice sprouted grains bread	5g protein
1 slice oatmeal bread	3g protein

PLANT-BASED "DAIRY" AND EGGS 101

Plant-based milks have been made for centuries by many cultures across the globe. In recent years, they've made a big comeback in the US as well. Common plant-based milks are made from almonds, coconuts, flax, hemp, peanuts, peas, oats, rice, and soy. You can find plant-based milks at the grocery store or easily make them at home. In addition to plant-based milks there are also plant-based butters, yogurts, ice creams, and even vegan eggs.

DID YOU KNOW?

When it comes to land use, water use, and greenhouse-gas emissions, conventional dairy milk is a worse offender than plant-based milk alternatives.

INTRODUCING PLANT-BASED "DAIRY" AND EGGS AT MEALTIME

Breakfast. Use plant-based yogurts in smoothies and parfaits or with granola. Switch from traditional eggs to vegan eggs when making quiches or baked goods. You may notice a slight difference in texture if eating scrambled, but most people find them undetectable in recipes.

Lunch and Dinner. Use olive oil or plant-based butter instead of traditional butter for cooking or on bread.

Dessert. You can always turn to sorbet, but if you're an ice cream lover, then plant-based ice creams are an easy, eco-friendly swap (and they're absolutely delicious).

Baking. Plant-based butter and milks are easy dairy substitutes when baking. You can also use avocado, applesauce, mashed banana, coconut oil, and pureed pumpkin in place of eggs or butter.

THINGS TO AVOID

Palm Oil. Some plant-based butters contain palm oil. Try to avoid it unless it's RSPO certified.

Almond Milk. Almond farming is pesticide-heavy, promotes monoculture agriculture, and is hurting the bee population. Despite its rising demand, consider trying other plant-based milks first.

High-Sugar and Low-Protein Plant-Based Yogurts. Check the labels for options low in sugar and high in protein, just as with traditional dairy-based yogurts.

Conventional Eggs. In conventional egg production, hens are inhumanely packed into cages by the dozen. Each bird has less space than a single sheet of letter-sized paper to stand. Instead, look for pasture-raised (it's better than cage-free or free range), organic, and "certified humane." Be wary of greenwashing terms like "humane" (it's not the same as "certified humane"), "hormone-free" (the use of hormones in eggs and chicken was banned in the 1950s), "farm-fresh," and "natural."

THE
CLIMATE
CREW

ECO-ACTION NO. 51
Buy Regenerative Foods

Imagine a productive agriculture system that sequesters carbon to fight climate change, rebuilds ecosystems, and promotes soil health and biodiversity—all while helping people fight disease and improve overall wellness. That is regenerative farming.

THE SCOOP ON SOIL

Topsoil is the outermost layer of soil, brimming with the highest concentrations of organic matter and microorganisms. Without it we wouldn't have food to eat, but it's rapidly disappearing due to conventional agriculture practices. Without focused efforts to rebuild and maintain healthy soil, humans could lose our ability to feed ourselves in the next 60 years. Modern conventional farming practices destroy soil health, contributing to desertification and the climate crisis. By supporting sustainable farming practices, which can regenerate the soil, we protect our food supply and planet while improving human health.

Nearly 80% of the carbon found in terrestrial ecosystems is held in the soil.

REGENERATIVE: THE BASICS

Regenerative farming keeps carbon in the ground, actively fighting climate change while feeding humans, nurturing the soil, and promoting biodiversity. Regenerative farmers grow crops, raise livestock, or do both—partnering with nature as indigenous people have done for thousands of years. Like organic farming, it does not use harmful chemicals or pesticides—but it takes these even further, leading the way as the most sustainable food system.

CONVENTIONAL AGRICULTURE	REGENERATIVE AGRICULTURE
Competes with nature, causing high environmental damage	Works with nature, resulting in regeneration of the soil and ecosystem
Contributes to the climate crisis and desertification	Fights climate change by sequestering carbon
Single-crop (monoculture)	Diverse crops (polyculture)
Destroys the microbiome of the soil, causes erosion, overuses water, and increases pest resistance and pollution through tilling and synthetic chemical intervention	Improves soil health, minimizes water use, reduces erosion, and increases production through minimal-to-no-till practices, cover crops, crop rotation, managed grazing, and composting
Demolishes biodiversity, clears land, and contributes to deforestation	Restores habitats
Chemical pesticides are used, negatively impacting farm workers, consumers, and biodiversity	No harmful synthetic chemicals or pesticides reduces workers' and your family's exposure to toxic chemicals
Supports industrial agriculture; puts many small farms out of business	Puts more money directly into the hands of smaller farms
Decreases food security and resilience	Increases food security and climate resiliency
Produces food devoid of nutrients	Generates nutrient-rich foods

YOUR FAMILY'S HEALTH

Our health and soil health are deeply intertwined. The community of microorganisms living in the soil where our food is grown reflects the health of our gut microbiome, impacting our ability to fight physical and mental illness, decrease inflammation, and maintain a healthy weight. Studies continue to be published showing how conventional agricultural practices, which strip the soil of nutrients, are a significant contributor to many prevailing modern diseases. Studies have also shown that we get a more nutrient-dense diet when we choose to eat foods grown in nutrient-dense soil. So by taking an active interest in supporting farms that regenerate the soil, we are taking care of our health as well.

GREEN READS

———

THE SOIL WILL SAVE US
by Kristin Ohlson

KISS THE GROUND
by Josh Tickell

GREEN ON THE SCREEN

———

Sustainable (2022)

Kiss the Ground (2020)

The Biggest Little Farm (2018)

GETTING STARTED

How to Spot It? Right now, there are two regenerative farming certifications: *Regenerative Organic Certified* and *Demeter Biodynamic Certification*, with more in the works. Regenerative farming is a philosophy that's existed for generations, so a regenerative farm may operate without one of these two certifications. Look for language like *no or minimal tillage, soil health restoration, rotational grazing, cover crops,* and *rebuilding ecosystem diversity.* Be sure to read packages, go to your farmer's market, and visit local farms so you can speak directly with farmers and ranchers about how they grow food.

It Doesn't Have to Be All or Nothing. If price stands in your way of purchasing sustainable foods, remember that there is no "all or nothing" rule. If you have access to organic or regeneratively grown food but cannot afford it all of the time, buying it just sometimes still has an impact. If you can't afford sustainably grown foods at all, there are other ways to reduce your food footprint and no reason to feel like you're not doing your part. Just do what you can, when you can, from where you stand.

ECO–FAMILY BITE–SIZE CHALLENGE

GET STARTED: PLANT-BASED EATING

As a family, pick three of the following tasks to kick off your
plant-based challenge:

○ Begin a "Meatless Monday" routine.

○ Test out one new plant-based recipe a week. Keep a list and repeat any family favorites.

○ Eat only plant-based during the week (but still eat meat and animal-based products on the weekends).

○ Eat entirely plant-based foods for breakfast and lunch but allow animal-based foods for dinner.

○ Strive to reduce beef consumption to one day a week (or cut it out completely). Opt for poultry if your family is not ready to give up meat entirely.

○ Research to see if there are any regenerative farms or ranches in your area. Plan a visit or support their business by buying food grown by them.

○ Try being a "vegetarian" or "vegan" for a month. Remember not to get stuck on labels. If you can't break up with one particular food (like yogurt, honey, or turkey sandwiches), don't let that hold you back from making other changes.

○ Buy a variety of plant-based ice creams and do a taste test with the family.

○ Get inspired! Follow plant-based influencers on Instagram for recipe ideas. Head to your local library and check out a few plant-based cookbooks.

○ Have each family member (your partner, teenagers, etc.) step up to cook one plant-based dish a week, so it doesn't all fall on your shoulders.

○ Build community! Host a potluck with families and ask everyone to make and bring a plant-based dinner so everyone can sample a variety of recipes in one sitting.

Note: For infants, in particular, be sure to speak with your child's pediatrician before introducing nuts, seeds, soy, and other plant-based alternatives (just as you would before introducing dairy or eggs). If you are concerned or have questions about eating a plant-based diet, it would be good to talk to your doctor or a dietitian for guidance, particularly for pregnant women, athletes, or children who are or are planning to become vegan.

ECO-ACTION NO. 52
Rethink Your Pet's Food

If American cats and dogs had their own country, they would rank fifth globally in terms of meat consumption. Many falsely believe that pet food is made up of the byproducts from meat production for humans, but in fact about 30% of farmed animals in the US are explicitly raised and killed to feed our furry companions. Turning your pet vegan is not advisable and could have health implications for your animal. But reconsidering your pet's diet can have a positive impact.

DID YOU KNOW?
A **quarter** of all meat in the US is eaten by our pets.

Better sources. Choose pet food companies that make sustainable choices, such as using renewable energy in their factories, or have an eco-certification like Marine Stewardship Council certified, Certified Organic, etc.

Rethink meat. Consider feeding your pet a beef-free diet. Focus on other sources of protein such as chicken or fish. (Some pet food companies are even branching into the insect world.) And according to the American Kennel Club, dogs can "thrive" on a vegetarian diet. However, it should be balanced and monitored closely.

GREEN READS

THE CLEAN PET FOOD REVOLUTION
by Ernie Ward, Alice Oven, and Ryan Bethencourt

Note: It's recommended to talk to your pet's veterinarian before making any changes to your pet's diet.

FOOD WASTE IS THE PITS

Food waste is an often overlooked yet significant contributor to climate change. Together we can make meaningful climate impact simply by shifting the way we plan, buy, store, and toss our food.

FOOD WASTE 101

> "Ranked with countries, food [waste] would be the third-largest emitter of greenhouse gases globally, just behind the United States and China."
>
> **—PROJECT DRAWDOWN**

WHAT'S THE PROBLEM? IT'S MESSY

Food waste is estimated to be responsible for 6–8% of global greenhouse-gas emissions. That's three times the global emissions from aviation. Additionally, 43% of all food waste in the United States happens in our homes—a figure that's hard to stomach. When analyzed against all of the world's most effective solutions to fight the climate crisis, reducing food waste is ranked third.

DID YOU KNOW?

The average American household throws away **31.9%** of the food it buys.

Organic matter, such as discarded food, used paper towels, and yard waste, does not break down in a landfill as it would in nature because landfills are anaerobic, meaning there is no oxygen present. So when organic matter breaks down, it decomposes anaerobically, producing methane gas—a greenhouse gas up to 34 times more potent than CO_2. But it's not just the greenhouse gases emitted during decomposition that are the issue. When we throw food out, we also waste all of the resources, like energy, water, labor, and transportation, it took to produce it.

FOOD WASTE + LANDFILL = CLIMATE CHANGE

When we keep food waste out of the landfill,
we are taking an active step to fight climate breakdown.

SIMPLE SOLUTIONS

There are two basic ways to reduce food waste at home: 1. Limit how much food you throw out, and 2. compost food scraps. Not overpurchasing food, meal planning, prepping, and properly storing food can reduce how much food your family throws away. There will always be some food waste, however—you're never going to eat peach pits or mango skins—so composting is an essential second step in diverting organic waste from the landfill. It's estimated that if composting increases worldwide, we could reduce our greenhouse-gas emissions by 2.28 gigatons by 2050, and you can be part of the solution.

───────────── **DID YOU KNOW?** ─────────────
According to the EPA, food is the single largest category
of material thrown in the landfill every day.

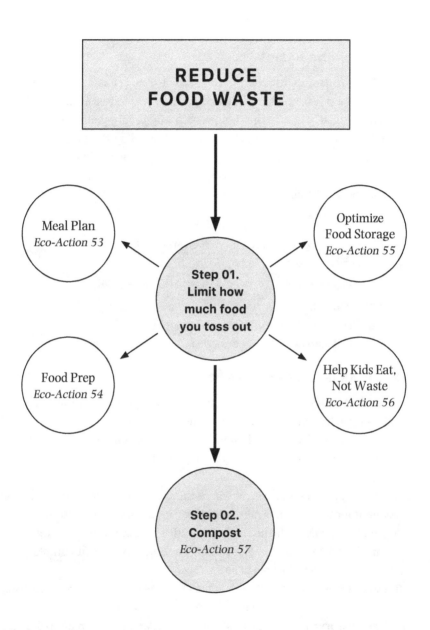

REDUCE
FOOD WASTE

Meal Plan
Eco-Action 53

Optimize
Food Storage
Eco-Action 55

Step 01.
Limit how
much food
you toss out

Food Prep
Eco-Action 54

Help Kids Eat,
Not Waste
Eco-Action 56

Step 02.
Compost
Eco-Action 57

ECO-ACTION NO. 53
Meal Plan

MEAL PLANNING BASICS

Meal planning doesn't just help reduce food waste and emissions; it's also essential to help your week run smoothly. Getting organized around food will relieve some of the day-to-day pressures of feeding your kiddos by streamlining grocery shopping, cooking, and avoiding the last-minute question of "What's for dinner?" So regardless who is in charge in the kitchen, adding meal planning to your weekly routine is better for both your family and the planet.

> **ECO-FAMILY TIP**
>
> **Plan Less.** Log on to websites like savethefood.org, where you can easily make a meal plan for free based on the number of people in your household and the foods you have on hand.
>
> **Hire It Out.** Don't have time to create a meal plan? No problem. Businesses like *Ends + Stems* will develop personalized weekly meal plans specifically designed to reduce food waste.

MEAL PLAN IN SEVEN SIMPLE STEPS

01. Keep a Master List. Make a master list of all of your family's favorite meals—it will help you as a reference when planning out recipes for the week. As you build your meal plan, look for overlapping ingredients. If two recipes call for rice, you can cook all of the rice the first night, saving you time.

02. Think Seasonally. Create a two- or three-week meal plan and cycle through it for the season. Then, after three months, change your meal plan to align foods with the new season (it's simpler than creating a new meal plan each week). With a seasonal meal plan, you can plan just four times a year instead of every seven days.

03. Look at the Calendar. What's going on this week? It will impact how many meals you need to plan for and will help you avoid overbuying.

04. Take a Survey. Do a quick kitchen survey, and make a plan to use any highly perishable ingredients right away. Making it a habit to look through what foods you have at home before heading to the store is an essential step in not letting food go to waste.

05. Consider Recipe Proportions. If you're a single parent with two small children, a recipe designed to serve four adults will leave a lot of extra food. Plan for smaller portions or incorporate leftovers into your weekly routine (or even freeze them for future meals).

06. Use Your Freezer. Busy nights are inevitable (and sometimes, watching a movie together as a family sounds so much better than cooking). Plan to double at least one recipe a week and freeze it so you can have a quick, easy dinner on hand.

07. Love Leftovers. Include leftovers in your meal planning—it will help ensure they won't get tossed.

Head to motheringearthproject.com for a free Meal Planning Template.

GREEN READS

———

THE ZERO-WASTE CHEF
by Anne-Marie Bonneau

THE ZERO WASTE COOKBOOK
by Giovanna Torrico &
Amelia Wasiliev

FAMILY FUN PROJECT
INVOLVING KIDS IN THE KITCHEN

Make time in the kitchen memorable by getting the kids involved in shopping, meal planning, prepping, and cooking. It's a fun opportunity to be together while also teaching essential life skills.

Littles. Young children always want to be involved, so allow them to spread seed butters on crackers or toast, shell peas and hard-boiled eggs, spin lettuce, knead dough, and gather dinnerware for their place setting.

Kids. As your child gets older, let them help with measuring, mixing, pouring, juicing, rinsing, peeling, scooping, cleaning, and making simple meals like sandwiches. Let them help you meal-plan, count quantities at the grocery store, and unpack groceries. Have them pick out and read recipes while you support them through the steps. Teach basic kitchen safety, and allow children to practice slicing with a knife appropriate to their age.

Tweens and Teens. During the preteen years, your child may be ready to work more independently in the kitchen, assuming they have already learned basic kitchen safety. Trust your gut. Work with them first to understand how to properly use the stove and other appliances. Teach basic recipes so they can gain independence. Make it a tradition to cook a meal together one night a week. Once they're ready, ask them to make one family meal on a regular schedule. Maybe it's once a week or once a month, but try to keep it consistent. It can be the same recipe over and over or they can get adventurous—either way, cheer them along in their efforts. And if they're up for it, maybe even make it a "date" to buy the ingredients together.

🌿

ECO-ACTION NO. 54
Food Prep

--- **DID YOU KNOW?** ---
The average family of four throws away **1,160 lbs.** of food annually, which totals approximately **$1,500**.

PREP FOOD TO REDUCE WASTE

Prepping food does not need to take hours. In fact, it can simplify your week, all while reducing food waste. Food prep can be narrowed down to one 10-to-20-minute session a week or woven into your everyday cooking routine. It's about being proactive and utilizing your time to its maximum potential. Here are five ways to help your family prep food with ease.

One-Touch Rule. If you're making a salad for dinner but aren't going to eat all of the lettuce tonight, go ahead and prep the entire head of lettuce anyway. It will save you time by not having to go through the entire routine each time want to eat your greens, not to mention using fewer dishes. The same goes for onions, carrots, or any other weekly recipe staples that requires prepping. For tips on storing produce for maximum freshness, head to the Mothering Earth website.

Don't Peel It. Skip peeling organic fruits or veggies. Peels are packed with nutrients and antioxidants and can help you feel full longer. Edible peels that are often discarded include apples, carrots, potatoes, cucumber, and eggplant. (Peels may need to be removed for small children or those with eating challenges due to choking hazards.)

Prep Once. Eat Twice. If you're making wild rice for dinner on Sunday night, double (or triple) the recipe, so you have rice on hand for lunches and dinners throughout the week. The same can be done for hot breakfast cereals and other meal staples. It saves you time and reduces your energy bill by not needing to make the same foods repeatedly. Just be sure you have a plan to eat it all, so it doesn't go to waste.

Cook a Big Batch. How often have you cooked a recipe, and you're left with extra ingredients? By making a large batch once, you can use up all of your ingredients in one go. Cooking a larger batch also means you can eat it for two or three nights (or freeze extras).

Double It Up in the Oven. Lasagna for dinner tonight and baked potatoes tomorrow? Put both in the oven now to save time tomorrow. Plus, doing so will reduce your gas or electric bill by only having to turn on the oven once.

ECO-ACTION NO. 55
Optimize Food Storage

IN THE PANTRY

Keeping a waste-free pantry isn't hard and requires minimal upkeep. The key is bringing attention to your routines when buying and putting away groceries.

Eat It Up. The first step to a waste-free pantry is to eat what you already own. If you find food lurking at the back of shelves that you aren't going to eat, donate it to a local food bank. They will generally accept expired shelf-stable food with undamaged packaging.

Organize. Next, get it in order. Consider how often you use the products when deciding upon placement. Set a limit to your pantry stock so you never have more than a few of anything on the shelf.

First In, First Out. When putting away groceries, place the newest items in the back of your pantry so you'll be sure to reach for older foods in front first. This applies to refrigerated goods and produce as well. The freshest milk should go behind the milk that will expire soonest. New oranges go on the bottom, and older ones go on top.

Label It. If you buy bulk bin items, label all jars with their contents (along with the date you filled it).

UNDERSTANDING EXPIRATION DATES

Understanding how expiration dates work helps with optimizing food storage while reducing food waste. According to the USDA, most shelf-stable foods are safe to eat long past their expiration date. (We're talking years in some cases for canned goods.) End-date labels are voluntarily put on products to help consumers understand when food may be best by. They do not indicate that a food is no longer safe to eat. Here's what each marker means.

- *Best by.* A "best by" label indicates when the food is at its freshest. It's about quality and taste, not safety.
- *Sell by.* A "sell by" date indicates how long stores should keep products on their shelves, but the food should still be fine to eat past the date. The labels are there to help ensure that people have time to

consume the food at home before it goes bad. Depending upon the item, it can last a few days and even weeks past the sell-by date and still be safe to eat. Milk can be consumed 5 to 7 days after the sell-by date; yogurt 2 to 3 weeks if unopened.

- **Use by.** A "use by" date is the last date the food maker guarantees the food will be at its peak.

If the packaging hasn't been damaged (no rust, dents, or swelling) and the food still smells and tastes okay, it's likely fine to eat it. The only exception is infant formula, where the expiration date is a hard deadline.

ECO-FAMILY TIP

When storing leftovers in the fridge, write the date you made them on a piece of compostable masking tape and sticking it to the container. Amid a busy week when the days blend together, you will know how old they are and won't throw edible leftovers out when they're still safe to eat.

IN THE FREEZER

It's pretty cool (no pun intended) that a freezer allows you to essentially stop time and save a meal for later. Yet freezers are often underutilized. Whether you need a quick meal or you're heading on vacation and don't want to toss out extra food, your freezer will save you time and limit how much food (and money) your family wastes.

FREEZING FOOD TIPS

Let It Cool. Let warm foods come to room temp before putting them in the freezer. (Just don't let them sit out for too long once they've cooled.)

Leave Room. When filling containers, be sure to leave room at the top for expansion during freezing.

Portion It. Dividing large meals out into smaller portions for freezing allows you to thaw single portions one at a time. This will speed up the time it takes to defrost your meal and will also reduce food waste by allowing you to defrost only what you need.

Airtight Is the Answer. An airtight container means less freezer burn on your food. Freezer burn won't hurt you, but it makes food taste funny.
Blanch It. You can freeze veggies without blanching them if you plan to use them right away. But if they will be in the freezer for a while, blanching them can help preserve the vegetable's flavor, color, and texture. To blanch, just clean your produce, put it in a pot of boiling water briefly (time varies depending upon the veggie), then cool in ice water.
Label It. Don't forget to put the date and contents on the container.
Safely Defrost It. Many people defrost food by leaving it out on the counter. Food safely experts agree this may not be the safest way, particularly for certain types of food. Putting your frozen food in the refrigerator overnight, placing the frozen container in a bowl of cool water, or microwaving on the defrost setting are all safe ways to thaw it out.

FOODS TO FORGO FREEZING

Meals like lasagna, soups, stews, and curries are freezer champions, with the majority of foods doing well in the freezer. However, there are a few foods that should be skipped.
Some Produce. Produce with high water content, such as cucumbers, potatoes, lettuce, melons, grapes, and cabbage, don't hold up well in the freezer. Strawberries aren't the same when brought back to room temperature after being frozen but are still great for baking and making smoothies.
Some Animal-Based Foods. Sour cream, mayonnaise, meringues, egg whites, and cream-based soups and sauces don't freeze well.
Fully Cooked Pasta. When freezing pasta, undercook it slightly; it will finish cooking when reheating it.

For tips on storing and freezing food plastic-free, see Eco-Action 42.

FRESH FOOD STORAGE

FRESH BREAD

If Eating within 2–3 Days. Keep bread fresh in its paper bag on the counter if you plan to eat it that day, or in a cool, dark space, such as a drawer or bread box, for two to three days after purchase. Bread should not be stored near heat or moisture sources (on top of the fridge, around the dishwasher or stove). Heat causes drying, and moisture leads to mold.

Long-Term Storage. Bread can last in the freezer for two to three months wrapped tightly in a reusable freezer bag. If you don't have one, use a large ziplock bag (which can be washed and reused) or a paper bag if you plan to defrost it within the week. You can cut slices before freezing, cut the loaf in half, or freeze it whole. The best way to defrost a loaf of bread is in the refrigerator overnight (out of the freezer bag) or if you plan to eat it right away, in the oven for 25 to 30 minutes at 325°F. Frozen slices can be put right into the toaster. Store defrosted loaves as you would fresh bread; it will last a maximum of two days. Defrosted bread should not be refrozen.

--- **DID YOU KNOW?** ---
Worldwide, **70%** of all fresh water is used to grow food. When you toss out food, it's not just food that gets wasted. You're also throwing away all of the resources it took to produce that food, such as water, land, energy, fuel, packaging, etc.

FRUITS AND VEGETABLES

Store "Friends & Enemies" Properly. Not all fruits and veggies are friends. Certain produce naturally emits ethylene gas, which causes produce to ripen. Produce can essentially be broken down into two categories: ethylene producers (generally fruits) and ethylene sensitive (generally vegetables). Ethylene producers, however, are also ethylene sensitive. So when storing ethylene-producing peaches, for example, you want to leave them out in the open (not in a plastic bag) so air can circulate. That's why berries are sold in baskets with holes to avoid early spoiling.

The Green Rule:
Be smart: Store fruits and veggies apart.
And bananas should stay far away.

When to Wash? Washing produce too early can encourage mold growth, so don't wash until you're ready to prep or eat the produce.
Got Limp Vegetables? Revive bendy carrots and celery by placing them in a container of cool water and then putting them in the fridge. Within a few hours, they'll have their crunch back. This is also a great way to store them after prepping; if you refresh the water every so often, they'll stay fresh for weeks.

For a complete Produce Storage Guide that you can put on your refrigerator, visit motheringearthproject.com for a free download.

Buy Ugly Produce. When buying produce, don't look for perfection. Supermarkets often throw out food that consumers have ignored because of its physical flaws. If it's molding, then, of course, skip it. However, if an apple isn't symmetrical or a carrot is crooked, don't be so quick to pass it up. Ask yourself if the cosmetic characteristics will impact its taste. If not, go for it!

Bruised produce, which also falls into the "ugly" category, can leave you with a mushy mouthful. Don't throw these softies out. If you're making a smoothie, French toast, muffins, or any dish where the fruit might be integrated into the dish, then bruised fruit is a less expensive and ideal way to get nutritious and perfectly edible food at a discount. You can also make guacamole or a salad dressing from mushy avocados or tomato sauce from bruised tomatoes. Ugly carrots and potatoes taste delicious roasted or in a soup recipe. Just because something isn't "perfect" doesn't mean it can't be eaten.

MEAT

Meat should be stored in the coldest part of your refrigerator, on the lowest shelf, in its original packaging, and on a plate or tray to contain drips or spills until you're ready to use. The more cut, cubed, or sliced the meat is, the quicker it spoils.

🍃

ECO-ACTION NO. 56
Help Kids Eat, Not Waste

Do you have a picky eater or child who barely touches their lunch? Then you're familiar with kid-related food waste. Even a ravenous teen can plow through the refrigerator but bypass food that needs to be eaten. No matter your child's age or food habits, waste happens. Here are some tried and tested ways to help keep bellies full while reducing what's being tossed.

Set Up an "Eat Me" Station. Too often food that needs to be eaten gets pushed to the back of the fridge or overlooked in the pantry. To solve this problem, set up an "eat me" station—a place to put any food that needs to get eaten ASAP. Locations could include the top shelf of the fridge or the kitchen counter. Use a low basket or tray so food is easy to see. Last night's leftovers, an overripe banana, and a half-finished yogurt are perfect candidates for the station. Hungry teens and toddlers can help finish up the food, which helps fight food waste.

Serve Little Ones Smaller Portions. Many parents of young ones find it a nonstop battle to get their kids to eat what's on their plates. It can be frustrating, worrying (are they getting enough of what they need for their growing bodies?), and also troubling (ah, so much food is going to waste!). Here are three tricks that help reduce food waste, encourage kids to figure out when they're actually full, and reduce mealtime battles.

- **Start with an Empty Plate.** When you sit down to eat leave your kid's plate empty, and put the prepared food on a platter in the center of the table instead. Being mindful that the food within reach can't burn them, allow your child to pick what they would like to eat. Perhaps they will ask for a little bit of everything or just want to indulge in one thing. That's okay, because everything you're offering has been selected by you and is a variety of healthy foods.

- **Serve Smaller Portions.** Once they've chosen what they'd like to eat from the prepared foods, give them a tiny portion. Children often get overwhelmed by a massive plate of food. For example, if you provide a two-year-old with 3 or 4 beans, they will likely gobble them all up and ask for more, but if you put 20 in front of them, they probably won't touch it. Even if they have a hefty appetite, giving them less and having them ask for more is a way to limit the amount of leftover food at the end of a meal. It will also encourage them to listen to their body to see if they're full before asking for more.

- **Save It.** If your child's leftovers include a few sliced grapes and two pieces of broccoli, don't toss it! It may seem like nothing, but that's half a meal for a little tike. Add a strawberry and a half slice of whole wheat toast with peanut butter, and you've got your toddler's lunch done for the next day.

FAMILY FUN PROJECTS
REUSING FOOD SCRAPS

Food scraps are a common form of food waste. While composting them is an important step to keep food waste out of the landfill, there are ways to reuse scraps that will reduce your overall food footprint.

01. MAKE SCRAP BROTH

Making broth from food scraps is a practical way to put your food waste to work. It saves money and packaging by not needing to buy prepackaged broths. Scrap broth can be used as a soup base or in place of water when cooking rice or grains.

Time: 5 minutes prep | 30 minutes on stove (plus time for cooling, if freezing)

Ingredients:
- Organic* food scraps such as carrot peels, celery tops, potato skins, onion skins and parts, corn cobs, and herb stems.

Optional:
- Peppercorns
- Herbs such as rosemary and thyme
- A bay leaf

Directions:
- Fill a large pot with water and food scraps. There should be enough water so that the scraps are covered.
- Bring to a boil, then turn down the heat and simmer for at least 30 minutes.
- Strain the broth and compost the scraps.

Storage

Use right away or cool to room temp; pour into airtight jars, leaving room at the top, and freeze. You can also pour cooled broth into an ice cube tray and freeze it. Remove frozen broth cubes and store them in an airtight jar in the freezer for when you need smaller portions of broth for cooking.

*Nonorganic produce, particularly peels and skins, increases exposure to food-related pesticides

02. REGROW FOOD FROM WASTE

Use ends and stems from food "waste" to grow new vegetables on your windowsill. You can do this with romaine lettuce, green onion, cabbage, celery, and more. Plus, kids love watching them grow.

Instructions:
- Cut a head of romaine or cabbage about 1 inch from the bottom. For green onion, cut the green leaves off and leave $1/2$–1 inch of the white bulb and roots at the base.
- Place the base in a shallow cup with water, leaving the top part out of the water.
- Put on a sunny windowsill.
- Change the water once a day.
- Watch your veggies grow!

When to Eat:
- **Lettuce.** For the lettuce and cabbage, grown in water indoors, it will reach about as big as it will get on days 10–12. It won't be as big as the original romaine/cabbage, but it will be enough for a lunchtime salad if you have two or three heads going. If your lettuce is growing well, it can be planted in gardening soil after eight days and will continue growing there.
- **Green Onions.** For green onions, wait until they are about 6" tall to plant in soil or continue growing inside in water until long enough to eat.

ECO-FAMILY TIP
Too Good to Go. Help divert food waste by downloading the Too Good to Go app. It connects you with food establishments that have more food than they can sell, so if a bakery makes too many muffins, you can get extras at a discount. Download the app to see if your local grocery stores, restaurants, ice cream spots, coffee shops, or bakeries participate.

ECO-ACTION NO. 57
Begin Composting

Composting is a pivotal way to fight the climate crisis by diverting food waste from landfills. It reduces methane emissions, improves soil health, reduces reliance on synthetic fertilizers, and improves soil's water retention. Composting speeds up the natural decay process by creating an ideal environment for bacteria, fungi, worms, and other helpful organisms to break down organic matter. So when food scraps, wet paper, and yard clippings are composted, they can be reused to make a nutrient-rich, dark soil fertilizer powerful enough to shift our world.

WHERE CAN I COMPOST?

Citywide Industrial Composting. If you live in a city with curbside composting, you've hit the food waste jackpot. Industrial composting works similarly to a weekly trash pickup. You collect your food scraps and put them in a separate curbside compost bin (similar in size to your trash bin) for the waste collection truck to pick up, usually on the same day as your trash. Some municipalities only allow garden waste in the compost can, while other cities will also allow food scraps.

Community Collection Points. If your city doesn't offer curbside composting, concerned citizens often work together to create community collection points. Locations often include the farmer's market or community gardens.

Share with Neighbors. Share Waste is an Earth-saving app that allows you to search by your address to find people in your neighborhood who will compost your food scraps at their homes.

Home Composting. If you have a backyard, fantastic! Outdoor space, however, is NOT necessary to compost. It's all about finding the right composter for your space.

COMPOSTING: WHAT DO I NEED?

No matter where you compost, these are the three basic elements you will need to begin:

01. Organic Matter. Food scraps, yard waste, compostable materials—here is a general guide of what you can put in the compost bin, depending upon how you compost:

YES, ANYWHERE! (home, community, or industrial)	INDUSTRIAL COMPOSTING ONLY* (not at home or community points)	NO-NOs EVERYWHERE
✓ Ends, peels, stems of fruits, vegetables ✓ Rice, pasta, grains ✓ Eggshells ✓ Coffee grounds and filters ✓ Plastic-free tea bags ✓ Cooked food without oil, dairy, and meat ✓ Flowers, plants, yard waste ✓ Hair, fingernails, pet fur ✓ Dust ✓ Dryer lint (only from natural fabrics) ✓ Wooden toothpicks, chopsticks ✓ Paper towels (not used with toxic chemicals), paper napkins, paper cartons, and newspapers	• Approved compostable packaging and to-go ware • Meat, fish • Dairy • Shells, bones • Cooked food with oil, dairy, and meat • Greasy pizza boxes *Be sure to check with your municipality to confirm what is accepted in your area.*	✗ Plastic produce stickers ✗ Liquids ✗ Recycling materials such as dry and clean paper, cardboard, plastic, glass, or aluminum cans ✗ Food packaging boxes and cartons ✗ Gum ✗ Yard trimmings treated with chemical pesticides ✗ Pet feces or litter ✗ Coal or charcoal ash

02. A Collection Container. If you compost through your city or at home, you will need a food waste collection bin for your kitchen to gather food scraps. Countertop options are popular as they're compact and can also be placed under the sink, hidden away. Stainless steel options are easy to clean, durable, and recyclable at the end of their life. You can even make one yourself by repurposing a coffee tin and drilling a few air holes in the lid (don't skip that step). To ease smells, you can add a charcoal filter. If you're collecting scraps that will be dropped off at a neighborhood collection point, you can store food waste in a compostable bag in the freezer until you're ready to take it.

03. A Way to Compost. When you sign up for curbside composting, you will be provided with a rolling sidewalk bin to dump all of your collected food waste that your municipality will pick up and compost for you. However, industrial composting tends to be more common in major cities than in the suburbs or rural areas. If composting at home, you will want to choose the right composter for your lifestyle, space, and family size. See page 246 for a guide to Home Composting 101.

ECO-FAMILY BITE-SIZE CHALLENGE NO. 10

GET STARTED: REDUCING FOOD WASTE

As a family, pick three of the following tasks to kick off your challenge to reduce food waste in your home:

- ◯ Create a meal plan for a month.
- ◯ Set up an ongoing "eat me" station.
- ◯ Prep once, eat twice. Double a recipe and make a plan for how you're going to eat it twice throughout the week. If you don't end up eating it, freeze it before it goes bad.
- ◯ Use your freezer to store leftovers that will not be eaten in the near future.
- ◯ Remove produce stickers before composting fruit and veggie skins and peels.
- ◯ Start an overripe fruit container in your freezer for any overripe bananas or berries. Use in smoothies or baking once you've gathered enough.
- ◯ Store fruits and veggies separately. Keep bananas separate from all produce.
- ◯ Participate in industrial curbside composting if it's offered in your area. If not, find a collection point in your neighborhood or start at home.

COMMUNITY

BEYOND THE EVERYDAY

Expanding our efforts beyond our day-to-day lives is an essential part of this regenerative and restorative process. Collective action, empowering and educating others, speaking up, and using your strengths hold the capacity to reshape the world and our future.

THE COLLECTIVE FOOTPRINT:
The accumulation of a million small things that add up to make a big difference.

THE CLIMATE CREW

ECO-ACTION NO. 58
Write, Call, Protest

USE YOUR VOICE

We need systemic change. However, businesses and the government are unlikely to leap on their own. We have to use our voices to turn up the heat, pressuring them to do better. It's a big task, but start small by paying attention to the eco-related challenges you come up against in your everyday life. . . .

- Are there no recycling bins at the playground?
- Do you wish you had curbside composting?
- Do you hate all the plastic mailers products come in?
- Do you wish your grocery store carried more sustainable foods and products?

Be vocal, get loud. It's time to demand change—now and unapologetically. Sure, your one plastic mailer might seem like nothing in the grand scheme of things, but how many packages do you think that company ships in a day? The small things add up.

Remember, "Think globally, act locally." Actions at a state, city, community, and business level add up. Given our nation's polarization in Washington, local efforts across our country, which are often less divided, can have a significant impact, even when top-down action sits at a standstill.

What Can You Do?

✓ Write a letter.
✓ Pick up the phone.
✓ Send an email.
✓ Call them out on social media.
✓ Sign (or even start) a petition.
✓ Boycott, and then be vocal about your choice.
✓ Rally others.
✓ Protest.

Hate Writing Letters?

Not sure what to say? Don't like making random phone calls? The Remark app makes it insanely simple to send feedback to businesses. Share both positive and constructive personalized comments to push businesses to do more (or continue doing the good they've already implemented).

ECO-ACTION NO. 59
Be an Influencer

THE CLIMATE CREW

RADIATE WHAT'S POSSIBLE

The term *influencer* comes with a whole host of preconceived notions—mainly involving being a hotshot on social media. However, to be an influencer, you do not need 100K+ followers on Instagram. The true meaning is to inspire action in others, and how you do that is up to you. Here are some ways to influence positive change with those around you.

Talk about It. Friends and family may be burnt out from listening to the news. With so many issues weighted with doom, a personal conversation can offer hope—and turn inaction into action. Simply talking about large-scale and local issues with those around you can have significant influence.

Lead by Example. People are much more likely to do things when their friends are doing them, so be the one to get the ball rolling.

Don't Lecture. There's no bigger turnoff than being told you're living life incorrectly. Avoid phrases like, "Oh my gosh, you're still using plastic baggies for your kid's snacks!" Finger-pointing will only turn others away. Instead, bring people into the fold with an inclusive spirit. Model what an eco-friendly lifestyle looks like so others can be influenced by the changes you're making. (An alternative script for the plastic baggie scenario could be, "We've recently started reusing resealable containers. It's already saved us money and keeps the kids' snacks from getting crushed in their backpacks. Plus, less waste!")

Listen. Influencers don't just share; they also listen. Hear what others have to say about their eco-challenges and roadblocks. You might not always have all the answers, but lending an ear and reminding them that there is always a place for them in the movement, even if they can't do everything, is imperative.

Post It. Share your sustainable swaps and tips on social media. Amplify the voices of others who are also doing the work. You don't need to have a public account or loads of followers to have an influence.

Continue Educating Yourself. As people begin to look to you as a leader, it's crucial to continue educating yourself on the issues and solutions. Books, films, lectures—there are many ways to keep learning.

🌿

ECO-ACTION NO. 60
Volunteer as a Family

In a fast-paced world, carving out time to spend together is precious. While bonding as a family, volunteering also allows you to connect with your community. It transmits important values to children and expands their world—taking learning beyond the classroom, teaching them new skills, building self-confidence, and showing them that they have the power to make an impact. Plus, studies show that giving our time and helping the world around us makes us happier—and who doesn't love a little extra joy? No matter your child's age, there's a way to roll up their sleeves and offer them a hands-on opportunity to make a difference. Whether you do it weekly or quarterly, folding volunteering into your routine will make the act of "giving back" part of your family's traditions.

Do Good, Feel Good, at *Any* Age.
- Plant trees together.
- Volunteer at a community garden or local farm.
- Host a food drive.
- Volunteer at a food bank.
- Walk (or ride your bike) for a cause.
- Clean up your community, beach, river, or park.
- Build a Little Free Library or community pantry.
- Rebuild ecosystems through local habitat restoration.
- Make and write postcards together advocating for environmental change. Send them to your local and state representatives.

ECO-FAMILY TIP
Organize a Pursposeful Playgroup. Get your child's friends (and their families) together and spring into action. Whether your child is 3 or 13, your kiddo's playgroup can participate in a beach/park cleanup or host a group bake sale and donate the money to a favorite cause. Volunteering with other families builds community and allows you to come together for a greater purpose.

ECO-ACTION NO. 61
Be a Change Maker at Work

THE CLIMATE CREW

START A GREEN TEAM
You do not need to work for an environmental nonprofit or have a sustainability-based job to be a change maker. All jobs have an impact. No matter your position, you can make a difference. And while making *greener* workplace choices on your own, such as shutting down your computer at night, is important, starting a Green Team can help make

systemic changes through better policies and practices while also building community.

401(K)s for the Future. To ensure you're paying into a more sustainable future, check with your HR department to see if your company offers a 401(K) plan that's not invested in fossil fuel expansion. If action needs to be taken, contact your HR plan administrator at work to get the ball rolling. The website investyourvalues.org has an "action center" for employees, which includes email templates and five basic steps you can take to help change the financial landscape of retirement planning at your company.

Elevate Your Energy. Inquire with your facilities department about embracing renewable energy. Look into heating, cooling, and lighting habits and infrastructure. Are LED ENERGY STAR lightbulbs being used? What happens when no one is there? Are there motion-activated light switches? Do major energy-hogging appliances like printers get turned off?

Fly Greener. Encourage your company to offer carbon offsets for all business travel or even better, find ways to plan meetings and events that limit air travel or distance traveled.

Bin Better. Set up recycling and composting bins in the kitchen and signage about what goes where. Add recycling bins under desks and in the copy room and other common places where trash cans are present. And don't forget to add a compost bin for paper towels in the bathroom!

Reusables Rock. Replace single-use cups, utensils, and plates with reusables in the office kitchen.

Recycle Electronics. Set up an electronic recycling bin to ensure that possibly harmful technology like phones, batteries, printers, and cords don't end up in the trash.

Go Paperless. Set up a paperless business for both customers and in the office.

Work with Eco-Friendly Vendors. Support other eco-conscious businesses. Work with vendors that use recycled or organic materials; are striving to reduce carbon emissions, plastic, and waste; use green energy to produce their products; and have ethical employment practices. When you do, you are shifting the market. Let unsustainable vendors know why you didn't go with them to encourage businesses who haven't adopted these practices to get on board.

ECO-ACTION NO. 62
Meet Like-Minded Families

EXPAND YOUR VILLAGE

"It takes a village" is not just a catchy phrase. Living in community with others is vital to our existence as humans. Yet in modern America we've become more and more isolated from one another. As we transition into parenthood, it only becomes more evident that the cradle of community, essential for raising children, is torn. Not only does this negatively impact our kids, it also affects our mental health. We are built to support one another when things get tough, celebrate and honor milestones together, and work in unison for the group's betterment. Parenting was not meant to happen in isolation!

Using sustainability as a tool to build community allows you to surround yourself with people who are also looking out for the well-being of each other and the world around them. Here are several ways to meet and gather with other like-minded families.

Join a Group. Use online organizations to search for family-friendly or parent-only gatherings in your area. Meetup.com, hikeitbaby.com, and Facebook groups are helpful tools to find other families interested in sustainability.

Start a Group. Start your own group for fellow families or parents and organize it around a theme like a sustainable book club, vegetarian supper club, or a vegan cookbook club (where everyone chooses a recipe to test out each month).

Go to Events. Attend local lectures and presentations in your area to meet others interested in similar topics.

Volunteer. Roll up your sleeves for environmentally related causes. It's a fun way to bond quickly with others over a shared experience.

Get Social. Use your preferred social media platform to follow, connect, and share with others on their sustainability journey.

Community is essential to our collective well-being.

COMMUNITY BUILDING		
IDEA	**DETAILS**	**GETTING STARTED**
Find an Eco-Buddy or -Crew	Commit together to go to meetings and speaking engagements (in person or virtually).	Call a friend (or group of friends) who might be interested in taking action. Then find your first event to attend together.
Start a School Buy Nothing Chat	Start a WhatsApp chat for parents at your school to post items they're ready to part with.	Reach out to class parents or send out a letter in your child's weekly take-home folder to gather interest.
Set up a Free Pantry	Start a free pantry in the foyer of your apartment building, at the entrance to your child's school, or in your office kitchen to help reduce food waste and inspire caring for one another.	Encourage tenants, families, or coworkers to share food that would otherwise go to waste. Attach a Free Pantry sign to a secondhand cupboard. Send out an email or post a notice to get others involved.
Host a Swap 'n' Social	A Swap 'n' Social is an event where friends can swap items they no longer use. It gives people an opportunity to socialize while getting rid of items they no longer need (and letting them pick up a few new goodies as well). *Theme ideas:* • *Kids' toys, books, & baby gear* • *Children's or adults' clothing*	Set a theme for your Swap 'n' Social. Invite friends to bring 5–10 items that are preloved and in good condition. Set them out so people can easily peruse items. The more people that come, the more variety—particularly when it comes to clothing and gear that pertains to ages and sizes.
Organize a Costume Trade	Host a costume trade at your child's school, community center, or home so Halloween costumes can be used again. (And bring kids joy.)	Gather costumes in advance of the trade by sending out a message to parents asking them to bring in costumes that their child has outgrown. Announce a date for the trade. Day-of, put out all of the apparel organized by size and invite everyone to pick out a new costume for trick-or-treating.
Build a Little Free Library	Place a Little Free Library station in front of your home to share used books with neighbors and passersby.	Head to littlefreelibrary.org for instructions on how to build and register your library. You could also go rogue and create a puzzle or game library too.
Join a Community Garden	Get your own little plot of land to grow fruits and veggies, while meeting others who are doing the same.	The American Community Gardening Association has a search tool to help you find a location near you.

ECO-ACTION NO. 63
Advocate

ADVOCACY: FOR ALL, BY ALL

There is a good amount of confusion about the difference between advocacy and lobbying. While a lobbyist is a professional advocate whose full-time job focuses on urging politicians to vote for or against specific legislation, advocacy work doesn't require a paycheck or a particular career.

Advocacy is about using your voice, money, and/or time to raise awareness and support people, politicians, businesses, or institutions that uphold eco-conscious and socially responsible policies, infrastructure, and practices.

WAYS TO ADVOCATE			
legislation* championing laws, policies, and regulations **what people usually think of when they think of advocacy*	**voting** mobilizing voters and personally participating in city, state, and federal elections	**direct action** protesting, signing/ sharing petitions, writing, boycotting, volunteering, voicing opinions publicly	**community** bringing together your neighbors and the larger public to take action
political supporting candidates who uphold strong environmental policies while actively encouraging all politicians to do so as well	**donating** giving money to organizations, activists, politicians, and educators that are engaged in fostering change	**business** supporting companies that align with your values while also urging businesses to implement and uphold sustainable systems and practices	**legal** taking legal action against agencies and businesses that aren't in compliance with environmental policies
education educating yourself and others to understand the issues and ways to take action	**events** organizing, attending, and supporting events that mobilize environmental efforts	**volunteering** offering your time to organizations that are fighting for change	**media** working with media outlets and posting factual information on social media to expand coverage on issues

Advocacy isn't just for grown-ups; kids can do it too. Support your kids in organizing grassroots advocacy efforts. Assist them in gathering ingredients and supplies to host an environmental fund-raising bake sale. Help get out the word that a portion of proceeds from the school musical will be going toward an on-campus teaching garden. Whatever the goal, assist and encourage your little advocates while letting them take the lead.

There are a lot of essential issues to advocate for. If you are having trouble narrowing it down, here are a few places to start.

ADVOCATE FOR . . .

- **Girls and Women across the Globe.** Supporting girls and women in education, business, and government expands collective mindsets, perspectives, and policies in the fight against the climate crisis. Educating girls reduces their susceptibility during natural disasters (over any other social or economic factor) into adulthood, helps decrease family size, and expands positions and opportunities to create change in their communities. Championing worldwide access to affordable schools and low-to-no-cost healthcare, buying from women-owned businesses and small cooperative farms, and voting for female leaders are all ways to advocate for women and climate action.

- **Food Equity.** Help others gain access to healthy, affordable food by supporting urban farming in underserved communities, living wages and fair working conditions, affordable citywide housing, and food equity policies, such as nutritious, free meals in public schools, particularly in low income communities.

- **Environmental Justice.** Environmental justice centers people, equity, and freedom from discrimination when addressing climate and environmental policy and action. It is a movement that was created in response to environmental racism. If you're not familiar with environmental racism, it is the disproportionate impact of climate disasters, environmental health-related problems, and resource/land appropriation and destruction on Black, Indigenous, and people of color (BIPOC) and low-income communities. These disparities are rooted in a history of colonialism and historical and current racist, discriminatory government and corporate practices. Tackling local environmental issues that specifically impact and exploit BIPOC communities, including water contamination, air pollution, toxic chemicals, e-waste dumping, and aiding in climate resilience can significantly reduce the risks put forth by environmental racism. If you are not part of the BIPOC community but would like to get involved, it's essential to listen to and elevate BIPOC voices, donate, attend events, and work as an ally to fight the injustices they are facing. Environmental racism is everyone's problem. Examples of environmental racism in the United States include:

- Lead-contaminated drinking water in Flint, Michigan, a predominately African American city.
- "Cancer Alley," an 85-mile stretch of 150 oil refineries and plastic plants in Louisiana, leaving the majority-Black neighborhoods in the area at a 95% higher chance of getting cancer from air pollution than other Americans.
- Pipelines, arctic drilling, and dams on or through indigenous peoples' land.
- Formerly segregated or redlined urban neighborhoods that were left treeless—resulting in residents having lower access to green spaces. These areas (whose populaces are still predominately people of color) are more susceptible to extreme heat, amongst many other environmental issues, putting residents at risk.
- Targeting hazardous waste disposal in or near BIPOC or low-income communities.

- **Indigenous Peoples and Conservation of Their Land.** Indigenous peoples make up less than 5% of the worldwide population, and yet they support about 80% of global biodiversity. If you are not indigenous, become an ally by supporting the rights of indigenous peoples and their land, both domestically and abroad. Listen to their stories and needs. Follow their lead. Elevate their voices. Back their rights to their land and against its destruction. Support their fight for clean air, water, and soil against corporate greed.
- **Access to Affordable Healthcare and Birth Control for All.** Domestic and worldwide family planning services like sex education, access to free-to-low-cost birth control, and affordable reproductive healthcare can improve the lives, health, and life expectancy of women and children globally while also having a ripple effect in reducing greenhouse gases.
- **Your City or Town to Set and Reach Net-Zero Climate Targets.** Get involved championing a net-zero climate policy for your town or city. Learn more about what is currently being done to reduce

carbon emissions and vote for local leaders who are spearheading these initiatives. Additionally, no business is too small to adopt these policies, so encourage companies to develop a net-zero plan (or add these ideas to your own business). For more on net zero, see page 39.

- **Citywide Composting.** If you do not have curbside composting in your area, strive to educate your community on the importance of composting while putting pressure on city officials.

Other areas you could advocate for include:

- Parks, trails, and open spaces
- Safe bike routes to school
- Land, water, air, energy, or animal conservation
- Solar panels added to parking lots in your town
- Voting rights
- School drop-off zones to be idle-free
- Electric vehicle charging stations in your community
- Access to sustainable food and clean water for all
- Bike racks outside your child's school or your office
- Communities on the front line of the climate crisis

THE CLIMATE CREW

ECO-ACTION NO. 64
Share What Makes You Sparkle

RISE AND SHINE

One of the most fulfilling ways to make an impact is to use your joys and passions as tools for change. Each and every one of us brings something special to the table, and when we harness our unique skills, not only do our strengths have the capacity to shift the needle on critical action, we also tap into our best selves.

What makes you tick? Are you a natural leader? Introvert or extrovert? Do you have a hobby? Do you like to make people laugh? Are you a teacher at heart or a lifelong student? Is your career something you're passionate about, or do you have interests outside of work that fill your cup? Are you connected to a community that brings you joy? Wherever your uniqueness lies, find what brings you happiness and allow it to fuel your action.

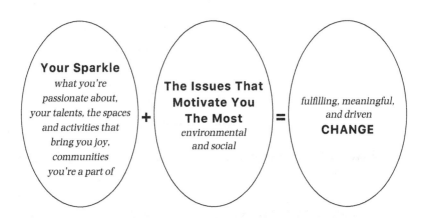

Your Sparkle
what you're passionate about, your talents, the spaces and activities that bring you joy, communities you're a part of

+

The Issues That Motivate You The Most
environmental and social

=

fulfilling, meaningful, and driven
CHANGE

YOUR SPARKLE

My favorite traits about my personality are _____
_____
_____

Three things that I am innately good at are _____
_____
_____

Five things that bring me joy are _____
_____
_____

In my free time, I like to _____
_____
_____

My passions include _____
_____
_____

Physical spaces where I enjoy spending my time are _____
_____
_____

The communities or networks I touch through my personal interests, work, family, etc., are _____

_____

_____

In my life, I am proud of _____

_____

and I have used these strengths to get me there: _____

_____

THE ISSUES THAT MOTIVATE YOU THE MOST

The issue(s) that motivate/interest me the most are (see pages 215–216 for ideas) _____

_____

_____

CHANGE

I can use my talents, strengths, and interests to begin making change in my world by _____

_____

_____

_____

_____

_____

_____

_____

_____

_____

_____

_____

_____

_____

_____

_____

_____

_____

A FINAL CALL TO ACTION

> "Look closely at the present you are constructing:
> it should look like the future you are dreaming."
>
> **—ALICE WALKER**
> *writer, social activist, and mother*

Congratulations! Upon finishing this book, I proclaim that you are officially an eco-parent. It is my greatest hope that this book has inspired you and given you and your family practical ways to begin making changes in your everyday lives. I want to remind you that YOU ARE POWERFUL, for so many reasons. And when it comes to environmental action, you now have the tools to transform the world around you.

We know the science. The facts are clear. Now is the time for action. What we do to the Earth, we do to ourselves. So when we heal the planet, we also hold the capacity to help heal humanity. Living sustainably has the power to connect, repair, and rejuvenate. It reminds us that we are enough and likely already possess all that we need. It gives us the discretion to unlearn harmful habits and build better routines. And it offers the tools, not to sustain the status quo but to heal and regenerate the world around us. Through sustainable living, the act of caring for the Earth, ourselves, and our communities is woven into the fabric of our lives. From large-scale action to the smallest of details, we practice the world we want to create—and through doing it, we bring it into being.

Parents, grandparents, caregivers—together, we can move toward a better tomorrow. We are all ingredients in the solution. As you put down this book and braid sustainability into your life, I invite you to use these five principles to navigate your way.

Dream It. The future is full of possibilities. As we repair our broken world, it's important to remember that healing our fractures opens up opportunities to restructure. Daydream about the possibilities of what could happen if we get our act together. What will the Earth look like if humans can live in harmony with the planet? What would it feel like to live in a society that values the Earth and each other? Allow these dreams to inspire you. By envisioning it, you hold the blueprint to start building it. The future we are fighting for is possible, and you are part of the story.

Consume with Care. You can significantly influence your footprint when you buy only what you need, consume carefully, and weigh what systems you are upholding through your purchases. And don't forget: the last step of consuming involves getting rid of things, so remain cognizant about how you dispose of items too.

Raise a Revolution. As parents, we shape the next generation by showing our children how to care for themselves and the planet. Your children are watching all that you do. Show them what hope looks like through action. With your choices, you are demonstrating that they too can have an impact, and that everything they do is part of a larger picture to which they are connected.

Be Gentle. Give yourself (and others) permission to make mistakes, be imperfect, and rest.

Let Love Fuel You. There is no stronger force than a parent's love for their child. It's potent, and we can use our love to propel and guide us to reconstruct the world we want to leave for them.

There is no better time than now to pick one place to start. Each of our individual eco-actions are a step in the right direction. And once we start taking enough steps, we begin to walk a new walk—leading to radical change. Let's look past our walls, zip codes, or whatever social or physical structures confine and divide us to come together as a united front. We can lift each other up and move toward wholeness as we march together toward a brighter future with our children by our sides.

The path to a brighter future begins with our actions today.

PART III
THE ECO-ACTIONIST
NOTEBOOK

___

THE 31-DAY
ECO-FAMILY CHALLENGE

Are you ready to dive into meaningful change but not quite sure what to do first? Begin with this 31-Day Eco-Family Challenge, designed to get you started in reducing your carbon, waste, and plastic footprint.

THE RULES

Before jumping in there are a couple of guidelines:

Don't Be Too Hard on Yourself. You are trying (hooray!), so keep reminding yourself of that. If you are doing this challenge as a family, be gentle with them as well. A complete lifestyle overhaul does not happen overnight. It takes small, intentional changes over time to create new habits that will last.

It's Okay to "Mess Up." Things will not always go as planned. You may eat out at a restaurant and ask for your drink with no straw—and it arrives with one anyway. Life happens. Even when you have the best intentions. Take each misstep as a learning experience and keep moving forward. Do not let mishaps derail you; just make the best choices possible with what life throws at you. One thing is certain: it will get easier. Practice makes a huge difference in rebuilding habits.

Don't Go in Order. You don't need to work your way chronologically through the month. The first three days are a good place to start, but after that do whichever action works best with your schedule. If you want to do Day 14 (wash your clothes on cold) on Day 4, go for it. Head to motheringearthproject.com to print out a copy and hang it on your refrigerator. Cross out the days as you go until you've completed all 31.

Start Today. Now is the time to begin. You've got this!

THE 31-DAY		
week 1: waste		
1 Aim to buy nothing (brand) new this month. *page 83*	**2** Do a trash tally: Get the kids involved. Where can you reduce? *page 47*	**3** As a family, assemble zero-waste kits for everyone in the house. *page 164*
week 2: climate action		
8 Begin composting, if you don't already. *page 58*	**9** Make it a Meatless Monday. *page 177*	**10** Switch your energy bill to green energy. If it's not available, write to your local representative. *page 41*
week 3: plastic		
15 Get the family invovled in fixing or mending something together. *page 127*	**16** Today, try following the 3/4 rule at the grocery store and see what happens. *page 157*	**17** Use a refillable water bottle instead of a plastic, single-use one. *page 94*
week 4: eco-swaps		
22 Browse a local second-hand shop. *page 78*	**23** Check out an online zero-waste store to research eco-alternatives to regularly used necessities. *page 234*	**24** Stash your paper towels and do without. Get the kids to cut up old towels and t-shirts to make rags. *page 58*
week 5: ripple		
29 Schedule an eco-gathering with friends. Think beach or park cleanup, clothing or toy swap, etc. *page 211*	**30** Use your voice. Reach out to a representative or company that you want to see make a change. *page 58*	**31** Research ways you and your family can get involved in environmental action in your community. *page 216*

ECO-FAMILY CHALLENGE

4	5	6	7
Just say no. Refuse all single-use items for a day. *page 86*	Download the Buy Nothing or a free marketplace app. *page 83*	Stop junk mail —both in your mailbox and your inbox. *page 81*	Dine out and bring your own container for leftovers. *page 157*
11 Unplug all devices in your home that are not in use. *page 43*	**12** Research online to see if your bank is using your money to fund fossil fuel projects like oil pipelines. *page 84*	**13** Walk, bike, carpool, or take public transport. If you must drive, can you carpool? Don't idle your car when parked. *page 72*	**14** Laundry day! Wash clothes on cold. Do laundry during off-peak hours. Hang dry what you can. *page 60*
18 Try packing a plastic-free lunch. *page 165*	**19** Double a recipe and freeze the second half instead of buying a frozen meal. *page 150*	**20** Make food that would normally come packaged in plastic. Stovetop popcorn for family movie night? *page 161*	**21** Together, check out your local farmer's market. Bring your own produce bags and containers! *page 167*
25 After finishing any single-use or plastic essentials, swap them out for reusable or sustainably-made options. *page 242*	**26** Browse the internet and discover the allure of online second-hand shopping. *page 101*	**27** Borrow something you need. Try checking out a book on plant-based cooking from the library! *page 187*	**28** Skip paper or plastic bags and instead gather reusable totes for your grocery store haul. *page 91*

NOTES:

YOUR PLANET PLANNER

A road map to sustainability in your area

_____

Welcome to your Planet Planner, a personalized way to keep track of the sustainable businesses and resources in your community. While you may not have all of these services in your area, you might be surprised to find new businesses and drop-off points that have been off your radar.

BUYING STUFF

Local Thrift Stores:

For adult clothing: _____

For home goods: _____

For kids' clothing and gear: _____

Local Flea Market: _____

Local Secondhand Bookstore: _____

GETTING RID OF STUFF

Recycling Situation:

○ Curbside

Day of the week: _____

○ Community Drop Point

Address: _____

Composting Situation:

○ Curbside

Day of the week: _____

○ Community Drop Point

Address: _____

○ Home/Yard

Donating and Tossing Less

○ I have downloaded a free marketplace app (see _The Motherboard_ resources guide for suggestions).

Closest Electronic Waste Drop-Off Point: _____

Closest Hazardous Waste Drop-Off Point: _____

REPAIRING STUFF

Neighborhood repair shops and services:

Electronics: _____

_____

Shoes: _____

_____

Leather: _____

_____

Seamstress/Tailor: _____

_____

Furniture: _____

_____

Lamps: _____

_____

Vacuum: _____

_____

EATING

Closest Grocery Store with a Bulk Bin Section:

Store name and location: _____

_____

Closest Farmer's Market:

Location and hours: _____

_____

Closest Restaurants with Vegetarian or Vegan Menu Options:

Restaurant No. 1: _____

Restaurant No. 2: _____

Restaurant No. 3: _____

SPEAKING OUT

Local

My mayor is: _____

phone: _____ *email:* _____

social media: _____

State

My governor is: _____

phone: _____ email: _____

social media: _____

Federal

My senators are: 1)_____ and 2)_____

1) phone: _____ email: _____

social media: _____

2) phone: _____ email: _____

social media: _____

My congressperson is: _____

phone: _____ email: _____

social media: _____

To find your elected officials and their contact details, visit www.usa.gov/elected-officials.

Tribal Land

My community exists on _____ land.

I can find ways to show support at:

tribe website: _____

contact: _____

For more information and contact details, visit native-land.ca to search by your address.

THE MOTHERBOARD

Your personal resources guide

🌿 PRODUCTS

SECONDHAND

Free + Used Marketplaces
Buy Nothing
Craigslist
Facebook Marketplace
Freecycle
Good Use
Nextdoor
Trash Nothing

Toys + Baby Gear
eBay
FiddlePiddle
GoodBuy Gear
reCrib
Toycycle

Instruments
Guitar Center

Clothing + Shoes
Bagsay
Bounce Mkt
Eileen Fisher Renew
Hand Me Up
Hanna Andersson
Kidizen
Mercari
Once Upon a Child
Poshmark
The Real Real
Rebelstork
Shop Tomorrows
Swap.com
Tea Rewear
ThredUp
Tradesy

Furniture
Chairish
EBTH
Etsy
Kaiyo
OfferUp

Books
AbeBooks
Better World Books
Chegg (textbooks)
Powell's Books
Thriftbooks

Outdoor + Active
Lululemon Like New
out&back
Patagonia Worn Wear
Play It Again Sports

RENTALS

Clothing
Armoire
Everlasting Wardrobe
Manymoons
Rent the Runway

Gear
BabyQuip
Baby's Away
Loop Baby

Toys + Books
Green Piñata Toys
NetBricks
Toy Library
Your local library

Kids' Clothing
Colored Organics
Hanna Andersson
Jackalo
Mightly
Mini Rodini
Monica + Andy
PACT
Tentree
Threads 4 Thought
Under the Nile
Winter Water Factory

Adult Clothing
Christy Dawn
Classic T-Shirt Company
Eileen Fisher
For Days
Free Label
The Good Tee
Knickey
Kotn
MATE the Label
Nudie Jeans
Outerknown
Reformation
The Standard Stitch
Swedish Stockings
Triarchy
Very Good Bra

Shoes + Socks
Arvin Goods
Cariuma
Conscious Step
Good Guys Don't
Wear Leather
Nisolo
Q for Quinn
Veja

Rain + Athletic Wear
Aigle
Cotopaxi
Faire Child
Girlfriend Collective
Kamik
Loop Swim
Patagonia
Reima

Toys
Haba
Hape Toys
Lovevery
Oli & Carol
PlanToys
Tegu
Tender Leaf Toys
Wishbone Design Studio

Diapers
BabeeGreens
Cottonique
Dyper
Eco by Naty
Esembly
Green Sprouts
GroVia
Healthybaby

Glass Bottles + Nursing
Dr. Brown's
Evenflo
Junobie
Lifefactory®
Mason Bottle
WeeSprout

Baby Gear
BabyBjorn
Bumbleride
Clek
Joolz
Nuna Baby
Snuggle Me Organic
Solly Baby
Sprout San Francisco
Stokke
The Swaddle Company

Zero-Waste Shops
EarthHero
The Good Fill
Helen Milan
Package Free Shop
Plastic Free Pursuit
Refill Revolution
The Refill Shoppe
Tiny Yellow Bungalow
Zero Waste Store

School Supplies
Cotopaxi
Decomposition Book
Pela Case
Terra Thread
Wisdom Supply Co.

School Lunches
Bambu
ECOlunchbox
PlanetBox
Pura Stainless
Stasher Bag
To-Go Ware by
ChicoBag
UKonserve
WeeSprout

Beauty + Body
Beautycounter
BLK+GRN
Diva Cup
Dr. Bronner
Elate Cosmetics
Fat and the Moon
Healthynest
Highr
Izzy
J.R. Liggett's
LastObject
Nopalera
Patch
Piggy Paint
Plaine Products
Raw Elements
Saalt
Terra Ties

Food
Gneiss Spice
Hive Brands
Loop
Sun & Swell
Thrive Market
Wally Shop

Kids' Dinnerware
Duralex
Life Without Plastic

Cleaning + Home
Ardent Goods
Cloud Paper
Common Good
Fillaree
Grove Collaborative
Hello Tushy
Marley's Monsters
Meliora Cleaning
Products
No Tox Life
Plant Paper
Redecker
Ten & Co.

Bedding, Furniture, Rugs
Avocado
Coyuchi
Earth Weave
Happsy
Holy Lamb Organics
Hook and Loom
Kindred Kid & Baby
LOOMY
Lorena Canals
Naturepedic
Pottery Barn*
Oeuf
Sol Organics
Under the Canopy
West Elm*
Willaby

*Look for their GREEN-GUARD certified, GOTS Organic, Tencel,™ Fair Trade options

TOOLS

SEARCH AND FIND
fees may apply for apps or services

Your Footprint
carbonfootprint.com
footprintcalculator.org
offset.climateneutral
now.org/footprintcalc

Carbon Offset Sites + Apps
Ecologi.com
Klima
Terrapass

Composting App
ShareWaste

Sustainable Fashion App
Good on You

Hair Salons
greencirclesalons.com

Recycling Sites + Apps
Best Buy (electronics)
earth911.com
Recycle Coach

Clean Product Finder Apps
Healthy Living (EWG)
madesafe.org
Think Dirty
Yuka

Food Share Sites + Apps
Flashfood
freeformula.exchange
Olio
Too Good to Go

Grocery Shopping Finders
app.zerowastehome.com
GreenChoice Grocery Shopping
litterless.com/wheretoshop

Palm Oil Apps
PalmSmart

Plant-Based Eating Apps
Feel Better
Food Monster
Forks Plant-Based Recipes
Garden Plate
HappyCow
Oh She Glows
Vegan Maps

Meal Planning Sites + Services
endsandstems.com
savethefood.com

Junk Mail Sites + Apps
DMAchoice.org
optoutprescreen.com
PaperKarma

PODCASTS

Browngirl Green
Climate One
Conscious Chatter
Good Together
Green Dreamer

The Green Dream with Dana Thomas
How to Save a Planet
Low Tox Life
A Matter of Degrees
Mothers of Invention

The Slow Home Podcast
Sustainababble
A Sustainable Mind
TED Climate

Animal

Certified Vegan

Global Traceable Down Standard

Leaping Bunny

PETA-Approved Vegan

Responsible Down/Wool Standard Certified

Appliances + Electronics

ENERGY STAR®

WaterSense

Better Business

1% for the Planet®

Certified B Corporation (B Corp)

Certified Carbon Neutral

Cradle to Cradle Certified® (C2C)

Green America® Certified Business and Gold Certified

MADE IN GREEN by OEKO-TEX®

Buildings + Furniture

EPA Lead-Safe

GREENGUARD Certified or GREEN-GUARD Gold Certified

Leadership in Energy and Environmental Design (LEED®)

Consumer Safety

EWG Verified™ (Environmental Working Group)

MADE SAFE®

OEKO-TEX Standard 100®

Forest

Forest Stewardship Council (FSC®)

Rainforest Alliance Certified™

Roundtable on Sustainable Palm Oil (RSPO)

Sustainable Forest Initiative®

Ocean

Marine Stewardship Council (MSC) Certified Sustainable Seafood

People

Fair Trade Certified (Fair Trade USA®)

Fair for Life

Fairtrade International

Plants

Demeter Certified Biodynamic®

Global Organic Textile Standard (GOTS)

Non-GMO Project Verified

Regenerative Organic Certified™

USDA Organic

FOLLOW

INFLUENCERS

Anna Sacks
@thetrashwalker

Anne Therese Gennari
@anntheresegennari

Ashlee Piper
@ashleepiper

Dr. Ayana Elizabeth Johnson
@ayanaeliza

Chelsea Murphy
@she_colorsnature

Greta Thunberg
@gretathunberg

Erin Boyle
@readtealeaves

Jane Fonda
@janefonda

Jane Goodall
@janegoodallinst

Joel Ussery
@sustainajoel

Kamea
@greendreamerkamea

Kathryn Kellogg
@going.zero.waste

Lauren Singer
@trashisfortossers

Leah Thomas
@greengirlleah

Lin + Toni
@plasticfreeto

Low Tox Life
@lowtoxlife

Amy | Low Tox Pharmacist
@lowtoxpharmacist

Nathalie Kelley
@natkelley

Nina Gualinga
@ninagualinga

Pattie Gonia
@pattiegonia

Ran Nomura
@zerowaste.japan

Rob Greenfield
@robjgreenfield

Shelbi Orme
@shelbizleee

Wawa Gatheru
@wawa_gatheru

Xiye Bastida
@xiyebaera

FOOD + GARDEN

Alex + Whitney
@plantbasedjuniors

Anne-Marie Bonneau
@zerowastechef

Ashlie Thomas
@the.mocha.gardener

Brooklynne
@beetsbybrooke

Char + Marv
@plantedinthegarden

Chris Chung
@fluent.garden

Humans Who Grow Food
@humanswhogrowfood

Karla
@vegan.kids.nutrition

Ron Finley
@ronfinleyhq

Slow Food International
@slowfood_international

The Edible School-yard Project
@edibleschoolyard

Toni Okamoto
@plantbasedonabudget

Veggie Mijas
@veggiemijas

FASHION

Aditi Mayer
@aditimayer

Aja Barber
@ajabarber

Dominique Drakeford
@dominiquedrakeford

Heidi Kaluza
@the_rogue_essentials

Jacki
@jacquitabanana

Marielle Elizabeth
@marielle.elizabeth

Orsolade DeCastro
@orsoladecastro

Sustainably Chic
@sustainablychic

MAKE + MEND

Arounna Khounnoraj
@bookhou

Clean Clothes Campaign
@cleanclothescampaign

Jamie
@thebarefootdyer

Katie Ng
@timetosew

Katrina Rodabaugh
@katrinarodabaugh

Lily Fulop
@mindful_mending

Recycle and Play
@recycleandplay

Suay Sew Shop
@suaysewshop

ECO-PARENTING

Ecoparent Magazine
@ecoparent

Mothering Earth
@motheringearth

SUPPORT

Circularity
@circularitycommunity

Climate Awakening
climateawakening.org

Eve Rodsky
@everodsky

Good Grief Network
@goodgriefnetwork

Parent Self Care
@parentselfcare

Skillshare
@skillshare

Therapyden
@therapyden

ORGS + MOVEMENTS

350.Org
@350org

Citizens Climate Lobby
@citizensclimate

Clean Air Moms
@cleanairmoms

Fossil Free
gofossilfree.org

Indigenous Climate Action
@indigenousclimateaction

Intersectional Environmentalist
@intersectionalenvironmentalist

Mothers Out Front
@mothers.out.front

National Black Food & Justice Alliance
@blackfoodjustice

Plastic Free July
@plasticfreejuly

Project Drawdown
@projectdrawdown

Queers 4 Climate Justice
@queersforclimatejustice

Project Regeneration
@regenerationorg

Remake
@remakeourworld

Seeding Sovereignty
@seedingsovereignty

Science Moms
@science_moms

Sunrise Movement
@sunrisemvmt

The Years Project
@yearsofliving

Union of Concerned Scientists
@unionofconcerned scientists

Women's Earth Alliance
@womensearthalliance

1000 Hours Outside
@1000hoursoutside

1000 Grandmothers
@1000grandmothers bayarea

HOME

Christine Platt
@afrominimalist

Diana Rene
@the.decluttered.mom

Heather Barta
@thebartahouse

Shira Gill
@shiragill

The Minimalists
@theminimalists

Zoë Kim
@raisingsimple

BONUS MATERIAL

SUSTAINABLE SWAPS 101
An everyday essentials checklist

Before you begin swapping out your plastic and single-use items for sustainable alternatives, remember to use up what you already own.

KITCHEN	
INSTEAD OF . . .	**TRY . . .**
✗ A plastic garbage bag	✓ Go bagless (when you compost food waste, your garbage isn't sticky or smelly)
✗ Paper towels	✓ A Swedish dishcloth, tea towel, or rag
✗ Paper napkins	✓ A washable cloth napkin
✗ Disposable coffee filters	✓ A washable coffee filter or French press
✗ Single-use coffee pods	✓ Reusable coffee pods
✗ Tea bags	✓ Loose-leaf tea in a strainer
✗ Plastic wrap	✓ A dishcloth with a rubber band, beeswax wraps, fabric bowl covers, or an upside-down bowl on a plate
✗ Freezer bags	✓ Stainless steel containers, glass jars, or silicone bags
✗ Plastic sponges	✓ A dish brush, bamboo pot scrubber, or Swedish dishcloth (depending upon the job)
✗ Liquid dish soap in a plastic bottle	✓ A dish soap bar or refillable soap concentrate
✗ Liquid dishwasher detergent that comes in a plastic jug	✓ Dishwasher tablets or powder that comes in a cardboard or metal container
✗ Using the trash can for all waste	✓ Compost and recycle more

BATHROOM

INSTEAD OF . . .	TRY . . .
✗ A plastic toothbrush	✓ A bamboo toothbrush
✗ Toothpaste that comes in a plastic tube or with microbeads	✓ Toothpaste tabs or toothpaste in a metal tube that's microbead-free
✗ Conventional floss (it's plastic and contains PFAS) that comes in a plastic dispenser	✓ Silk floss that comes in a glass or metal refillable dispenser
✗ Plastic-bottled shampoo & conditioner	✓ Shampoo & conditioner bars
✗ Liquid hand soap that comes in plastic	✓ A bar of hand soap
✗ Plastic-bottled body wash	✓ A bar of body soap
✗ Plastic-bottled face wash	✓ A facial cleansing bar
✗ Plastic-bottled face cream	✓ Face cream that comes in a glass or metal jar
✗ Exfoliators with plastic microbeads	✓ Exfoliators with natural exfoliants such as oatmeal, salt, coffee, nutshell powders, and sugar or manual exfoliants like 100% plastic-free cleansing brushes, face sponges, and dry body brushes
✗ Plastic loofah	✓ Natural loofah (you can even grow them in your backyard)
✗ Body lotion that comes in plastic	✓ A body moisturizer bar
✗ A plastic razor	✓ Stainless steel safety razor
✗ Canned shaving cream	✓ A shaving soap bar
✗ Deodorant that comes in a plastic applicator	✓ Deodorant stick that comes in a compostable paper tube, bar, or cream form. (Don't worry. It works just as well.)
✗ Tampons or single-use pads	✓ A menstrual cup, period undies, or washable pads
✗ Cotton balls	✓ Washable facial rounds
✗ Cotton buds	✓ Washable, reusable cotton buds or compostable ones made of bamboo

✗ Traditional toilet paper	✓ Recycled or bamboo TP that comes wrapped in paper, or use a bidet
✗ Tissue	✓ A handkerchief or bandanna
✗ Makeup in disposable cases	✓ Refillable, reusable makeup cases
✗ Makeup remover wipes or liquid that comes in plastic	✓ Natural oils, such as jojoba oil, that come in a glass jar
✗ A plastic brush or comb	✓ A bamboo brush or comb
✗ Traditional hair ties (they're plastic!)	✓ Compostable hair ties made of organic cotton and natural rubber
✗ Plastic bath toys	✓ Natural rubber or sustainably harvested wood bath toys
✗ Conventional sunscreen	✓ Mineral, coral reef–safe sunscreen that comes in a compostable paper tube, metal pump dispenser, or metal tin

NURSERY	
INSTEAD OF . . .	**TRY . . .**
✗ Traditional diapers	✓ Cloth diapers
✗ Single-use wipes	✓ Cloth (or compostable) wipes
✗ Plastic diaper pail bag	✓ Reusable, washable cloth diaper bag
✗ Conventional diaper cream	✓ Diaper cream that comes in a metal tube or glass jar
✗ Plastic teething toys	✓ Pacifiers and teething toys made from medical-grade silicone or natural rubber, and wood teethers with a nontoxic finish
✗ Plastic baby bottles	✓ Glass or stainless steel baby bottles with a natural rubber nipple or medical-grade silicone
✗ Plastic breast-milk storage	✓ Food-grade silicone trays and Mason or Bell jars
✗ Disposable nursing pads	✓ Washable nursing pads
✗ Stuffed animals made from synthetic materials	✓ Stuffed animals made from natural materials

✗ Plastic toys	✓ Eco-friendly toys made from sustainable materials like FSC wood, natural rubber, food-grade silicone, or organic cotton that's also free of flame retardants and toxic glues and dyes
✗ Vinyl bath mat	✓ Natural rubber mat

LAUNDRY ROOM

INSTEAD OF . . .	TRY . . .
✗ Laundry detergent in a plastic jug	✓ Powder laundry detergent in a cardboard or metal canister or strips that come in paper. Look for refillable options as well.
✗ Stain remover in a spray bottle	✓ Stain remover bar
✗ Bleach in a plastic jug	✓ Oxygen brightener that comes in metal or cardboard packaging
✗ Dryer sheets	✓ Wool dryer balls

OUT + ABOUT

INSTEAD OF . . .	TRY . . .
✗ Single-use water bottle	✓ A refillable water bottle
✗ Single-use coffee cup	✓ A reusable thermos
✗ Disposable plastic cutlery	✓ Carry a set of metal cutlery in your bag
✗ Ziplock snack bags	✓ Reusable containers or silicone bags
✗ Plastic straws	✓ Carry a metal, bamboo, or silicone straw with you
✗ Plastic-bottled drinks and juice boxes	✓ Aluminum can or glass bottles
✗ Getting takeout that you'll eat while you're out	✓ Dining in a restaurant that uses real plates and cutlery

HOME COMPOSTING 101

Whether you have a backyard, side yard, porch, deck, or no outdoor area, you can compost at home. It's simply about finding the right composter for your space and lifestyle.

COMPOSTING INGREDIENTS

When composting, you need only four basic ingredients:

01. BROWNS: CARBON-RICH MATERIAL

Browns are dry things such as fallen leaves, small twigs and sticks, shredded paper, and egg cartons.

02. GREENS: NITROGEN-RICH MATERIAL

Greens are generally wet, like vegetable or fruit scraps, fresh leaves, flowers, nutshells, and coffee grounds.

03. WATER

Water aids in decomposition and helps regulate the temperature of your compost. Too dry or too wet can lead to problems.

04. AIR

The organisms that break down your compost need air to live. Vents and rotation (movement) help the compost "breathe."

There are different recipes (browns-to-greens ratio) depending upon the type of composter you're using. A general rule is to layer your greens and browns like lasagna with browns always on the top and bottom with layers of browns and greens sandwiched in between. The number of layers you add will depend upon the size of your composter and the amount of material you have, but no matter what, browns will always be the first and last layers you add. The browns are there to allow water and air to flow through and will also help prevent smells from escaping (and keep flies away).

Once an ideal condition is created, your compost will heat up! That's right. Heat is a by-product of the organic materials breaking down. If it has the correct ratio of browns, greens, water, and airflow, it should reach 135°F–160°F.

While rare, if not properly managed, compost piles can become so hot they can pose a fire danger, so it's important to tend to your compost as directed.

WHAT TO DO WITH THE FINAL PRODUCT?

Once your food waste is done breaking down, you will be left with a dark soil-like material. If you don't have a garden where you can use your finished compost, you can add it to indoor potted plants; supply to neighbors with gardens; offer it to a community garden, farm, or school; or give it away on any free online marketplace sharing platform.

FIND THE BEST COMPOSTER FOR YOU

Ready to figure out which composter is right for you? Take the test on page 248.

COMPOSTER TYPES

TRADITIONAL OPEN COMPOST PILE

What is it? Traditional open compost piles can be done two ways: hot or cold. Cold composting is essentially creating a pile of yard waste and leaving it to decompose, while hot composting decomposes faster but requires turning and care.

Where? Outside. Best for yards.

Pros:

✓ Free to low-cost to buy or build containers to house the pile(s) of waste

✓ A great option if you have space

Cons:

✗ Requires more space than other methods

✗ Some cities and counties require permits

✗ Food waste in an open pile is more likely to attract pests if not tended to regularly

✗ The breakdown process can be slow if done cold

STAND-ALONE ENCLOSED BIN

What is it? An enclosed bin sits on the ground and has a lid at the top where you can add new scraps. Some have a bottom that can be opened to remove your final compost. The walls on all 4 sides have holes which help aerate the compost.

Where? Outside. Best for back or side yard.

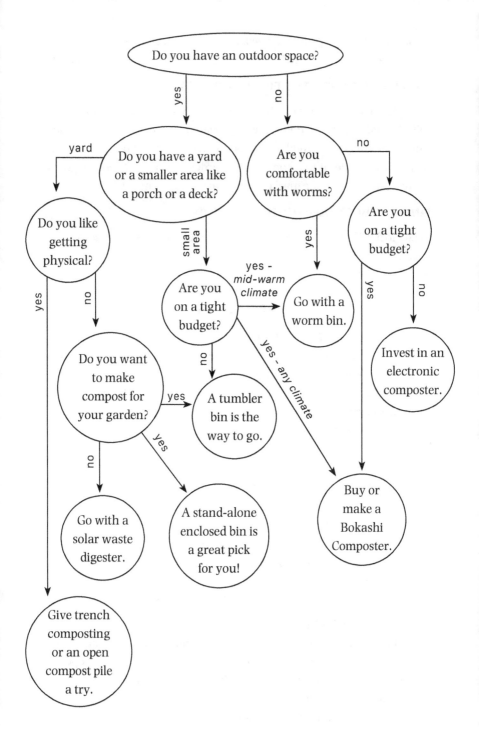

Do you have an outdoor space?

yes → Do you have a yard or a smaller area like a porch or a deck?

no → Are you comfortable with worms?

yard → Do you like getting physical?

small area → Are you on a tight budget?

no (worms) → Are you on a tight budget?

Do you like getting physical?
- yes → Give trench composting or an open compost pile a try.
- no → Do you want to make compost for your garden?

Do you want to make compost for your garden?
- yes → A tumbler bin is the way to go.
- yes → A stand-alone enclosed bin is a great pick for you!
- no → Go with a solar waste digester.

Are you on a tight budget? (small area)
- yes - mid-warm climate → Go with a worm bin.
- no → A tumbler bin is the way to go.
- yes - any climate → Buy or make a Bokashi Composter.

Are you comfortable with worms?
- yes → Go with a worm bin.

Are you on a tight budget? (worms)
- yes → Buy or make a Bokashi Composter.
- no → Invest in an electronic composter.

Pros:

- ✓ Keeps outdoor composting tidy
- ✓ Comes in multiple sizes depending upon family size and waste amounts
- ✓ Low maintenance, as some enclosed bins do not require any turning
- ✓ Minimal odor
- ✓ Good for both food scraps and yard waste

Cons:

- ✗ Mid-range to expensive ($50–$400+)
- ✗ Some bins are open on the bottom, which could allow for pest problems

TUMBLER BIN COMPOSTER

What is it? A compost tumbler is a stand-alone bin that's sealed and can be rotated with a handle to easily turn the compost—making the process easier and faster than composting in a pile.

Where? Outside. Best for back or side yard, balcony, or patio.

Pros:

- ✓ Some are raised off the ground which makes for easy turning and also keeps out pests
- ✓ Takes 3+ weeks to create compost (longer in cold months)
- ✓ Minimal odor
- ✓ Keeps outdoor composting tidy
- ✓ Comes in multiple sizes depending upon family size and waste amounts
- ✓ Minimal effort (just spin it for a few seconds 3–4 times a week or when you take food scraps out)

Cons:

- ✗ Mid-range to expensive ($75–$500+)

SOLAR FOOD WASTE DIGESTER

What is it? A solar food waste digester, also known as the Green Cone, is comprised of two parts: a nearly 2.5-foot cone that sits above ground and a lower basket that's buried under the dirt. Food scraps are put in the cone and left to be "digested." Nutrients return to the soil through the basket below the cone.

Where? Outdoors. Best for yards.

Pros:

- ✓ Great if your main goal is to keep food waste out of the landfill but you're not interested in making compost that can be removed
- ✓ Easy to use and requires little attention to maintain

✓ Takes almost all foods

✓ Odorless

✓ Can be used year-round

✓ Less likely to attract pests

Cons:

✗ Does not produce removable compost for you to use

✗ Cannot use for yard waste

TRENCH COMPOSTING

What is it? Trench composting is when you dig a hole in the backyard and bury your food at least 12" deep in the ground so critters won't dig it back up.

Where? Outdoors. Best for yards.

Pros:

✓ Free (after the cost of purchasing a shovel)

✓ Enriches soil within a month

✓ Odorless

✓ Doesn't require turning

✓ No effort after the hole has been dug

Cons:

✗ Requires space

✗ You have to dig holes regularly

WORM BIN

What is it? A worm bin, also known as vermicomposting, is a method of creating compost with earthworms. The worms eat the food scraps, helping to break it down quickly and efficiently to create compost.

Where? Indoors or outside. If outside, mild to warm climates (55°F–77°F).

Pros:

✓ Inexpensive to mid-range cost ($30 DIY to $150 new)

✓ Takes up little space

✓ Less likely to attract pests

✓ Requires little attention

✓ Can be used year-round (indoors in winter depending upon climate)

Cons:

✗ Worms will die if climate is too cold

✗ Can attract fruit flies if not properly cared for

✗ Not ideal for children and adults with tactile sensitivities

✗ Not great if you have a lot of yard waste

BOKASHI COMPOSTER

What is it? Bokashi is the Japanese word for "fermented organic matter." As the definition suggests, it's a fermentation process that breaks down food waste. It's done in a bucket and takes about 2–4 weeks.

Where? Outside or indoors in either an apartment or house.

Pros:

✓ Inexpensive ($30 DIY to $50+ new)

✓ Most are small and take up little space

✓ Easy to use

✓ Requires little attention

✓ Takes almost all foods

✓ Odorless

✓ Can be used year-round

✓ Less likely to attract pests

Cons:

✗ Most bokashi composters are small and thus not great if you have a lot of yard waste. Larger options are available but are pretty pricey.

ELECTRIC COMPOSTER

What is it? Add an electric composter to your kitchen and create compost in a matter of hours. Devices range in size from countertop dimensions to trash can proportions.

Where? Indoors. Best for apartments or houses with no yard waste.

Pros:

✓ Takes up little space

✓ Less likely to attract pests

✓ Easy and effortless

✓ Odorless

✓ Can be used all year

✓ Takes almost all foods

✓ No extra collection bin is needed

Cons:

✗ Expensive ($300+)

✗ Not great if you have a garden with a lot of yard waste

✗ Requires electricity

✗ Extra regular cost of filters

THE GREEN GLOSSARY

Biodegradable. Capable of decay through the action of a living organism, such as bacteria. For a product to be labeled biodegradable it must quickly decompose. However, many products designated to be biodegradable can still leave behind toxic chemicals and/ or harmful substances. Additionally, many products labeled biodegradable cannot degrade properly unless they're in a human-controlled environment. Also see *Compostable.*

Biodegradable Plastic. Just because a plastic is labeled biodegradable, doesn't mean it's eco-friendly. It simply means that it can break down faster into smaller pieces than conventional plastic. The term biodegradable can be misleading because not all biodegradable plastics are compostable. Unless the product says "compostable" on its label, then the biodegradable plastic should be thrown in the trash. If recycled, it risks contaminating conventional plastic recycling. If littered or composted, it can add harmful toxins or microplastics to the environment. Also see *Compostable Plastic.*

Biodiversity. See page 171.

Carbon Dioxide. Carbon dioxide (CO_2) is a naturally occurring part of the carbon cycle in which carbon cycles through the soil, atmosphere, oceans, plants, and animals. While carbon is essential for all life on this planet, in the past century human activity has put too much CO_2 that was trapped below the Earth's surface into the atmosphere, throwing things off balance and triggering climate change. Carbon dioxide is the most common human-generated greenhouse gas. Through the carbon cycle, carbon dioxide can be taken out of the atmosphere and put back into the earth, with the ocean, forests, and soil being the largest carbon sinks—part of the reason why maintaining these ecosystems is vital.

Carbon Emissions. Carbon emissions refer to the release of carbon dioxide (CO_2), a greenhouse gas, into the earth's atmosphere through human activity—mainly the burning of fossil fuels. Carbon pollutants then get unleashed in our atmosphere, trapping heat from the sun and causing the temperature of the Earth's surface to rise. Thus, carbon emissions are one of the main drivers of the climate crisis.

Carbon Footprint. The total amount of greenhouse gases, including carbon dioxide, that are generated by an individual, a company, a country, or a product.

Carbon Neutral. 1. A science-based designation that is the same as net zero except it only aims at reducing carbon and not all greenhouse gases. (See *Net Zero.*) 2. A loose term for when a business or organization buys carbon credits to help offset their emissions. Often, this is done instead of identifying and implementing carbon reduction strategies within the company.

Carbon Offset. Countering emissions with another action that reduces greenhouse gases, including carbon, in the atmosphere. Examples include planting trees oneself or funding projects such as reforestation. When buying carbon offsets (aka carbon credits), you can fund projects that sequester carbon to reduce your footprint in areas of your life where emissions are unavoidable. However, transparency and efficacy are still lacking in the carbon offsets market. It's likely that the offsets purchased (by an individual or business) aren't an equal conversion to what is being offset by many programs. This isn't to say that no offsets are happening. It just might not be equal to the credit promised by the offset program. Thus, the first step is reducing emissions before trying to negate any inescapable emissions through carbon offsets.

Carbon Sequestration. The process of capturing and storing carbon dioxide from the atmosphere back in the earth.

Climate Change. Historically, a term for natural climate change, such as ice ages. Currently, a term for climate change that has been proven unequivocally to be caused by human activity. Right now, the Earth's atmosphere is heating 100x faster than it has in previous periods of warming. Climate change and global warming are often used interchangeably. Global warming, however, is actually a side effect of climate change. The term climate change includes global warming but also encompasses other byproducts such as extreme weather-related disasters; changes in weather patterns; biodiversity loss; warming oceans; melting glaciers; rising sea levels; increased disease, etc.—resulting in compromises to infrastructure, ecosystems, agriculture, transportation, energy, and human health.

Collective Footprint. The cumulative action of individuals that collectively has a large impact on larger structures.

Compost. A nutrient-rich soil-like mixture made from decomposing organic matter, which can then be used to promote soil health.

Compostable. Organic matter such as food scraps, yard waste, and soiled paper that can be made into compost. A municipal composting facility is often required for some materials to break down, such as compostable plastic (see *Compostable Plastic*). Not all compostable matter tossed in the landfill will break down properly and will emit harmful greenhouse gases during decomposition. Thus, it is essential to dispose of compostable matter correctly.

Compostable Plastic. Compostable plastics are made from vegetable matter like potato or corn starch and are designed to fully break down when placed in a human-controlled environment. Some compostable plastics can be composted in a home composting system (and will be labeled as such), while others require industrial composting, such as compostable bags labeled as "certified compostable." They will not break down properly if littered. And like all compostable items, compostable plastics that are thrown in the landfill can be harmful to the environment, so they should be composted properly instead of being put in the garbage. Also see *Biodegradable Plastics*.

Degradable. Something that is capable of breaking down into smaller pieces. While it may take hundreds or thousands of years, technically, everything degrades.

Disposable. Anything designed to be thrown away after short- or long-term use.

Eco-actionist. Someone who uses their daily habits, choices, and routines as tools for change.

Economies: Linear, Recycling, and Circular
- **Linear.** In a linear economy, raw materials are collected from the Earth, transformed into products that we use, and then thrown away either immediately or in time.
- **Recycling.** In a recycling economy, some items get recycled to help limit the natural resources taken from the earth. While some materials get repurposed, a lot still ends up in the trash.
- **Circular.** In a circular economy, after an item gets used, it's either reused, remade, repaired, returned, recycled, or repurposed, with the landfill taken out of the equation, which significantly reduces the strain we put on natural resources.

Ecosystem. A geographic area in which living organisms (plants, animals, decomposers, etc.) interact with nonliving elements (weather, water, rocks, etc.) in community.

Endocrine Disrupter. See page 130.

Environmental Justice. Environmental justice is a movement begun in the United States in the 1980s as a response to environmental racism. It centers people, equity, and freedom from discrimination when addressing climate and environmental policy and action.

Environmental Racism. Environmental racism is the disproportionate weight, both domestically and abroad, of climate disasters, environmentally related health problems, and resource and land appropriation and destruction, on BIPOC and low-income communities. These disparities are rooted in a history of colonialism and historic and current racist discriminatory regulations and practices. These injustices have put people's health and lives at risk.

Food Waste. Food waste is any food that gets thrown away. It includes edible food that goes uneaten, spoiled food, and also inedible parts such as pits and rinds. It also refers to the wasted food that occurs within the supply chain.

Fossil Fuel. Oil, coal, and natural gas are fossil fuels, formed by the remains of decomposing prehistoric organisms underground, which are then extracted and burned for energy. Fossil fuels are carbon sinks, holding carbon underground. When they are extracted and burned, they are released into the atmosphere, throwing naturally occurring greenhouse gases off balance. Eighty-one percent of the total energy used in the United States comes from fossil fuels, including 90% of our fuel for transportation.

Global Warming. Global warming refers only to the heating of our earth's atmosphere, caused by greenhouse gas pollution. Global warming is one side effect of climate change.

GMOs. Genetically modified organisms (or GMOs) refer to organisms whose DNA have been altered through genetic engineering. GMO plants are common in our food system. Starting January 1, 2022, the FDA is requiring GMO food to be labeled, but it's now called "bioengineered." There are gaps in the classification of these foods, so if you're avoiding GMOs, look for the Non-GMO Project or 100% USDA Organic labels.

Grassroots. People coming together at the community level to collectively act by addressing and fighting issues and injustices locally or on a larger scale.

Greenhouse Gases. Greenhouse gases (or GHGs) are gases in the Earth's atmosphere that trap heat. Greenhouse gases include carbon dioxide, methane, nitrous oxide, and fluorinated gases. They're produced by burning fossil fuels (such as coal, petroleum, and natural gas) for power, heat, transportation, and manufacturing, as well as being generated by organic waste sent to landfills, animal agriculture, air conditioning, refrigeration systems, and much more.

Greenwashing. When a company markets themselves or their products as *green* without truly sustainable goods or business practices.

Landfill. Landfills are giant holes in the ground where trash is compacted and then covered with soil or alternative materials. Landfills are typically anaerobic, meaning no oxygen is present. When food and other organic waste break down in the landfill, they emit gases such as methane, a greenhouse gas that is up to 34 times more potent than carbon dioxide.

Microplastic. Plastic debris measuring 5 millimeters (.2 inches) or less are microplastics. (That's about the size of a sesame seed.) Microplastics come from many sources, including shedding from synthetic clothing and furniture (also known as microfibers), vehicle tires, city dust, and microbeads used in cosmetics and cleaners.

Net Zero. Net zero aims at removing greenhouse gases from the atmosphere in amounts equal to those that we contribute to the atmosphere. To stop climate change in its tracks, we must reduce our greenhouse gas emissions to net zero. Scientists internationally agree that we must reduce all seven greenhouse gas emissions 45% globally by 2030 and reach net zero by 2050 in order to have a habitable planet for future generations. Companies, businesses, and governments can all adopt a net zero policy of making clear infrastructure changes to dramatically reduce emissions, counterbalance any emissions that cannot be eliminated, and set science-based targets to reach the goal of net zero by 2050.

Nonrenewable Resource. A finite resource that gets depleted upon use, has a limited supply, and replenishes slowly—meaning it cannot be replaced at the same speed at which it's used. Common examples of nonrenewable resources are oil, natural gas, and coal (fossil fuels). Additionally, plastic, groundwater, slow-growing trees such as redwoods or old-growth forests, earth minerals, etc., are sometimes also considered nonrenewable resources.

Organic. The growth of plants or animals without the use of chemically formulated, human-made fertilizers, pesticides, antibiotics, or growth stimulants.

Organic Matter. Matter composed of organic compounds and cycled within ecosystems through decomposition. When it comes to our waste streams, organic matter such as food scraps, yard waste, and paper towels is often sent to the landfill, where it cannot properly break down. It can be used to make compost—a far more effective and sustainable way to manage organic waste—which also aids in soil carbon sequestration.

Overabundance Blues. When excess stuff leaves us feeling overwhelmed and like we have nothing—making us want to buy more.

PFAS. See page 132.

Plant-Based. See page 174.

Plastic. See page 86.

Pollution. The harmful contamination of air, water, soil, etc., by natural or human-made substances (solid, liquid, or gas) or energy (light, sound, heat, etc.).

Recycling. Converting "waste" such as paper, plastic, metal, and glass into new materials or objects. Some materials are infinitely recyclable (meaning they can be recycled endlessly with no loss in quality), such as glass and aluminum. In contrast, other materials, such as plastic and paper, can only be recycled a few times before they're waste.

Regenerative Agriculture. A holistic approach to agriculture that focuses on land conservation and rehabilitation. Regenerative farms and ranches grow food or raise livestock (sometimes both) using the natural ecosystem cycles, which include plants and animals to sequester carbon and keep soil and life thriving. It currently leads the way as the most sustainable food system.

Renewable Energy. An energy source, such as wind, solar, or tidal, that is naturally recurring and not depleted when used. It's also sometimes called clean energy. Natural gas, a type of fossil fuel that is often burned to create electricity, is not a renewable energy source but often gets misinterpreted as one due to the word "natural" in its name.

Renewable Resource. A natural resource that can be used repeatedly without running out because it's replenished either through quick natural reproduction (bamboo, hemp, etc.) or an infinite recurring process (wind, sun, hydro, etc.).

Single-Use. Something designed to be used once and then be disposed of either by recycling, composting, or going in the trash.

Sustainable Living. See page 11.

Volatile Organic Compounds (VOCs). VOCs are emitted as gases from solids or liquids such as household sprays and cleaners, air fresheners, dry-cleaned clothes, furniture, rugs, mattresses, building materials, and paints. VOCs can be carcinogenic and cause a number of serious health issues. They can be odorless or scented, with formaldehyde being one of the most well-known VOCs. In addition to creating indoor air pollution, they also contribute to smog formation in outdoor air.

Wishcycling. See page 51.

Zero Waste. 1. Zero waste is the goal of not producing any waste (including trash, recycling, and compost). 2. Cutting out waste while also looking at the total environmental impact of an item through its entire life cycle (from the design and materials all the way through to its disposal) to ensure the conservation of resources and limit the risk of harm to land, water, air, ecosystems, animals, and people.

ACKNOWLEDGMENTS

To my husband, your endless support, love, and encouragement have been instrumental in writing this book. You are my rock. C and T: life's greatest gift is being your mom. I love you to the end of the universe and back. To my parents, thank you for always believing in and supporting my dreams. Ann and Peter, thank you for hosting summer camp for the kids so I could get this book finished. It really does take a village. Liz, for being my mentor through the entire book proposal process. Thank you to my family and Allison, Ann, Bella, Elizabeth, Ellen, Juno, Lauren, Leighna, Nisha, Nnamdi, Rohan, and Theo for literally lending a hand for the cover. A shout-out to all of my teachers, particularly from high school and the World Arts & Cultures department at UCLA, for helping me find my voice and hone my grassroots activism during such formative years. To my agent, publisher, and editor for believing in this project.

And to YOU! Thank you for reading my book and becoming part of this movement. We are in this together.

INDEX

To access The Mothering Earth Project,
free printable materials, and book sources,
please use the QR code or link below:

www.motheringearthproject.com

ABOUT THE AUTHOR

Julia Rockwell is a mother and sustainable-living expert, educator, and writer. She is the founder of *The Mothering Earth Project*, an organization dedicated to helping other people live sustainably through community and connection.

A lifelong lover of healthy and mindful living, Rockwell holds an arts activism–based BA in World Arts & Cultures from UCLA. She lives with her husband and two children in San Francisco, where they lead a sustainable lifestyle.

Mothering Earth is her first book.

FOLLOW

Julia Rockwell | @juliasustainably

motheringearthproject.com | @motheringearth

#motheringearthproject